11.95

South East Essex Coll
of Arts & Technology

CREATING HARMONY
Conflict Resolution in Community

Edited by
Hildur Jackson

Gaia Trust, Denmark
in association with
Permanent Publications

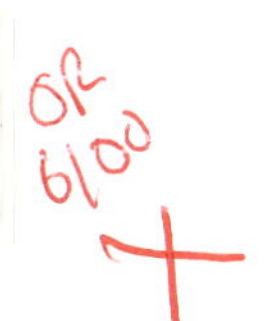

C/R
STL
303.6
CRE

Published by:
Gaia Trust
Storkevaenget 8, 2840 Holte, Denmark
Tel: +45 45 42 55 11 Fax: +45 45 42 55 91

In association with:
Permanent Publications
Hyden House Ltd., The Sustainability Centre
East Meon, Hampshire GU32 1HR, England
Tel: +44 (0)1730 823311 Fax: +44 (0)1730 823322
Email: hello@permaculture.co.uk

© 1999 Hildur Jackson

Project co-ordinated by Maddy and Tim Harland

Design by Tim Harland

Typeset by Lucy Dollery and Tim Harland

Cover evolved by Tim Harland from a photograph by Patch Adams

Printed by Biddles Ltd., Guildford, Surrey

Printed on 75% post consumer recycled totally chlorine free paper

British Library Cataloguing in-Publication Data
A catalogue record for this book is available from the British Library

ISBN 1 85623 014 7

All rights reserved. No part of this publication may be reproduced, stored in a retrieval system, rebound or transmitted in any form or by any means, electronic, mechanical, photocopying, recording or otherwise, without the prior written permission of The Gaia Trust.

Whilst reliable sources have been sought out in compiling this book, neither the authors, publisher or distributor can accept any liability for the accuracy of its contents nor for the consequences of any reliance placed upon it.

CONTENTS

Note

The book is divided into three parts. The first part is dedicated to ways of creating harmony and preventing conflict when establishing or rebuilding settlements. The second part documents the life stories of different communities and the conflict resolution culture they have developed. The third part is devoted to specific conflict resolution techniques. There is, however, no sharp dividing line between the various parts.

Part II
Conflict Solving: Lessons From Communities All Over The World

This section opens with four contributions from the Third World. Here, many traditional cultures still have valuable indigenous and cohesive communities from which we have much to learn. Now, however, their way of life is being threatened by globalisation and urbanisation creating environmental devastation and mass disaffection with traditional values.

0005324019 001

Part III
Conflict Resolution Techniques

THIS BOOK IS DEDICATED TO DIANE GILMAN

She planned and was the soul of the Findhorn conference:
Eco-villages and Sustainable Communities – Models for 21st Century Living.
She brought many of the authors of this book together
and thus inspired the contributors.

More than anyone she had a dream about community.
We often shared that dream together.
She left her body in January 1998.

Acknowledgment

I want to thank Maddy Harland and Permanent Publications for the incredible work they put into editing this book. Thanks a lot.

Hildur Jackson

Introduction
by Hildur Jackson

Humans must make peace with each other and create harmony with the whole biological system that is part of the cosmos. As Thomas Berry, America's Grand old man of deep ecology puts it, we have to develop a kind of literacy which allows us 'to read the Great book of the Universe and in particular to develop the ability to read the book of Nature as it is presented to us in the local setting of our lives'. 'The ability to read the book of Nature' means to learn to feel and unite with nature, to be in harmony with it, and feel its resonance (see Part I of this book). As for 'the local setting', we must recognize that we have a need for a relationship with the land where we live, and that we can understand and evaluate our lives in the light of this relationship.

One way of doing this is to learn to live in sustainable communities in harmony with fellow beings (Parts II and III). This book centres on this vision of harmony and love, as opposed to conflict and control, as the fundamental principles of life. We all need to learn how to apply these principles.

The Eco-village Vision

Reading the Book of Nature has resulted in the emergence in many parts of the world of a new vision of how we might solve the global, ecological and social problems that face the world and threaten our survival: that vision is the eco-village (or Cities of Light or eco-habitats – the preferred name will crystallize with time). Living in an eco-village is a way of living in harmony with the natural world, with the land, plant and animal kingdoms, as well as with our fellow human beings.

An eco-village is a sustainable community in an urban or rural setting, in either the North or South, which tries to respect and restore the circulatory systems of the planet at all levels, in both people and nature, thereby enabling us to live in harmony, love and solidarity, and to read the book of Nature wherever we live.

A fully fledged eco-village is the integration of:

- Earth: physical structures.
- Water: infrastructure.
- Fire: social structure.
- Air: culture.

Using these four elements to define an eco-village has several advantages: It builds on ancient wisdom from all over the planet; all the various spheres of life are given equal importance; and, lastly, it gives us a definition of what real development is. In this sense we are all developing countries. In order to help develop a definition of the eco-village and clarify goals for sustainable settlements, I have developed the following model based on the four elements.

SELF AUDIT FOR ECOVILLAGES AND COMMUNITIES

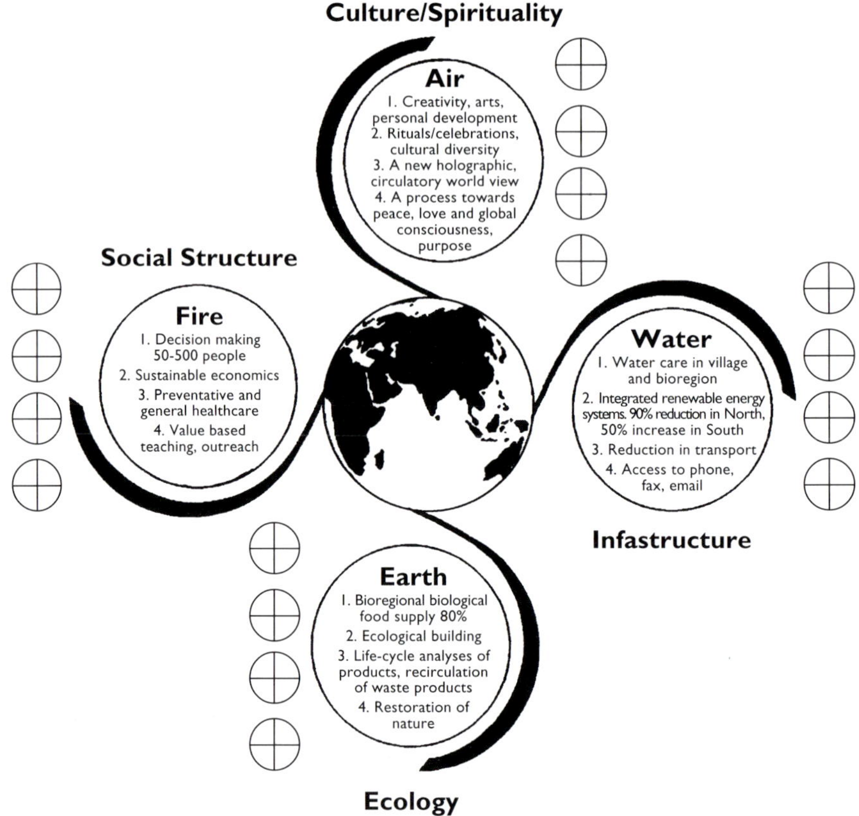

Self Audit User Guide

1. Colour 0-4 quarters in the circles above according to the following scheme:

   No colour means: No interest in this topic in the eco-village.

   One quarter coloured: Interest in the topic, but have done very little.

   Two quarters: Quite interested. Have come half way.

   Three quarters: Very interested. Almost there, but room for improvement.

   Four quarters: Main area of concern. No room for improvement.

2. Add up your scores. Number of quarters that it is possible to colour ranges from 0-64. Notice where you can still improve. Scores above a certain level, which will have to be agreed upon, e.g. 48 points and higher would be a qualified eco-village, with at least 2 of the points in each element.

This is the self audit of:

Name of eco-village here...points...........

Each element has 4 dimensions, and each individual community can choose how important each element is for the group by filling out one, two, three or four of the quarters. This should be done by the community itself, not by somebody else wanting to classify it. The 'perfect' eco-village will thus score 64 points and will probably never exist since groups will always have some preferences.

An eco-village can be either an existing village, or part of one, a suburban area or even part of a city. But its main constituent will be a group of people prepared to commit themselves to co-operating towards a vision – one which hopefully the whole planet will eventually choose to share.

The first step, however, is to clearly express that vision through the setting up of a number of eco-villages, so that we can demonstrate that the vision is possible and that it is, in every respect, a better way of living. We need, in short, to create a positive myth as an alternative to the American Dream which, for some, has now turned into a nightmare.

Some people have already been working on this for many years, trying to build from scratch a new culture by consciously creating eco-villages founded on this new world view. Many of these visionaries came together at a meeting on Findhorn, Scotland in October '95 and it was from this meeting that the beginnings of a worldwide network of eco-villages originated (GEN, the Global Eco-village Network), and that the idea was born for this book which would share the experience.

The first meeting of the Global Eco-village Network, Findhorn 1995. Photo: Hildur Jackson

Conflicts – The Greatest Challenge

Probably the biggest problem that faces eco-villages is that of learning to solve conflicts. Many people are afraid of entering a community for fear of not being able to solve conflicts, and it is this aspect of social sustainability which is one of the most important facets of sustainable living.

The industrial society has 'stolen' conflict from us in a variety of ways: legislation and other rules laid down by society are meant to minimise conflicts and, in doing so, they regulate much of our behaviour: in schools, in work life, when building, in economics etc. We are born into a society where everything is over regulated. Influencing and changing these rules becomes increasingly difficult as legal power is transferred from nation states to conglomerates of nation states, and from companies to transnational corporations. We feel victimised by a system that doesn't need us for anything but consumption.

When a conflict arises, courts or other administrative bodies decide, according to given rules, who is right. Conflict resolution never becomes a learning process which is part of our personal development or our acceptance of responsibility, but instead is assigned to the established power structures and formal legal systems which leads to even greater alienation.

We must reclaim the right to solve our own conflicts and to live full lives as human beings.

One of the aims of this book is to show that resolving conflict can be fun, and that, if we can change our view of it, it can also be one of the most exciting challenges for eco-villages. Conflict resolution offers opportunities for personal growth, for getting closer to other people, and for really living our lives.

Conflict solving, which is essentially the social aspect of sustainability, is a skill that can be learned. It is something we used to know, but have forgotten, and yet an immense body of knowledge is still available to us from all the wisdom and tribal cultures of the world. Many communities, among them Findhorn, which began this process more than thirty years ago, have had to re-learn effective ways of solving conflict in order to be able to live sustainably.

Who Is This Book For?

- This book has been put together for eco-villages and/or communities already in existence, or for people who want to set one up. Hopefully it will inspire such people to create a harmonious lifestyle which in itself will limit conflict. And when conflicts do arise they may then be seen as a challenge and an opportunity: "Hey, here is a chance to learn and to grow. Let us welcome this challenge."

- It is also intended to help and inspire those who are trying to reconstruct local communities anywhere on sustainable foundations. This should be our ideal for all local communities and local groups, including schools.

- It may be a useful tool for any group currently working with conflict resolution. New institutions for resolving conflict are being created in many countries in response to a growing wish to handle dissent peacefully. But the literature on conflict resolution seldom covers the broader concept of living in harmony with the cosmos, nature and fellow humans in harmonious communities.

- A new discipline is gaining ground in the academic field. Known as environmental ethics, human ecology or bioregional studies, depending on which country you live in. This book adds new concepts and actual case studies to the body of knowledge covered by a theoretical course on social sustainability.

This is a very practical book which is best used like a handbook. Draw on it for ideas, or to find out whom to consult for a seminar or workshop. Take away from it the realisation that conflicts can be a gift, a chance for growth, an opportunity for developing real friendship, even for having fun together. You could plan your next holiday as an experience week in a community, or as a training course in conflict resolution – something which many eco-villages now offer. Above all, remember that the fear of conflict should never keep you from participating in a community or an eco-village. For those of you already involved in communities and eco-villages, you have embarked on a journey to leave a dying culture and create a new one. You need all the strength possible from the divine, from the group and from the land in order to succeed, because even if you are a group of relatively well-functioning human beings you may still encounter problems. In the following pages you will find ideas as to how to get this strength. Hopefully you will be inspired by the contributions of the many experienced pioneers whose wonderful ideas have proved effective in many other communities. Find the ways that suit you best and be part of what may be the most exciting development of our time.

A big thanks to all the contributors to this book. They have all worked without fee so that you the reader can have this at an affordable price. Any profit will be donated to GEN – the Global Eco-village Network.

Hildur Jackson
February 1999

Part I

Learning to Live in Harmony With All Creation

Towards a New Renaissance

by Hildur Jackson

Photo: Suste Bonnén

Hildur Jackson is trained in law and cultural sociology. She is a long time grass roots activist, and initiator of one of the first Danish cohousings established some 30 years ago. For 7 years she has been involved with the Nordic Alternative Campaign, a movement of 100 Scandinavian grassroots groups who have aligned themselves with the scientific community to build a vision of ways to solve the major global, ecological and social problems. Writer, permaculture designer, co-founder of Gaia Trust and instrumental in the development of an eco-village strategy, she also leads courses in the setting up of sustainable eco-villages. She has been married to Ross Jackson for 32 years and is the mother of three grown sons and a happy grandmother.

Address:
Storkevaenget 8
2840 Holte
Denmark
Tel: +45 45 42 55 11
Fax: +45 45 42 55 91
Email: hildur@gaia.org

The Vision

The vision is to honour the cycles of nature and live as beautifully and in as dignified a way as possible with them; to respect the soil, the plants, the animals and our fellow human beings in an earth centred world view to follow the pulse of life.

It is at the same time a spiritual world view honouring physical matter and mind, which are born of the divine. We are both cosmic and earthly beings, and there is no contradiction in this; contact with divine love is our natural inheritance. Matter itself is nothing more than a different, external form of mind. And mind and matter are both manifestations of spirit. But we are here in physical form to learn to understand this unique level of external manifestation, to live with it and to live with it gracefully.

The Earth – Physical Structures

To live with the soil and its cyclic system means to understand the building up of matter by photosynthesis and its breaking down again to humus by worms, bacteria and fungi; to create farming systems which respect this cycle and give back to the earth what we have taken from her by creating healthy, local foods for everybody in abundance; cycles like these can continue indefinitely.

It means to build ecologically and restore what has been destroyed. To learn to resonate with the land and restore nature wherever we happen to be. To give room to wildlife. We are made up of earth, not of dirt. If we pollute the Earth, we pollute ourselves.

Water – Infrastructure

We are here to live with water which represents infrastructure and to learn to understand the cycles of water being driven by the sun and the wind. To use it efficiently without polluting either surface water or underground water and to clean it biologically in as gentle a way as possible when we have used it for washing, cooking or production, always respecting it as a precious gift; the water in us is the life giving flow: blood, lymph, nerves, sexual and etheric energies. We have to remove blockages so that the energy can flow freely and so that life can unfold at its optimum.

Fire – Social Structure

We are here to learn to live with fire, which in people is the aspect of communication through words, pictures, symbols and dreams. We have to work on our capacity to communicate, to remove blockages and create non hierarchical structures where the right of everybody to be part of community and communication is recognised and where 'mindful living', as Thich Naht Hanh puts it, is the goal. A world where old people, the handicapped and women can live full lives. We have to learn to make economy and technology supportive of this mindful living and to create a health system that reflects this knowledge and builds on prevention, meditation, and healing by natural means. Living with fire encompasses the creation of a lifestyle in harmony with nature so that conflicts are fewer, and learning the skills to solve them when they do arise. These are the social aspects of sustainability which is sometimes called social ecology in Denmark.

Air – Culture

We have to learn to live with air, to learn to breathe freely and thus to get in deep contact with our hearts. The openness of our hearts and the depth of our love will be reflected in the culture. A loving culture has a world view which accepts the interconnectedness of all life; it creates a vibrant, creative culture where everybody takes an active part, a culture which allows us to cherish true individuality as opposed to the growing uniformity of our industrial society. It will be a truly global culture supporting and cherishing cultural diversity and working for love, peace and the restoration of nature.

The Eco-village Vision

The vision is therefore to create settlements and neighbourhoods that are the unfolding of circulatory consciousness and will develop on the lines of the model we have described. The eco-village is a circular non-extractive system, where living, production, food and recreation are brought together locally. Where matter circulates instead of being part of a linear system that pollutes our environment, and where 'waste' is seen as a resource for new production. Where land is set aside for wildlife and people to explore daily the spirit of nature. The eco-village as a vision lives up to the recommendations of the Rio conference and to Agenda 21 planning for the next century. We are talking here about a new global culture so it feels right to use the term 'a new renaissance' for what is being born.

From Seeds Sown in the Renaissance

But the seeds were sown long ago in the first renaissance, when Bruno and Campanella, Bacon and Andrea Valentin wrote their utopias of the good life respectively entitled *Civitas Solis*, *The New Atlantis and Christianopolis.* Not only did they create utopias, they also advocated groups for personal development and for the creation of a 'religion of love' (Bruno). They intended to create a science and ethics in which spirituality was to play an integral part, expressed through a vast literature (e.g. Shakespeare, Bacon, Campanella, Bruno). All this was part of a great spiritual and democratic awakening throughout Europe in the Renaissance period. Since the burning at the stake of Bruno in the year 1600 by the Catholic Church the seeds have been resting and maturing. They were reawakened in the environmental, peace, women's and social movements of the 1960s and 70s and in the work begun at Findhorn over 30 years ago. They have continued in the cohousing movement in Denmark, and in the creation of intentional communities all over the world such as Auroville, Camphill, Emissaries and Ananda. The whole world now seems ready to share this age old vision of actually creating paradise on Earth.

Birthing a New Renaissance

The metaphor we need for the new age should have the following characteristics:

- It should express a reverence of the feminine as of the masculine.
- It should link us to our past.
- It should integrate science, spirituality and art, which were separated after the renaissance.
- It should be non cataclysmic and yet hold some new visions – enough to channel all the liberated end-of-the-millennium energies.

Many have been working on personal development and on learning to feel more love, to become an expression of love and this process has to continue. We are all on our way. But we also have to make ourselves ready for the next step:

learning to live in a group, and learning to live together may be the single most difficult part of the vision. But we have no choice other than to relearn it. Either we learn to live harmoniously and to solve conflicts in sustainable habitats, or we perish as a species. We can, nevertheless, help and support each other in this process and learn from each other. And it can be fun.

Obstacles to Creating Eco-villages

The eco-village is a harbinger of a whole new culture, and a new way of designing and organising human settlements. But none of the projects currently under way has as yet developed the idea to its full potential, so although many elements of the eco-village can be seen in different combinations in projects the world over, the fully functioning eco-village has yet to be created.

Since we are dealing with a whole new concept of group living, it is not surprising that a whole variety of problems can arise. Think of what new villagers in the North have to cope with:

- Gathering together a group of like-minded, motivated, capable people.
- Creating and forming a vision of the community.
- Outlining this vision in a physical design, in words or in concrete ideas which can be acted upon.
- Designing ecological buildings, renewable village-based energy systems, high levels of self-sufficiency and new systems of agriculture, all of which constitute a major research task.
- Tackling all the problems arising from laws, rules and administrative practices based on a system of finance geared towards a very different structure.
- Holding down a job in order to make a living and possibly raise a family at the same time.
- Learning to work, co-operate and live together, while building a new society.

Keys to Success for Eco-villages

For an eco-village to work successfully there are four major tasks which must be fulfilled and which in themselves can give rise to conflict:

1. The shared vision must be clear and members must be committed to it.

2. Materialisation of the overall vision must be agreed in a concrete form (organisation, design, finance, etc.), and approval has to be obtained from the necessary authorities.

3. The participants have to take responsibility for their own personal problems concerning work, children, partners, and their emotional and spiritual life.

4. Community processes for decision making and conflict resolution must be agreed upon.

Creating a Clear Vision

In order to help eco-village projects clarify their common vision I have developed the illustrated model based on the four elements.

A community may choose how important each element is for the group by filling out one, two or more quarters, but the perfect eco-village will probably never exist. Eco-villages seem to be created mainly from one of three motivations: spiritual, social or ecological. Some communities define themselves as ecological as a way of making them more 'mainstream' or acceptable. This can lead to endless discussions with part of the group defining themselves as spiritual. But the definition of ecology is then often from a global perspective, considering the global eco-system and the interconnectedness of life. And where then is the difference to a spiritual village? The major difference is in language and understanding, and perhaps a lack of focused spiritual practices.

Since language often separates unnecessarily, inventing new language can be part of solving some of the problems. When ecological, spiritual and social eco-villages in Denmark set about creating a common organisation, it was language which most hindered them in their attempts to define a common goal. Finally a very old, yet new, terminology of a circulatory world view restoring the natural cycles in people and nature on all levels was agreed upon (the cyclic model as described above), and suddenly ecology and spirit met and became one.

A two week permaculture or eco-village design course is a good way of creating a clear vision and can save a lot of problems and time later on. Problems coming out of a confused vision or marked differences in vision between participants can be difficult to solve, and the group may even have to split, but you will be surprised at how similar are the visions all over the planet, and how much the different kinds of eco-villages learn from each other and appreciate each other. So trusting in the good intentions of others is an important ingredient for success.

Materialisation of the Vision

Making the vision a reality may take years, and a lot of the detail will probably not have been thought through in the vision phase. The early years will see many problems in realizing the vision of creating a new culture. And no wonder; the participants are inventing something radically new, and it often helps to see it as part of a huge experiment. Do not despair and turn your colleagues into enemies, call a meeting or conference, get the problems sorted out properly and decide on conflict resolution techniques.

The Danish cohousings have – after 25 years of experience – found a formula for creating communities that reduces friction to a minimum. The same will probably happen with eco-villages. Four areas that often cause debate are mentioned below so that people will realize just how common they are.

The Food Ethos

The first decision is whether you want a meat-eating, vegetarian or vegan community. Maybe you only want vegetarianism in the communal kitchen? Can you then accept animals in the fields? Are the members mainly vegetarian because of the way our society treats animals, or do they oppose killing animals for consumption even if done respectfully? If you are vegetarians can you then accept cows for milk and dairy products only, or also raise the cattle to enjoy the good grass and enjoy the sight of them? And what about sheep for wool? Who doesn't wear a woollen sweater or use woollen blankets? But if you have them for wool you still have to slaughter the males in the autumn. Is this acceptable when done in a respectful way on the farm, so that the animals don't have to suffer transportation?

How about pigs which are good at ridding an area of difficult weeds? And perhaps the community wants to earn a living from the production of high quality food. Clearly even the smallest details of our culture need re-examination, and changing from one culture to another is no easy task. It takes tolerance. And time.

Agriculture

The system of agriculture as a whole will also need careful consideration, as it is going to be a totally new system which is village-based, self-sufficient and probably of an organic/permacultural design. It is likely to be a further development from organic farming, which in the long run is not sustainable.

Organic farming is still a linear system where matter is taken from the countryside, brought to the cities and then poured into the ocean. The solid waste when composted is often so polluted that nobody wants it back. Our goal must be a circular system where matter returns to the fields after consumption (see chapter 6 on permaculture; 'Reconnecting with the Earth').

The system will be different from organic farming though, as it is likely to:

- Contain a high degree of self-sufficiency.
- Not produce primarily for a market.
- Be based on group effort.

A permaculture or eco-village design course will help enormously and is strongly recommended for new communities. Many disputes further down the road may be avoided if everyone joins a two week permaculture design course, since this forces people to visualize the reality. But there are no easy solutions. How do we establish a proper economic base for one or more farmers or gardeners when prices for food outside the eco-village are so low (although the true cost of agri-farming will be paid for by future generations), and when people in the eco-village are reluctant to pay over the odds for what is just outside their door? One solution could be to take farming out of the sphere of economy and to create land trusts instead. Another is community supported agriculture (CSA) which is gaining momentum in the US and USA.

Building Ecologically

Building costs will undoubtedly be high even if you undertake a lot of the work yourselves. They will include waste water treatment systems, alternative energy systems, energy conservation, greenhouses, animal housing, and in addition such facilities as a common house, meditation hall and health centre. So how do you get the money for all this? Of course this will present considerable problems, and they won't be solved by communal dancing even if that may give you the courage to begin tackling them. Our society's current financial system is not geared towards eco-villages, but in Denmark a national organisation was set up which negotiated with the government and finance organisations to agree special funds, and to make a bigger percentage of public loans available for financing eco-villages.

Dealing with Authorities

In 1997, a national competition was held in Denmark to find the best sustainable settlement for the 21st century. 53 groups took part and it was supported by 5 government ministries. A wealth of exciting ideas showed that people are ready for change, but the judges in their report pointed to the need for a cross ministerial group to help communities through the legal jungle, and allow up to 100 projects special status as experiments.

Many politicians are aware of this growing movement, but are not yet ready to act. Since most laws and administrative practices are geared towards the industrial society, politicians and administrators will need your knowledge and support, so be patient. This may require time and energy from the project as a whole, but, make no mistake, you are breaking new ground and you may expect difficulties, even though your are doing a wonderful, important job.

Personal Problems

In addition to all this, initiatives creating something new often attract individuals who are unhappy with the existing society. They can be wonderful people with a lot of determination and desire to contribute, they may become your best friends. But be careful, they can also project their problems onto the group and cause misery and confusion. Likewise if you move into an eco-village to solve personal, marital or financial problems then you have made the wrong decision. Being there will not solve them, but simply make them more visible and project them on to the group as a whole.

What is the solution to this? While not wishing to exclude particular individuals the group must have a policy for handling situations such as this or it may end up spending considerable time and energy on it, to the detriment of other needs.

One way is to make it a precondition that those joining the project be involved in a process of personal development or have some spiritual ethos. This at least gives a language with which to handle difficulties. Other groups are happy to have a spiritual master or teacher to consult. Yet another strategy may be to find relatively strong, practical people as the base for the project so that the group has the capacity to handle these problem situations.

Decision Making and Conflict Resolution in Communities

Try to find generally accepted ways of making decisions: majority or consensus decisions, or something in between qualified majority decisions. Another possibility is listening to the minority and the importance of the decision for them. Sit in a circle where everybody can be seen. Use a talking stick or choose one or more people to be 'keepers of the heart'. After each session listen to their experiences of how the group worked. Make meetings fun and accept that we think with the whole body and that all levels of the body must be nourished during meetings. Take moments of silence before every new session, and come to a consensus upon which way to handle conflicts when they do arise. This book will hopefully give you a lot of ideas of how to deal with them.

Conclusion

Most people think of spiritual work and personal growth movements as opposed to the more practical work as environmental activist or building of an eco-village.

Experiences from eco-villages show that these two are not in opposition; on the contrary. Being part of building an eco-village is a short-cut to personal and spiritual development. All your basic assumptions are being tested, nothing in your personality can remain hidden, too big ego's or wrong thinking will be exposed!. In this process you must not only serve Gaia – Mother Earth and future generations, but you live your life, you have fun – you become truly yourself as the unique being you were meant to be. Eco-village people are the freedom-fighters (or birthers) of our generation; the most free people I know. Thanks to all of you for birthing a new culture and to all new-comers: learn from the experiences of others and have a safe journey.

TOWARD AN ECOLOGY OF THE HEART

by Will Keepin

William N Keepin, PhD, is Co-Director of the Colorado Institute for a Sustainable Future, a non-profit training and activist organization that cross-fertilizes ecological leadership, spiritual practice, and sustainable community. He was formerly consulting physicist to the Energy Foundation, and has 16 years experience in environmental science and sustainable energy. He has been research scholar at the Royal Swedish Academy of Sciences, the International Institute for Applied Systems Analyses, and the Rocky Mountain Institute. He was a Hewlett Fellow at Princeton University, and his environmental work has influenced energy policy in several countries. Will holds a PhD in mathematical physics and an MA in East-West psychology. He is widely published and is a Consulting Editor to the journal *ReVision*.

Address:
The Colorado Institute for a Sustainable Future
PO Box 17904
Boulder
Colorado 80308
USA
Tel: +1 303 440 4153
Fax: +1 303 444 1274
Email: ecosustain@aol.com

> *"It is possible that the next Buddha will not take the form of an individual. The next Buddha may take the form of a community; a community practising understanding and loving kindness, a community practising mindful living."*
> Thich Nhat Hahn

The enthusiastic development of ecological villages, or 'eco-villages' across the globe offers new hope for creating practical solutions to the diverse problems facing our culture today. This chapter reviews the emergence of a new eco-spiritual world view, and the forces driving its widespread appeal. The practical implementation of this world view is then examined in the context of the exciting synergistic benefits offered in eco-villages, with particular emphasis on spiritual practice in community life and the implications for conflict resolution in community.

The Emerging Eco-spiritual World View

Daily we read in the newspapers about the destruction of the natural environment. Rain forests are levelled, pollution spews forth from fossil fuel combustion, biological diversity is disappearing – the litany of devastation seems endless. Yet what drives this crisis, and how can we address these underlying forces?

Human Roots of the Ecological Crisis

Today's environmental movement focuses largely on protecting natural ecosystems and reducing physical pollution released from our industrial economy. Vital as this mission is, the underlying forces of consumerism and materialism that drive consumption are only just beginning to receive serious attention. Even in the United States where materialistic lifestyles have long been celebrated, a recent study commissioned by the Merck Family Fund finds that Americans are concerned that "materialism, greed, and selfishness increasingly dominate American life, crowding out a more meaningful set of values centred on family, responsibility, and community."[1] A whopping 88 percent of respondents agreed that protecting the environment will require most of us to make major changes in the way we live. When asked what would bring greater satisfaction in their lives, non-material aspirations outstripped material ones by huge margins. People want less 'stuff' and more meaning in their lives; they want less frenzy and more time for family, friends and community service.

These trends point to the deeper roots of the ecological crisis. The problem is not just 'out there' in the natural environment; our internal environment is also in crisis. The outer malaise in society reflects an inner turmoil in our psychological and spiritual identity. Our culture is grappling with a profound crisis of values and ethics – a collective spiritual crisis that we can no longer afford to deny.

This raises urgent questions: How can our cultural values and practices be transformed to become genuinely sustainable and simultaneously restore meaning and fulfilment to our lives? In short, how shall we live? These questions call forth a yearning for practical visions of a win-win future for humanity and the Earth, in which human beings live sustainably in material terms, and richly in the intangibles of life. This calls for a new cosmology that focuses not only on the outer environment of the natural world, but also on the 'inner' environment of soul and spirit.

The Eco-spiritual World View: Scientific and Spiritual Foundations

A new world view is emerging today in which the cosmos is seen as a single interconnected process in creative manifestation that unfolds from moment to moment. This view posits a fundamental interconnection between all constituent elements in the universe as an essential characteristic that is beyond understanding in purely material terms. As Thomas Berry puts it, the universe is not a collection of objects, but rather 'a communion of subjects'. This new cosmology is having profound impacts on our understanding of the cosmos, the human being's place in it, and our relationship to our planetary home.

Even Western science is beginning to embrace this expanded cosmic perspective, and many of the extreme limitations in the orthodox scientific world view are being lifted. A growing body of new discoveries points to a broad consistency between the Western scientific world view and spiritual teachings down through the ages. Contributions from leading thinkers such as David Bohm in physics, Stanislav Grof in psychology, Rupert Sheldrake in biology, Ken Wilber in spiritual philosophy, Joanna Macy in deep ecology, and a host of others is pointing the way toward an exciting circulatory and participatory view of the cosmos and our role in its unfolding evolution.

Unification of Science and Spirit: The Work of David Bohm

The work of physicist David Bohm provides an illustrative example of this emerging cosmology. Bohm was a close colleague of Albert Einstein's at Princeton University and later settled in London, where he developed a profound interpretation of the foundations of modern physics – his theory of the implicate order.

Based on extensive theoretical work in quantum theory and relativity theory, Bohm proposes that reality is not a collection of separate objects (as it appears to us), but rather it is an undivided whole that is in perpetual dynamic flux. This undivided whole, which he called the 'holomovement', is not static, but rather in a constant state of flow and change. In the holomovement, even mind and matter are united: "In this flow, mind and matter are not separate substances. Rather they are different aspects of one whole and unbroken movement."

Bohm proposes that this flow consists of two fundamental aspects: the 'explicate order' and the 'implicate order'. The explicate order refers to the physical universe that we perceive with our five senses and scientific instruments. The implicate order refers to an invisible subtle realm from which the explicate order appears.

At first blush, it is tempting to assume that the implicate order refers to a subtle level of reality that is secondary and subordinate to the primary explicate order, which we see manifest all around us. However, for Bohm, precisely the opposite is the case: the implicate order is the fundamental and primary reality, albeit invisible. The explicate order – the vast physical universe we experience – is but a set of 'ripples' on the surface of the implicate order.

The radical implications of Bohm's implicate order take some time to grasp, especially for Western minds that have been steeped in the Newtonian-Cartesian paradigm of classical physics that still dominates today's science. The implicate order refers to a kind of ultimate realm beyond matter and thought – the well spring of true knowledge and wisdom. Bohm emphasises that the existence of an 'implicate' or invisible realm is essentially the same in several traditions including Taoism, Yoga, Buddhism, and in the teachings of the Indian sage Krishnamurti, with whom Bohm had extensive dialogues.[2] The implicate order may be seen as representing the realm of Mystery, the unknown, the Unseen, the spirit world, or any of a number of other names for the absolute or un-manifest dimensions of existence referred to in the world's spiritual and mystical traditions. Yet Bohm's concept of the implicate order is rigorously consistent with the mathematics of modern physics.

Bohm's postulates of the holomovement and implicate order have profound implications for the whole of science. Prior to Bohm, science had generally regarded the universe to be a vast multitude of separate interacting physical particles, and questions about the existence of anything beyond matter, space, and time were dismissed as meaningless. However, Bohm offers an altogether new view of reality that is consistent with spiritual teachings down through the ages, and is also consistent with the rigorous data and equations of modern physics. Moreover, Bohm demonstrates that there is no experimental evidence in physics to justify the conventional materialist world view over his; the data support either interpretation equally, and the choice is a matter of subjective beliefs and predilections.

Bohm's work provides theoretical underpinnings for a revitalised science in which the world is not merely a vast cauldron of matter/energy interactions, but is richly imbued with meaning. For Bohm, meaning is the stuff of the implicate order, and is every bit as real as matter and energy. Indeed, Bohm was deeply troubled by the suffering in the world, and his vision calls for a complete restructuring of our fragmented collective consciousness in a new Renaissance:

> *"What is needed today is a new surge that is similar to the energy generated during the Renaissance but even deeper and more extensive... the essential need is for a 'loosening' of rigidly held intellectual content in the tacit infrastructure of consciousness, along with a 'melting' of the 'hardness of the heart' on the side of feeling. The 'melting' on the emotional side could perhaps be called the beginning of genuine love, while the 'loosening' of thought is the beginning of awakening of creative intelligence. The two necessarily go together."*[3]

Genuine love and creative intelligence were indeed the hallmarks of David Bohm's life-work, and they are the forces driving today's emergence of a more balanced and compassionate science - one that draws insights from the heart as well as the mind. The mystical poet Rumi sums up the challenge for science quite succinctly:

> *"If you are in love, that love is all the proof you need. If you are not in love, what good are all your proofs?"*

Principles of Eco-psychology and Deep Ecology

The work of Bohm and a host of other leading scientists and philosophers offers a new understanding of the world and our place in it. Some of the basic foundations of this understanding may be summarised as follows:

> The Earth is a living system, as evidenced by the Gaia hypothesis developed by James Lovelock. Human beings are fundamentally interconnected with the Earth and with all life. The Earth is our larger body, and deserves to be treated with the same care we give to our own bodies. Neither ecological problems nor humanity's problems can be resolved without taking full account of this interconnection. What we do to the Earth, we do to ourselves. Hence a major task of our time is to bridge and heal the alienation between person and planet, and establish a healthy relationship between the two.

In this understanding, the ecological crisis takes on a whole new meaning. Rather than viewing it as a crisis 'out there' in our physical environment, we are now recognising that human consciousness is intricately involved in creating and sustaining this crisis. This demands an altogether new understanding of who we are. Today's dominant models of human consciousness define the human being as an isolated and fragmented entity living in a mechanical, purposeless universe. This model of human reality is a product of an outdated cosmology, that of the scientific industrial era that now weighs heavily on the planet.

In contrast, the new eco-spiritual world view calls for a new cosmology that embraces not only scientific models and understandings, but also spiritual teachings, ancient wisdom, and the non-western knowledge of indigenous cultures. This world view cultivates a rich pluralistic epistemology and methodology, drawing on mythological and archetypal understandings, intuitive and emotional modalities, scientific approaches, and spiritual practices. It also embraces the goals of gender equity (equality between women and men; masculine and feminine), racial equity (equality for non-white races), and cultural justice-honouring non-western cultures and indigenous peoples of the world.

Recently a new discipline called 'eco-psychology' has emerged, which bridges the fields of ecology and psychology to address the psychological, social, cultural and spiritual roots of the ecological crisis. Eco-psychology calls for a profound revisioning of mental health and suggests that the drive to live in harmony with the natural world and its rhythms is primal and innate. Suppression of that drive is just as disorienting and damaging as suppression of other human needs. As emphasised by Theodore Roszak, today's psychology and psychotherapy "stop at the city limits, as if the soul might be saved while the biosphere crumbles". Indeed the very notion of sanity must be redefined to include our planetary home.

Eco-villages: Building a Win-Win Future for Humanity and the Earth

What does all this mean in practice? The major challenge is easy enough to state: How, then, shall we live? This is rapidly becoming one of the burning questions of our time, and the development of eco-villages is one of the most promising pieces of the solution.

Ecological Benefits of Eco-villages: Ameliorating Humanity's Conflict with Nature

Eco-villages provide a wealth of vital ecological benefits that help human beings to live in greater harmony with the Earth. Clustered housing and pedestrian-based infrastructure reduce transportation needs and enable efficient distribution of supplies and resources, while also enhancing community social interactions. Water usage can be reduced with new water-saving technologies, coupled with innovative cistern collection systems that can greatly reduce water pumped from wells, even in semi-arid climates. Constructed wetlands utilise natural ecosystems to convert input sewage into flourishing gardens and high quality effluent water which can be restored even to drinkable standards.

Energy-efficient infrastructure in eco-villages can greatly reduce energy demand, and integrated renewable energy systems can provide pollution-free power and heat at reasonable cost. On-site employment, pedestrian and bicycle commuting and computerised 'smart shuttles' for deliveries and transportation to nearby cities can minimise highway traffic and congestion. Ecological building materials such as straw bale and rammed earth construction offer inexpensive construction using indigenous materials, with fire-resistive ratings that are at least four times superior to conventional wood frame homes. Permaculture principles and biodynamic farming enable local organic food production.

In sum, eco-villages offer practical ways to ameliorate our society's negative impact on the natural environment by providing comfortable living conditions with an 'ecological footprint' per household that is far smaller than in traditional suburban settings.

Social Benefits of Eco-villages: Reducing Social Roots of Human Conflict

Phenomenological research has shown that people living in community groups tend to experience intensified personal growth and at times profound transformation – even in communities that do not emphasise these aspects as explicit agendas. A broad range of well-developed human qualities and capacities are universally reported for people living in community, regardless of the size, location, focus, or governance structure of the community. These characteristics include:[4]

- Increased self-confidence.
- Better communication skills.
- Clearer thinking.
- Broader perspectives.
- Less idealism.
- Increased responsibility.
- Broader set of skills.
- Broader general (useful) knowledge.
- Increased awareness of personal limitations.

Other profound differences from mainstream society include a sense of physical safety in eco-villages. Reports of attacks or physical violence in eco-villages are extremely rare, which means greatly enhanced safety for women and children. Alienation and isolation are also relatively rare, as community members tend to engage and challenge each other, while at the same time accepting individual idiosyncrasies and celebrating diversity. Social relationships are innately more intimate and intense, and people come to see each other very clearly: both their unique gifts and glaring imperfections. This tends to cultivate a tolerance for imperfection, and a release from self-loathing for one's own failings.

In summary, eco-villages can provide vibrant, healthy social settings in which many of the most desirable human qualities are naturally cultivated. Life in a healthy community tends to cultivate well-rounded compassionate human beings, while also ameliorating systemic social causes of human conflict so prevalent in modern urban culture today.

Spiritual Practice in Eco-villages

In the dominant secular materialist culture, people are strongly conditioned to seek gratification and fulfilment through material means and acquisition. Yet it is becoming painfully clear that industrialised societies will not be able to maintain their current level of material consumption in the future. This is particularly true in the United States, which accounts for only five percent of global population yet consumes over one-fourth of the world's resources. The average American watches 21,000 television commercials every year. Each advertisement holds out a false promise of happiness and fulfilment if the consumer will just buy this next widget. The time has come to reclaim the spiritual dimensions of human life, and outgrow our culture's shallow, futile attempt to fulfil spiritual yearnings in material terms.

Living in community can greatly accelerate inner spiritual development. Communities provide powerful cauldrons for burning through egoic blockages and personal limitations. Even if there is no explicit spiritual intention, each person in a community serves as a mirror for every other person, and these multiple reflections can quickly unmask ego attachments and personality flaws, sometimes with brutal accuracy and swiftness.

When conflicts arise in community, they can serve as alchemical fuel for the transformation of each party to the conflict. It becomes virtually impossible to hide away and live in one's ego fantasies in a community of people who are committed to living in truth. Furthermore, as people go through powerful transformative changes, they often discover gifts they didn't know they had.

Integrating Spiritual and Ecological Consciousness

Spiritual development may be viewed as a process of self-transcendence, in which a narrow identity is continually transcended and replaced by a broader sense of self. Informally speaking, this self-transcendence may proceed in at least two different directions, which could be called lateral and vertical. Lateral transcendence is more ecological, referring to an emerging identification with other living beings and life forms, and is the focus of disciplines such as deep ecology and eco-psychology. Vertical transcendence is more 'spiritual', referring to the development of ever more subtle and refined states of higher consciousness, and is the focus of disciplines such as transpersonal psychology and various schools of spiritual teachings.

An overemphasis on vertical transcendence (without lateral) leads to traditional monastic life, effectively disengaged from the manifest world. Similarly, excessive focus on lateral transcendence (without vertical) leads to secular ecological activism, which often results in burn out and loss of soul, due to the absence of a connection to the deeper dimensions of life.

The beauty of a spiritual eco-village is that it provides a unique, practical context for integrating lateral and vertical transcendence – combining the ecological and spiritual in mutually reinforcing ways. Both are essential; a spiritual community that is ecologically destructive is no more sustainable than an ecological community that lacks spirit and vitality. The emergence of spiritual eco-villages answers a vital need for new communities that bridge spiritual practice, community living and ecological infrastructure.

Beyond Romantic Love: Reclaiming our Relationship to the Beloved

Spiritual experience is often denied in our culture as a legitimate aspect of human experience. Hence we are conditioned to mistrust the authenticity and value of spiritual experiences. The result is that many people enter spiritual realms only at relatively rare moments in their lives, such as the death of a loved one, or when they fall in love. Indeed, perhaps the most common initiation to spiritual experience in our society is 'falling in love' with another human being. While this experience offers a legitimate glimpse into the spiritual or 'divine' realms, it is only temporary because it is accessed through the focused attention and presence of another human being. Nevertheless, having once tasted this divine consciousness, however briefly, we seek to recreate it and we tend to associate this experience of divinity with the object of our love; that is, we project our own divinity and spiritual needs onto the relationship with our lover.

Over time this leads us to habitually seek spiritual fulfilment in intimate relationships with other human beings. This is a natural tendency in our secular culture, in which the experience of being 'in love' is for many people the most readily comprehensible form of spiritual experience. Yet this places impossible demands on intimate human relationships, and robs us of our deepest spiritual treasures, which can only be found within. A spiritual yearning cannot be satiated in mental, emotional or physical terms – it is born of a different dimension entirely, and must be addressed in its own domain. This is not to deny the tremendous blessing and power of intimate human relationships, but rather to affirm the priceless gifts that come from developing an inner spiritual life.

Rather than yearning in vain for the 'one and only' beloved person who could fulfil all our desires, we can instead reclaim an appropriate relationship to the 'divine' or invisible 'oneness' that permeates all of creation. Instead of having to choose which flower in the garden to love, we focus our love on the source from which all flowers come; the radiant sunlight itself. As we engage in practices to reawaken this awareness of ubiquitous divinity in our lives and communities, we begin to love the ONE in the many. This enables us to live in state of loving grace much more of the time, as the futile search for a 'one and only' is replaced by the continual experience of the ONE shining out from everyone and everything we encounter. This consciousness of the 'Beloved' in all beings is naturally cultivated in a community of people living in loving kindness and spiritual intention together.

By learning to turn inward for spiritual sustenance – where it is eternally present and available – we become more realised as agents of cosmic or 'divine' will. This makes us more effective in our communities and less dependent on others in a needy way, and hence more able to give and receive freely. This teaching can be naturally cultivated by living in spiritual community, where our experience of love can be transformed from being a need to becoming a blessing.

ECO-VILLAGES' SERVICE TO THE LARGER WORLD

The healthiest eco-villages generally embody a larger purpose that extends beyond fulfilling the needs of the community itself. This larger purpose or service to the world draws vitality and energy into the community, keeping it fresh and alive. This larger purpose might be anything from simple cottage industries, organic food production, ecological activism, training and education, permaculture, spiritual growth workshops, health services, or many other possibilities. The principle is that the gifts generated in the community – the products, services, positive energies, compassion and love – are not ultimately for the community members only; they are for the world.

As the eco-village nurtures its larger purpose, then its internal needs and goals are also fulfilled. "It is in giving that we receive." Directing positive energy outward to serve the larger good keeps the community engaged and creative. On the other hand, if the benefits of the community are limited to the community members themselves, over time the community will become insular and begin to wither. There is a saying: "What you attend to, you become." When a community commits itself deeply to a larger noble purpose, it will in due course become transformed into a living manifestation of that purpose.

Sceptics steeped in Western conditioning and the ideal of individualism often fear that living in community will require giving up their uniqueness and individuality. The concern is that living in a community of people with shared values and a larger purpose necessarily requires surrender of individual identity. In fact, what must be surrendered is not one's uniqueness, but one's ego. In a healthy functioning community, the uniqueness of each community member is not only honoured, but is an essential contribution to the organic whole of the community and its service to the world.

A powerful synergy emerges in a community of people who work closely together in commitment to a common purpose. There is a kind of multiplier effect, whereby a close-knit group of people can contribute far beyond their numbers. Eco-villages offer a remarkable opportunity to harness this power and apply it to transform our dying culture into healthy, sustainable forms. The diverse knowledge, skill, resources, and multiplicity of perspectives available in community creates a powerful 'temenos' or cauldron of truth and transformation. It enables community projects to unfold rapidly as mistakes are quickly detected and corrected, or avoided altogether. This adds a richness and depth to life that is often missing in modern Western society, and it costs nothing in material terms; it is a wealth born of the innate splendour of the collective human psyche and spirit.

Transformative Conflict Resolution: Conflict as Spiritual Transformation

When conflicts arise in eco-villages, there is a profound opportunity for the deepening of community. Our cultural conditioning teaches us to shun conflict, not recognising the potential gifts that lay hidden therein. When conflicts arise in groups, we typically respond in one of three ways:

- Repress the tensions and try to be nice to each other.
- Analyse the tensions and try to change ourselves or others.
- Act on the tensions and hurt one another.[5]

Yet there is a fourth way, which might be called 'transformative conflict resolution', in which conflict is embraced as a form of spiritual practice and transformation. This requires all parties to the conflict to enter into the unknown together, knowing that a resolution is possible in which each party undergoes some form of learning or transformation of consciousness. This approach recognises the very presence of conflict as a sign that each disputant has only a partial view of the situation, and that the conflict has arisen necessarily as a challenge to forge a deeper unity and harmony in the community.

In transformative conflict resolution, creative solutions to the conflict emerge organically from the community as it moves into and through a transformative group process, taking account of all voices and perspectives in the group. For this to succeed, cognitive approaches and dialogue methods alone are generally not adequate. Experiential modalities of group process are needed for working through powerful emotional and psychic energies. In our culture we have generally been conditioned to suppress challenging emotional energies in order to foster peace and harmony, yet this often creates a powder keg of repressed energies that greatly exacerbate conflict. Rather than being repressed, anger, grief, despair, fear, sadness and vulnerability can be embraced directly in their own terms, with powerful and transformative results.

The most effective experiential modalities for group process allow each participant to work with her or his own inner process, while simultaneously participating in the community process. An example is the Holotropic Breathwork developed by Christina and Stanislav Grof, which has proven invaluable for transforming gender conflicts between women and men.[6] Another key example is the process oriented psychology developed by Amy and Arnold Mindell.[7]

Facilitation of transformational conflict requires a broad range of skills, including a solid core of authenticity coupled with a delicate balance of openness, flexibility and knowing when to act. A key requirement is that facilitators stand for all sides in the conflict and hold a strong intention for the group process to unfold in its own natural manner so as to bring forth the inherent wisdom in the group. This means that the outcome is not predetermined, and the agenda emerges organically from the community process itself.

As Arnold Mindell describes this process:

> *"Once a community gets together in an open forum and deals with its most difficult issues, it knows itself from a new angle. The atmosphere improves. The community proceeds to work on action plans, business goals, contracts and social issues...*
>
> *"Organisations and communities do not fail because of their problems, nor do they necessarily succeed because they solve them. Problems will always exist. Communities that succeed open up to the unknown during periods of crisis... Instead of becoming rigid and breaking apart when faced with a challenge, they are transformed in the direction of greater flexibility. Previously unheard-of solutions are created...*
>
> *"When trouble knocks, the possibility for a new kind of community is at the door. The new community is not based only on understanding one another, but on the common decision to enter into the unknown, into trouble – into that fire that is the price of liberty."*[8]

In summary, the beauty of transformative conflict resolution is that it provides a vehicle which requires community members to go deep within themselves and tap the source of unconditional love and creativity that resides within every human being. In reconnecting to these inner wellsprings of insight and forgiveness and truth, remarkable transformations take place in communities that could not be foreseen beforehand or orchestrated by outside facilitators. In this way, a community can re-invent itself as needed over time, and maintain an evolving identity that allows it to become truly sustainable.

Conclusion

In these time of urgent cultural crisis, we are called to serve in two capacities simultaneously: as hospice workers to a dying culture, and as midwives to an emerging new culture. While this dual role is challenging in the face of impending ecological doom, the emergence of eco-villages across the globe offers tremendous inspiration and hope for a win–win future for humanity and the Earth. Indeed, the good news may be better than the bad news is bad. Eco-villages offer practical possibilities for integrated solutions to long-standing social and ecological problems simultaneously.

Life in a vibrant eco-village of 300 people can be far richer than life in a bustling metropolis of 300,000. Within easy walking or bicycling distance, eco-villagers can find close friends, basic services, health care, entertainment, meaningful employment, social and community functions, celebrations, theatre, art, dance, and spiritual practice – all provided with minimal impact on the natural environment. Eco-villages can serve as living incubators for birthing a new culture, offering fresh vision and practical fields in which to sow the seeds of a sustainable society.

Sources

[1] Report prepared by the Harwood group for the Merck Family Fund, July 1995. *Yearning for Balance – Views of Americans on Consumption, Materialism, and the Environment.*

[2] Bohm, D., and Peat, D., 1987. *Science, Order, and Creativity.* London: Routledge. pp. 255–7.

[3] Bohm, D., and Peat, D., 1987. *Science, Order, and Creativity.* London: Routledge. p. 265, p. 271.

[4] Keenan, 1995. *More Confident, Less Idealistic: How We Grow In Community Communities*, Spring 1995.

[5] Mindell, A., 1992. *The Leader As Martial Artist.* Harper: San Francisco.

[6] Keepin, W., 1995. Gender and Planetary Healing: A New Approach. *ReVision*, Winter 1995.

[7] Mindell, A., 1995. *Sitting in the Fire.* Portland, Oregon: Lao Tse Press.

[8] Mindell, A., ibid.

Turning to Natural and Spiritual Law

by Hanne Marstrand Strong

Hanne Marstrand Strong is President of Manitou Foundation, a non-profit private foundation founded in 1988, and Manitou Institute, a non-profit charitable organization created in 1994. These organizations are guided by Hanne Strong's desire to establish an ecumenical, sustainable teaching community in the Rocky Mountains of Colorado, which now includes the Spiritual Life Institute, Crestone Mountain Zen Center, Haidakhandi Universal Ashram, Karma Thegsum Tashi Gomang Project, Sri Aurobindo Learning Center, Samten Ling Retreat Center, Atlanta, Yeshe Khorlo, Naropa Institute, EDUCO and the Baca Center for High Altitude Sustainable Agriculture.

In 1992, she founded the Earth Restoration Corps, an international educational program designed to provide an outreach program to the world by training youth and adults in Natural Law, leadership, and practical skills to live sustainably and in harmony with Nature. The program prepares participants for employment opportunities in fields such as environmental restoration, alternative energy and building technologies, sustainable agricultural techniques and preventative health care practice. Based on many of the ideas presented in this chapter, the Earth Restoration Corps is designed to empower the young people of today to become conscious citizens living in harmony with themselves, each other, the environment, and the universe.

Over the last 20 years, Hanne Strong has also worked extensively with indigenous peoples worldwide to help in their struggle for the preservation of their spiritual and cultural values. She has received extensive spiritual training from North and South American Indian shamans, Tibetan Buddhist Lamas, Hindu masters, Taoists and other mystics. Hanne Strong, born and educated in Copenhagen, Denmark, is married to Maurice F Strong and has two daughters and seven grandchildren.

Address:
Hanne Marstrand Strong
Manitou Institute
PO Box 118, Crestone
CO 81131–0118, USA
Tel: + 1 719 256–4265
Fax: + 1 719 256–4266
Email: spirit@manitou.org

In my travels around the world, I am often asked if there are any new solutions to immediate problems concerning humanity. How can we resolve social and environmental deterioration? Is there any possible remedy to what is ailing our planet? The new solution is the old solution, one which returns us to balance using the knowledge and wisdom of ancient traditions. The answer lies in Natural and Spiritual Laws which have sustained all life since the beginning of time.

Our ignorance of these basic laws is the root cause of the imbalance in the modern human mind, resulting in imbalanced actions which create conflict. It is critical to recognize the root cause of conflict, and its resolution on a fundamental and individual level through the wisdom of these laws. If every human being on this planet acknowledged the wisdom in Natural and Spiritual Laws, then we would begin to take responsibility for our lifestyles, actions, and behaviour, and to develop the highest aspect of being human, find new meaning in life and create strong enlightened societies.

It is critical that spiritual leaders and world leaders assume a significant role in this process. The tremendous human and financial resources, and high level of organization, training, and infrastructure of the government, military, and industrial corporations globally have the potential to be a formidable force for positive change. Two billion young people will be entering the job market in the coming years and we must direct this generation to create a sustainable future through employment in jobs that do not destroy our planet.

At this point in history, in the midst of an explosion of information, population, and technology, we have created a lifestyle that perpetuates self destruction. We have transgressed very basic laws that govern nature. There may be philosophical, ideological, and political differences between cultures, but in terms of our environmental needs for survival there is a fundamental Natural Law that sustains and unifies the symbiotic relationships of life on Earth. One means for understanding Natural Law is to consider the human body. If one damages one's lungs, the integrity and function of the body is severely compromised by the lack of life-giving oxygen. The rapidly perishing forests and coral reefs are the lungs of the atmosphere and ocean. Just as it is in our own interest to remain physically healthy, it is also imperative that we preserve the health and diversity of our environment through alignment with Natural Law.

Having transgressed Natural Law through disregard and ignorance, we need to reawaken the innate awareness that our ancestors had of the laws that govern life. Natural Law seems quite obvious and apparent at first glance. What spiritual traditions introduce is the sacredness and preciousness of all life, and this brings with it a sense of value. A recognized fundamental tenet of world spiritual traditions is the concern not only for one's own welfare, but also for the world as a whole. The ancient traditions provide a wealth of wisdom concerning Natural and Spiritual Law. The spiritual masters emphasize the understanding of these laws through personal integrity and awareness, and through living in accord with Nature.

Numerous masters from around the world have expressed their insightful understanding throughout time. These teachings were beautifully illustrated by Lakota Chief Luther Standing Bear when he wrote, "The old Lakota was wise. He knew that man's heart away from nature becomes hard; he knew that lack of respect for growing, living things soon led to lack of respect for humans too. So he kept his youth close to its softening influence." He also wrote, "The man who sat on the ground in his tipi meditating on life and its meaning, accepting the kinship of all creatures and acknowledging unity with the universe of things was infusing into his being the true essence of civilization. And when native man left off this form of development, his humanization was retarded in growth."

The dynamic of interdependence speaks to us of the importance of learning how to live harmoniously with ourselves as well as the world as a whole. Here the question arises, how do we relate to ourselves and others in these trying times? This entails recognizing the law of cause and effect, which is shared by all the world's spiritual traditions. Jesus recognized this when he said, "As you sow, so shall you reap."

The Essenes were an extraordinary spiritual culture that studied and practised Natural and Spiritual Law to a remarkable degree. Edmond Bordeaux Szekely, author of *From Enoch to The Dead Sea Scrolls* says, "The Essenes expressed an exceptional knowledge of psychology in their practice of Communions with natural and cosmic forces." Szekely writes of how they were also aware of the significance of interdependence and its correlation with Natural Law, "If man fails to become consciously aware of the Law, he deviates from it unknowingly... These deviations create all imperfection in his world, all the limitations and negations in his thoughts and feelings and physical well being, in his environment, in society and the entire planet." The Essenes recognized negligence of Natural and Spiritual Law as a source of conflict, and that resolution of conflict depended on the understanding and practice of the laws in every aspect of their lives.

The contemporary author and visionary Sri Aurobindo illustrated the interconnectedness and interdependence of individual spirituality when he wrote, "To grow in the spirit is the greatest help one can give to others, for then something flows out naturally to those around that helps them."

Karma is the Buddhist term for interdependent causation. It is the law that every development and happening in life has a cause, and this law of Karma is inescapable. Buddhist teachings identify selfishness as a source of conflicting internal emotions, which in turn leads to conflict in the outer world. The great Buddhist master Shantideva of ancient India says, "All the violence, fear, and suffering that exists in the world comes from grasping at self... If we will not let go of the self, we will not be able to put an end to our sufferings, just as if we do not let go of fire with our hands, we cannot avoid being burned." If our actions are motivated by our egocentric desires and conflicting emotions such as greed, jealousy, and aggression, they lead to exploitation of the Earth and others. The world's spiritual traditions are unanimous that we must not allow our conflicting emotions to reign over us, but that our emotions need to be transformed, liberated, or disciplined. The conflict that originates in these emotions is consequently resolved through wisdom in action. As the *I Ching* comments beautifully, "This refers to a man who... must not seek his own salvation and abandon the world to its adversity. Duty calls him back once more into the turmoil of life."

In this dire time of turmoil, living examples are imperative in conveying the importance of wisdom in action. Living in accordance with Natural Law in Taoist tradition is eloquently expressed by the term 'Ki'. Sueng Heun Lee, founder and master of the Korean Dahn Hak tradition, tells us that, "'Ki' is the basis of all existence and phenomena in the universe. It is the inexhaustible source of life. Disease is being out of the flow of 'Ki'. How can we cure people of disease, physical or mental? We help them bring themselves back into line with 'Ki' and become one with the true source of their vital energy. Being cured is a small acquisition compared with the other blessings they will get and Spiritual Law and to resolve conflict."

Our disregard for the environment positions us on the brink of disaster. A fundamental need of society is not being met, which has led to a level of indiscriminate consumerism unprecedented in history. In this 21st century it is critical that each of us develop our own awareness. We can no longer afford to perpetuate our current state of ignorance without aggravating an already severe situation. Our future is dependent on our actions today, and because of technological advances our capacity for continuing devastating effects is greatly amplified. We must implement the sustainable technology we already have at our disposal in order to progress without further damaging the environment. We are immature spoiled brats of the post-Industrial Revolution wielding lethal weapons in our infancy while disregarding the repercussions of our actions. We ignore the guidance of our parents, the earth and the universe, and the traditions of wisdom. If we continue in our youthful folly, Mother Nature will teach us all a lesson we won't forget. So we must grow up, mature, and become aware.

What we are being presented with is a pressing need for conscious discernment in order to create a better future through the cultivation of self-awareness. The message conveyed here is not one of simply reverting to the past, but of integrating the enlightenment of the past with present technology so we may progress into a sustainable and enlightened future. We have a blueprint of sacred laws which can help guide us in our relationship with the world. Re-learning, integrating, and living by these laws in the present offers a remedy to conflict. Without these changes in consciousness, there will be no future.

Meeting the Land
Doing Science, (Art and Religion) Goethe's Way
by Margaret Colquhoun and Christopher Day

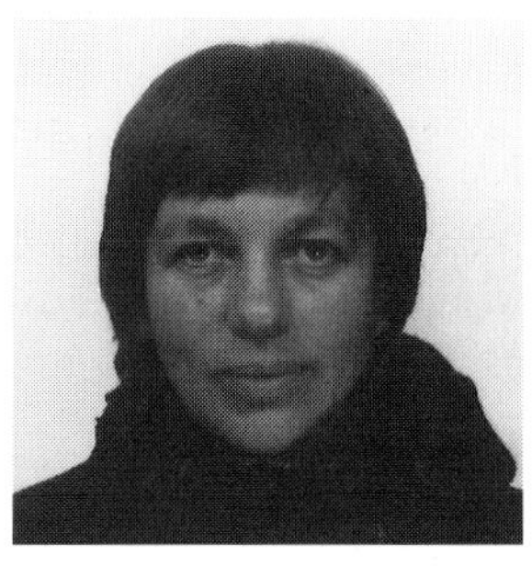

Margaret Colquhoun is an evolutionary biologist based in Scotland and working freelance in Goethean Scientific research and education all over the British Isles. She is co-founder of the Life Science Trust and Seminar (running since 1990) and is currently involved in the establishment of a small eco-village in South-East Scotland, the Pishwanton Wood Project, as a centre for Goetheanism in the English-speaking world. She teaches regularly at Schumacher College, at Emerson College and elsewhere, is co-author of the recently published book, *New Eyes for Plants* by Hawthorn Press and co-creator of the touring landscape exhibition "Creative Encounters with Nature". Her main interests are in landscape and medicinal plants but she is concerned to work in any way to help people come into closer communion with nature in order to help heal themselves and the earth.

Christopher Day trained as an architect and sculptor. In addition to designing buildings in accordance with ecological principles, he offers worldwide consultancy on the development and rescue of places both indoors and outdoors.

Address:
The Life Science Trust
Kirk Bridge Cottage
Humbie
East Lothian
EH36 5PA
Scotland
Tel/Fax: +44 (0)1875 833654

The Life Science Trust is a Scottish Charity Reg. No. SCO20705 November 1992

Harmony: "a combination of simultaneously sounded musical notes to produce chords and chord progressions especially as having a pleasing effect" says the *Reader's Digest Wordfinder*. Translated into 'Harmony in/with Landscape' this might then mean that each part of the whole sounds its tone in pleasing accord with all the other parts, and would assume a Oneness in a chord of parts 'in accord with one another' in a landscape 'in all creation'.

"It is the Universal Oneness in numerous manifestations revealed" says Goethe in a small poem entitled '*Parabase*'. These words of J W Von Goethe introduce a method of holistic science which has been named after Goethe himself and which lies at the basis of a multitude of creative and social processes today dedicated to living and being 'in harmony with all creation'.

The process of studying nature in a Goethean way involves a striving towards and working out of that experience of 'being at one with' all that is around us and of which we are a part. 'All creation' and the landscape includes ourselves. But being a part we are also apart – in that we think, judge and are capable of choice – a choice of whether or not to act in harmony or in disharmony with our surroundings. This seems to be unique to the human species. Choosing to act in harmony or even knowing the experience of 'being in harmony' do not come naturally to we humans at our current stage of evolution. The *Oxford Dictionary*, perhaps surprisingly, describes harmony as "a pre-established agreement between body and soul before their creation". Are we now striving to find an original pre-birth agreement between us and all creation and might this perhaps be one answer to our problems of conflict emergence, let alone conflict resolution?

Since the paradisiacal days of Eden we have lived through millennia of strife and conflict and we have achieved a remarkable degree of freedom in our mastery of the material world. This achievement appears to have been won coincidentally with a loss of the capacity to live and create in harmony with the living world. Ever since the time of the middle of the Millennium when Francis Bacon was able to say: "we need to torture Nature in order that she reveal her secrets", we have been on a path of progressive estrangement from the rest of creation – and hence from each other? We have lost our capacity to live in harmony with Nature – in less than 500 years! Now surely it is time to offer our highly developed intelligence in freedom and transform it, before it's too late, to aid Gaia in her healing.

Embarking on such a process of personal integration with the world would seem to involve the necessity of our being conscious of the way that we integrate with every level of being from the most superficial physical appearance to the life which forms us and the spiritual essence of all that is. Only then can we sacrifice ourselves in the service of the other, be it plant, place or person, stone or animal, landscape or the earth as a whole – once we've found the way to an experience of the 'pre-established harmony'.

Goetheanism and Beyond

The following is an exposition of a scientific and artistic journey (which turns out to be a deeply religious or spiritual one) based on Goethe's approach to the world, developed into a clear and conscious path by the philosopher and scientist, Dr Rudolf Steiner, and subsequently modified according to place, process and people involved. It involves an inner and an outer journey in the development of ourselves as beings capable of living in harmony with the rest of creation.

In editing Goethe's scientific works, (which Goethe himself as Germany's most well-known poet deemed to be more important than any of his artistic achievements), Rudolf Steiner said that Goethe's greatest offering to humanity lies in the fact that his Art and Science spring from one source – from the

'Primal Source of all existence'. Goethe developed a method of listening to this 'Heartbeat of the Universe' as it sounds in all creation and what he heard there he then expressed sometimes in an artistic, sometimes in a scientific medium. What interests us in his method in this particular context is that, if we are able, through our own inner efforts and personal development, to attain to a level of being able to listen together to the heartbeat of the Universe, to the Primal source of all existence as It expresses Itself in this particular plant, person or place (in all of the 'numerous manifestations' in which It is revealed) then surely this will render conflict unthinkable, even impossible? This is 'an accomplishment yet to be achieved' and what follows is a condensed summary of something of the beginning of our journey towards such a striving.

Over the last five years many groups of people within the Life Science Trust, a charity in Southern Scotland, have been working hard to develop a technique of 'listening to the land' and to sounds of it through each other. To date, when people have been truly engaged in the process and have managed to 'let go of their own stuff', we have experienced no conflict whatsoever and only consensus concerning our experience of the needs of the place. We have been practising this in smaller and larger groups at regular intervals on a piece of land in the South East of Scotland as the foundation of our research and development work in the formation of a Life Science Centre for the research, practice and teaching of Goetheanism in the English speaking world. We have also offered it in many other places, including our workshop at Findhorn in October 1995 in the Eco-villages conference ('Listening to the Land' – Christopher Day and Margaret Colquhoun). Here is a condensed summary of some of our experiences in south east Scotland.

Meeting the Land

We arrive to a flurry of rooks, wind in the pines, sun sinking slowly over a majestic panorama of hills in the distant west – the Pentlands, Arthur's Seat and then the Ochils across the water beyond Fife. In the lightening north the Paps of Fife stand strong and dark against the grey sky; silver grey mirrored in the shining strip of sea stretching her finger inland to form the Firth of Forth. The plain of Lothian is bathed in rising mist and one can 'see' how it once was sea, then marsh and, only recently (in geological terms), dry productive land – 'the Garden of Scotland'. Igneous intrusions rise out of the plain – Berwick Law, the Bass Rock, Garleton Hills and Traprain Law, each conversing in dark form language with Arthur's Seat to the west, the king of this kingdom, as did once perhaps the dwellers of those hill forts or sacred places on their summits, commune with one another in days gone by. The stillness draws us into reverie; past becomes present; future, part of the same.

We attempt to let go of all our preconceptions, our woes and worries of the day; to walk in silence for an hour or two, letting this place speak its soul into our hearts. We are walking through the house of nature drinking in the contents of each 'room'. Here is a cosy, dark, closed corner for quiet contemplation; there an expanse of light and windswept brightness; in one place a lot of animals; in another, burgeoning bracken or thickets of birch and willow. Light and darkness, moods of cold and warmth, play together and form a pattern in the whole. These first impressions are valuable and can be sketched as a mood map of inner soul experience evoked by the place. Each individual's first impression is unique. And yet they have much in common: 'an oasis in a desert of modern agriculture', 'a haven', 'a sanctuary', 'a precarious balance between human abuse and healing potential'.

This exercise also has the effect of allowing us to let go of our own feelings in order to be able to see more clearly exactly what is there now: sixty undulating acres of neglected woodland full of springs and scrub regeneration called Pishwanton Wood, a name which means, in Scots, 'capricious water' or a 'wood of bountiful water'.

Pishwanton Wood – The Earthly Facts

Next day we recall the place from memory in its physical facts and make a map of what our senses reveal. This map is a picture of the outer physical journey of discovery – and hence 'objective' in the conventional sense. But there is a paradox here in that what each person sees is what they know; and therefore a reflection of the inner of the subject – hence perhaps not entirely objective! Doing this together, and sharing at each stage of scientific discovery, enriches each person's possibilities to see, and widens their perceptual horizons. The sensory observation of the 'here and now' is deepened as each of us chooses an area to study in detail. This first 'getting to know' a place in all its facts and characteristic details is an absolutely essential part of any scientific process. One cannot note and describe enough, nor move on, until the facts of the phenomena are firmly grounded in consciousness and recorded in whatever way is deemed appropriate. Annotated maps, sketches and species lists accompany lots of drawing in this 'earthly mode of observation'. The very activities of drawing, measuring and note-taking enable us to see more, to know more. Goethe called this initial grounding in reality 'Exact Sense Perception' and, like getting to know someone you love, the physical exploration is never over.

Entering the 'Stream of Time'

Sharing our findings of the different areas of study allows us slowly to build up a picture of the whole place together with its history. Evidence on the ground of past activities (such as tree felling, ditching, a mill lade, an old track) plunges us into 'the stream of time' of Pishwanton Wood's 'becoming'. We have crossed a spatial boundary and, leaving the earthly facts which support us, we enter a region of temporal fluidity.

We find that now we are using that within us which is characteristic of the element of water as a tool for perceiving. Living in between all the facts, we find ourselves swimming along in our imagination in the process which has led to the development of this place in time; an activity which Goethe called 'Exact Sensorial Fantasy'. We cannot think this logically. Our minds start to dream between the facts we know – an act, in Goethe's words, of 'recreating in the wake of ever-creating nature'. Thinking then becomes a living force at our disposal and we find ourselves using our fantasy or imagination as an organ of apprehension.

The place begins to grow within us – like an inner garden – and it's very difficult to hold back from being swept along into the future by this onward flowing stream of time. After a day or so of 'growing our places' we find we've become so 'embedded' in the land (and it in us) that it feels painful to leave bits of wire lying there, to suffer the felling of a tree or to allow choked up water courses to go on being 'constipated'.

Airy Revelation – Of the Genus Loci

Now the joys and sufferings of the land start to become our own. We find we've crossed another threshold – to an activity of perceiving where feelings seem to appear in us in crystal, light-filled, airborne clarity, almost despite ourselves, from 'out of the place itself'. We find we 'know' with a kind of inner knowing or a non-rational way of understanding, what is right and true for the place. We start to recognize within ourselves the Being of this place, how it expresses itself in all its physical phenomena. There is an experience of 'seeing as if for the first time'. The Genus Loci has begun to speak. And what is so remarkable at this stage on the journey is the consensus or communality of experience amongst all the people involved. One has the experience of reaching a true objectivity – via a subjective route! The 'personality' of the place is read and translated through our own personalities which we use as tools in the service of its expression. Goethe described this as 'Seeing in Beholding'.

Fire of Oneness

The experience of being 'inspired' by the Genus of Place leads naturally into a state of being described as 'becoming one with', of melting with or melting into the landscape. All the experiences so far are gathered up and their essences distilled. Einstein described this state as one common to all great lovers and all great artists (as well as great scientists!) when they 'know' that which they love. Perhaps this is what love is? It is the state that Merlin led the young Arthur towards as he encouraged him to experience 'becoming one with' members of the different kingdoms of nature in order that he be prepared as a suitable vessel for the kingly status that was his destiny. It is the state that all of us long and strive for if we want to be true kings and queens in our dealings with the earth – to deal with the realms of nature in ways which are compatible with their essential being and its fulfilment; in ways which acknowledge the sacred in the smallest flower.

'Becoming one with' and experiencing such a communion with Nature is an uniquely warming experience. We feel the Oneness between each other in such moments of overcoming the greatest conflict of all – that of our estrangement or separation from nature. The fire of common union once experienced can drive, inspire and empower a person for many years ahead. This can change lives. We may experience a new sense of responsibility – for our selves, for our own destiny and for the future of the earth.

This, then, is the beginning of the Pishwanton journey – new for us and yet not new. Has our way – Goethe's way – something to do with the way of those who used the hill forts all those years ago? Was their spiralling journey up three levels of volcanic intrusion (harder rock amongst the surrounding softer sandstone) an echo of our journey through the elements but one appropriate to their consciousness? And is all that belongs to our Celtic heritage the predecessor of Arthur's way which has been inscribed into the landscape all over the British Isles?

CELTIC CHRISTIANITY NOW

Our journey is mapped out, one might say, in the Celtic invocation:

Christ! King of the Elements
Hear Me.

Earth, Bear me
Water, Quicken me
Air, Lift me
Fire, Cleanse me
Christ! King of the Elements
Hear me.

I will cleanse my desire through love of Thee
I will lift my heart through the air to Thee
I will offer my life renewed to Thee
I will bear the burden of earth with Thee
Christ! King of the Elements

Fire, Water, Air and Earth
Weave within my heart this day
A cradle for Thy birth.

A Celtic Prayer

So perhaps one could say Goethean Science in the 20th/21st Century is a kind of 'reawakening of Arthur' and a direct link to our Celtic past as in the first half of the invocation – an answer to a call to become one with, to deal wholesomely and in harmony with the world around us.

> *"A 'Wholeness Science' would include and emphasize more participatory kinds of methodologies; it would assume that, whereas we learn certain kinds of things from the subject studied, we get another kind of knowledge from intuitively 'becoming one with' the subject. In the latter case, the experience of observing brings about a sensitisation and other changes in the observer. Thus a willingness to be transformed himself or herself is an essential characteristic of the participatory scientist"*
> Willis Harman, President of the Institute of Noetic Sciences in *Newsletter of the Scientific and Medical Network, 1992*

Perhaps you can get a sense, dear reader, of the enormous steps awaiting us as scientists (of life) if we are to move towards a holistic experiencing of the world. And science is for all of us if we define it as "that essentially human activity of finding out about the world around us" – not just the physical facts of what something is in all its unconnected bits, but how they fit together, how they function and, indeed, what aspect of the World Spirit is here being expressed in which relationship to the rest of the world.

All this in such a way that it is satisfying to each of us as an independent human spirit. One of the definitions of 'satisfaction' (in the *Reader's Digest Wordfinder*!) is "Christ's atonement for the sins of mankind". If we take this seriously, then perhaps it is understandable that when we are able to open ourselves to some aspect of nature and allow the spirit within it to have its place – to marry with the echo of that spirit deep within ourselves – we might approach some kind of atonement for all those generations of non-acknowledgment of the divine, of the sacred in nature and reawaken our connection to Gaia.

Goethe's way of doing science then, is a science which allows, of necessity, for each human being of today (as did our Celtic forebears) to unite the outer physical journey with an inner spiritual one. It is a journey which can lead to a glimpse of the Logos; as that shining dream of reality that can flower within us if we penetrate deeply into the phenomenological world of nature's things. Entering deeply into something 'out there' opens the doors to deeper layers of our own inner world. We find we cannot go further without a certain inner transformation. Thresholds are encountered – both in nature and in ourselves – and overcome. Science, and the quest of daily life becomes a pilgrimage – on the inner as well as the outer path. Not only is our way of knowing the world transformed, but also our ability to act and to transform the world; the Art of Life. Our daily deeds start to be changed as we find we are able to act for and with the World Spirit – the second half of the Celtic invocation.

From Pure Perception to Healing Action

Going back to Pishwanton, you may recall the different stages of encounter on our journey through the elements to meet this particular piece of land. When we began to study Pishwanton Wood as a place – now nearly seven years ago – we had a question: "Is this a suitable place to build a Centre for Goethean Science and Art?" We asked the land to tell us about itself. The question "Who are you?" stood there all the time as we sought the answers first to "What are you?" in all your parts; hilltops, bogs, streams and dry pine woodland; birch scrub and glowing gorse. A threshold was reached in the accumulation of earthly facts, and the development of Pishwanton as a place crowded in as the facts started to be understood in terms of the very fluid 'becoming' of the place. Switching from 'exact sense perception' (of facts) to the fluidity of 'exact sensorial fantasy' demands an essential change of gear on the inner path.

Living into the development of Pishwanton through ages of time and into the relationships between all its parts we started to appreciate 'who' this place is, carried towards us as an airy inspiration. That which it is trying to express of itself in the world started to become apparent as something of the precarious and flexible nature of its being came to meet us. We became aware of a tremendous peace and healing potential within the land itself, right down to the gestures of the land forms round about. We realised the effort involved in understanding such a varied place so full of transformations (it is not called 'capricious water' for nothing!) would make, and was already showing it to be an ideal place for practising, demonstrating and teaching the very method of study we were trying to do there. We had begun to 'become one with' this place – to be purged by its being and fired to act ourselves.

The Creative Process

Bringing to consciousness what a 'Life Science Centre' would involve, we tried to find those places within the landscape which might welcome or provide a home for the activities we could envisage. There then began a long process of 'listening to the land' again and again; of trying to find the right forms in the natural world and in the design of new buildings and landscape features to clothe our own human activities. This has been, and still is a tremendously creative process, oscillating between scientific listening and creative design. Each step of the way leads to some kind of inner step within the individuals involved and a further clarity about the nature of this bit of the earth along with a renewed reverence for handling and caring for it into its future.

The proposed first building which was designed (in its third attempt) in October 1995. It will be made of Pishwanton earth. This will allow grey-water purifying ponds to be dug as the house is built. The roof will be of turf, rising out of the field into which it is partially dug. The form of the roof echoes the lines of the distant hills in Fife and the building itself offers an embracing open gesture to the curve of the Lammermuir Hills to the south, towards which it faces.

Seed for the Future

This 'Seed Building' will house all the proposed activities (in simple sketch form) which are needed for developing an integrated centre for teaching, demonstrating and researching into how to meet the land in a healing and sustainable way for the future of the earth. The second half of the Celtic invocation has begun.

The Pishwanton Project is attempting to grow out of a process of sensitive and artistic integration of proposed human activity and need, (coming from the future), with a careful scientific listening to the given natural world, (which has grown out of the past). The art of transformation of the earth – of horticulture, agriculture, silviculture, architecture, technology and life in general is growing out of a listening science – out of Goethean Science, an 'accomplishment yet to be achieved', which can allow each individual to reconnect with 'The Way, the Truth and The Life' in every aspect of daily life, life which itself is an active conscious journey of scientific discovery and creative deed.

Place, People and Consciousness

by Peter Dawkins MA, Dip. Arch.

Peter Dawkins is Founder-Director and Principal of the Zoence Academy. He is also an internationally known author, lecturer and teacher of the Western Wisdom Traditions and Zoence (Science of Life), Zoence consultant and healer, geomancer and cosmologist.

Photo: Jane Withers

Peter is a pioneer in the rediscovery of landscape, temples and the healing of the Earth through geomantic pilgrimage and Founder-Director of the Francis Bacon Research Trust and Founder-member and Elder of the Gatekeeper Trust. He is the author of several books, his latest being, *Zoence – A Science of Life*.

Address:
Roses Farmhouse
Epwell Road
Tysoe
Warwick
CV35 OTN
England
Tel: +44 (0)1295 688185
Fax: +44 (0)1295 680770

Zoence Academy

Zoence Academy organises and runs the Training Course in science and practical application of Zoence.

The Francis Bacon Research Trust

The Francis Bacon Research Trust is an educational charity established especially to research and make known the lives, work, philosophy and wisdom teachings of Sir Francis Bacon, the Rosicrusians and Shakespeare, inheritors of the Western Wisdom Tradition and practitioners of an earlier version of Zoence.

Note

This chapter is adapted from a presentation in October 1995 at the Eco-villages Conference, Findhorn.

We are all striving to do the same thing, which is to make this world a better place to live in, and ourselves better people in the process. I hope that as we learn to live more harmoniously with each other and with the land, with the world, we will appreciate the sense and the spirit of place much more. We will come to recognise its needs, come to recognise its purposes. Because it is the landscape which supports everything else: it is the foundation of everything else – the foundation of all the vegetable, animal and of the human kingdom. It is our home that we live in and depend on. It is there with its intelligence, its spirit: it is there with its purpose. It has its needs. When we get it right, when we have joy in the landscape and give joy back to the landscape, the landscape rejoices.

I've seen many seeming miracles that happen when you get it right and celebrate where you are and not just who you are. When you celebrate where you are, and you give joy to the landscape, something happens, miracles occur. Sometimes we dismiss them as coincidences, but I think coincidences can be defined as two different realities coinciding at the same time in a meaningful way.

I have also noticed that if we abuse the landscape we don't just pollute it physically, we also pollute it mentally and emotionally. The landscape, as well as a physically built environment, can take on an aura, an atmosphere, which is negative and difficult to cope with. For instance, if there's been a lot of sorrow lived by previous inhabitants of a house it gets into the fabric of the building and affects the consciousness of the building itself; and the next people who come into that building have to deal with that and change it, otherwise they can get sick. Many people are sick because they go and live in sick houses. This also spreads to the outer environment and environments can become sick too from what we do.

I also think environments become sick of their own accord because something in nature is not quite balanced. Nature has also its problems. Nature is evolving like we are, and I very much believe in the old teaching that humankind was created to be the gardener of the world, the gardener of the planet. So we help the plants to grow in the right places, we help the mountains in their evolution even. You help shape the land to make it even more beautiful than before and tune into that process.

A great key is to attune very carefully to the intelligence of the land and listen to it. So one of the main things for us to remember is that our environment, our landscape, is an intelligent entity with its own life, which is allowing us to participate in that life and in that consciousness. It has some similarities with ourselves: like us it is composed of patterns of energy. If you could see the landscape with different eyes you'd see it as all energy. We're all energy: we're forms of energy, containing focal points of energy which focus consciousness in us as well. The landscape is very similar.

We each have polarity: top and bottom. If you think about it, we could not exist without polarity. Our manifestation occurs because of polarity: top and bottom, left and right, front and back, inside and outside. The landscape is the same: you find polarity, for instance, in the hills and the valleys, the mountains and the lakes, what's above and what's below, hot and cold, wet and dry, and so on. And these polarities enable creation and manifestation to take place. In fact it is possible to discover that the greater the polarities, the greater is the potential for the creativity of that place to happen. Or in ourselves, like in our relationships, if two very different people come together and make a good relationship – a loving, kind, friendly relationship – their creativity can be enormous; rather than if you have two very identical people coming together, when it is easier to get on with each other but it is not so dynamic and easy to be creative. The landscape is the same.

Also like us the landscape manifests within its pattern certain places that have a distinct character, purpose and power. We have them in our own body. I mean we have a head, focus of our thinking, we have a chest, focus of our feeling nature, our emotions, and we have an abdomen, for all the assimilation, procreation and the generative willpower for getting things done. This is lovely architecture – threefold architecture, manifesting the trinity of life. The landscape is not dissimilar from us. There is an art in this, because once you have recognised these three locations manifesting then the next thing that manifests is what is called in tradition the sevenfold nature. In our body it appears as the seven focal points called the seven chakras on the spine: crown, brow, throat, heart, solar plexus, sacral and root. This comes quite naturally as a progression from the three initial spaces. The three initial spaces come naturally from the polarity: top and bottom and the heart balanced between the polarity. We have this pattern in our body and the landscape has it, and there is always evolution trying to manifest it more and more in the most harmonious and beautiful way possible.

Flowing between all these areas of consciousness and purpose is energy, flowing energy, which is our life force – our very life force. If it gets blocked in us we have problems and can get really ill, and a lot of the therapies that take place now are simply to unblock these energy flows in us, often caused by emotional trauma. It can be caused through physical things and mental hang-ups too. The landscape can also be blocked in its energy flows. Our buildings can be blocked in their energy flows, creating sickness; ill health occurs and causes changes in people's behaviour.

For centuries, sacred architecture has been trying to deal with this subject: so natural, universal design is incorporated into the architecture itself. This threefold, sevenfold design is found throughout the world. The sacred buildings are great universities and 'books' for us to study and to appreciate. Most sacred churches and temples are located very carefully on chakra points in the landscape, the focal points of consciousness and purpose in the landscape. These buildings are located in a meaningful way, in an attempt to try and enhance the landscape, and for the landscape to enhance whatever we do. It is very possible to work in co-operation with nature in this way. That is what the ancient sages tried to do, and hopefully what we still try to do today.

At the top of the next page you will see a rough diagram of a human body, showing approximately the seven major chakra points. Sacred architecture has tried to imitate this – to imitate our own structure, as also the structure that is in the landscape itself, recognising that there are similarities there. There is

The Chakras

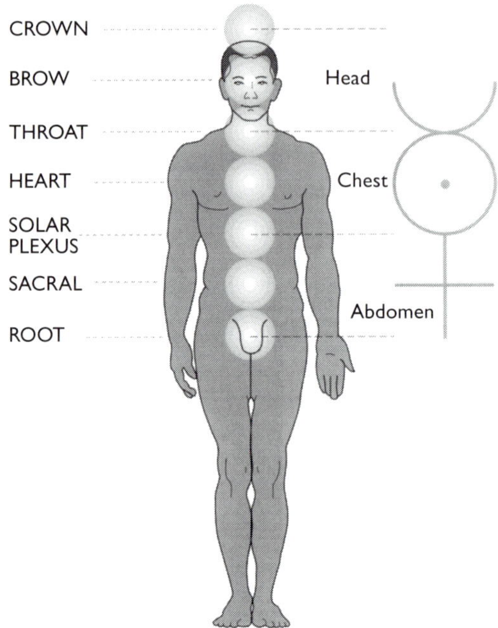

Plan of Cathedral

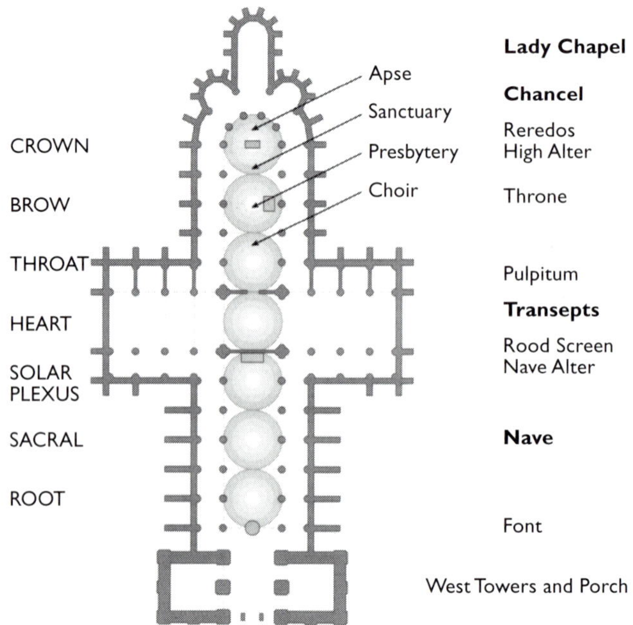

a harmony and a harmonic that takes place. Just as an example, the second diagram gives an archetypal plan of a cathedral. You can see how the architects of these sacred structures tried to make a cathedral like a person lying on the ground, with their back on the ground and face up to the sky. The Church calls it the 'crucifixion' form: I like to think of it as embracing the universe in love, in joy, in wonder.

You can see how the nave, where most people sit, contains the chakras that belong to our abdomen. Then, where the transept crosses the nave (called the crossing), is the central tower rising up, marking the heart centre. The heart centre is based at that central place. The heart is actually the most important part of the building, just as it's the most important centre in our body. From the heart the polarities are set up, and everything else. It is the seat of our divinity, our life. In the church that heart centre is recognised as being the centre of the cosmic cross. You can stand in that crossing, in a cathedral, and you can look up towards the east end, you can look back to the west end, look to your right and to your left in the transepts, and then you can look above, up the tower, and you can feel below your feet the foundations going deep into the earth: a wonderful cosmic cross, with yourself standing in its centre, the heart of the cosmos.

Then, if you go up further up the church into the place called the chancel, you find the chakras associated with the head: the throat where the choir sing and the Word is spoken; the brow chakra where the bishop sits on a throne (called the cathedra), from where he can see and be in charge of what goes on in the church (the brow or ajna chakra is the chakra of perception and command); and then right at the east end the crown chakra in which the high altar is placed, providing the place for that final wonder or joy (communion is pure joy) to manifest.

Church services are designed to work with the energies in a creative way in that form of architecture. These things you can also find in the environment. For example, if you go round looking at churches you'll find that most churches dedicated to St. Michael are placed on high points in the landscape: you don't find them low down, you find them high up. In terms of the landscape chakra system, you'll find that these are usually on crown chakras in the landscape, and they are dedicated to St. Michael for that reason – it is like a code, a language, a myth if you like, that tells you what is going on. Myths are very important – myths are ways we use to describe things that are otherwise very difficult to describe to each other: and myths are related to the landscape. You find that every myth has a relationship to people and to landscape: you cannot separate the two. Myths are a great way to learn and a great way to convey teaching: so the myth of St. Michael with the Dragon tells a great deal about what is going on in us and in the landscape.

You find that churches dedicated to St. Mary, the mother, are usually either at the root chakra, associated with water, or in the heart, symbol of the heart centre. Mary signifies the purest and most loving part of us, located in the heart, out of which the light of love is born. You will find St. Peter churches, for instance, usually in the throat chakra. St. Peter was known as the spokesman or hierophant of the apostles: he was the speaker, and so St. Peter churches were usually placed on throat chakras in the landscape.

So it is a whole knowledge and a whole language being shown in our sacred tradition. The architecture was an attempt to enhance these places in the landscape in ways that helped the landscape and helped our own society to evolve in a good way, so that each has joy in the other. It was also very carefully guarded knowledge. It's a knowledge that we all need to learn now but it was once a very carefully guarded knowledge because it was misused, and when misused could lead to terrible hardship and crimes.

An example of this is the Normans who were the first to build castles to dominate the English countryside. They found in the landscape the brow chakra points and built their castles on these brow chakras. In that way they were able to dominate the psyche of the people as well as being physically in control, because they knew how to do this. There are more modern examples of misusing its knowledge in order to dominate and control the psyche of whole nations – the Nazis being one. There is a real danger in the unwitting or deliberate misuse of such knowledge; and yet at the same time it is so imperative that we have a good knowledge of it so that we do the right things in the right places for the right reasons – for then we can live in harmony with nature and with each other, enhancing all life.

There are different ways of discovering patterns in the landscape and working with them. One way is simply by instinct: or, to take that a step further, by intuition. Many wonderful places were built or developed in the past, which manifested the chakra systems (and still do), which were built quite intuitively. Then there is a step further where a certain amount of conscious inner guidance comes into it as well, which is certainly the case with Findhorn, Scotland. Knowledge is gradually added to that.

The map of Findhorn Park (*opposite*) is an example. I don't know whether the community were conscious of creating chakras or not, but they are manifesting, and manifesting rather wonderfully! The Universal Hall, although not built first, has a very important function.

There's a double scheme in process of manifestation at Findhorn – a smaller scheme laid on top of a larger scheme in such a way that the head of the one scheme lies on the heart of the other. Now this isn't unusual – it happens in nature and is often built into sacred architecture. It is expressed, for instance, in the icon of the Madonna and Child – a very old icon – where the Christ child, or Horus in the Egyptian Mysteries, has his head on the heart of the mother, so the head and heart relate to each other.

Now there is a very deep mystery in this. One of the ways, for instance, for coming in tune with our own higher self, or guardian angel as some people call it, is to actually become aware that standing behind you is a beautiful being, a loving being, and you can just rest your head gently in the heart of that being. It is a beautiful thing to do. Try it if you haven't tried it – have a go. Some traditions call the angel or 'Mother' the Comforter, because she bestows such comfort in this way. This works because at the nape of your neck there is an

FINDHORN PARK

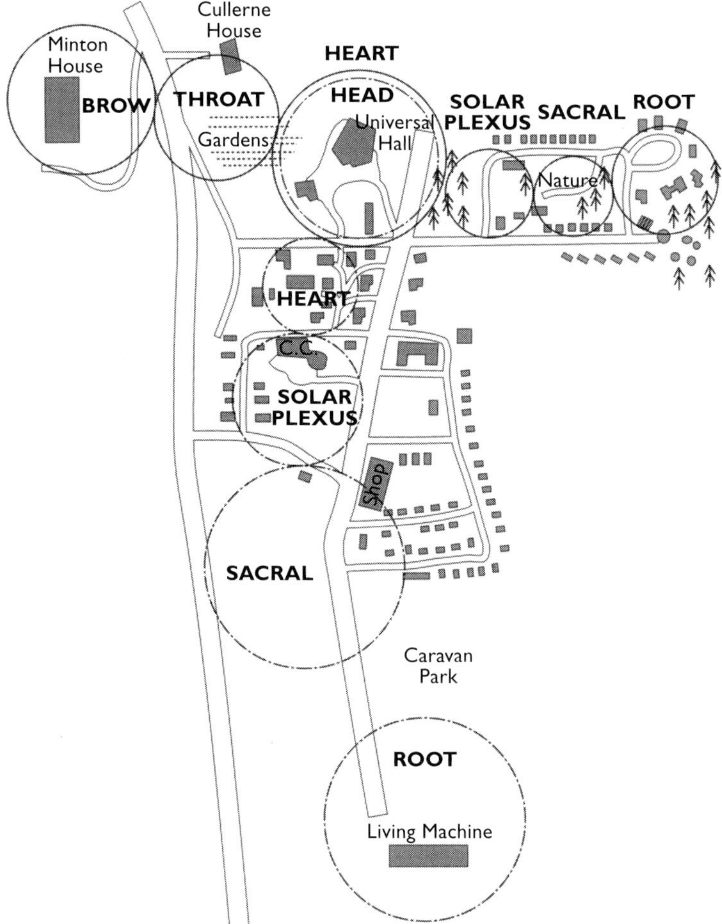

eighth chakra – referred to as the alta major chakra – which is linking with that angelic heart centre and uniting with that higher heart centre in a special way. It allows inspiration and divine love to enter into our hearts from the heart of the angel, our higher or 'Madonna' self; and the angel keeps this aflame in our hearts by continually breathing into us further inspiration to fan the flame of our heart. We do it, the landscape does it, and at Findhorn it is happening.

The foundation of the Findhorn community, the first caravan, with the original garden around it, marks the first heart centre. The first landscape chakra system of the Findhorn community is derived from this centre, extending north-south. The head of this first pattern, which is still in the process of manifestation, is marked, it would seem, by the Universal Hall and its surrounding gardens, to the north of the Caddy's caravan.

The chakras of the landscape abdomen are to be found emerging to the south of the caravan: so, for instance, you can obtain your good food in the solar plexus (or stomach) part of the body, and this is where we find the Community Centre with its dining facilities – an absolutely appropriate place to have restaurants and food making. Also, for the general population, the solar plexus chakra is where most people feel happiest. It is the area where in cities and towns most of the successful shops and restaurants appear. Then you get down more into the nitty gritty of trading and industry and so on when you get to the sacral chakra area. In this Findhorn pattern that is emerging the sacral area contains the shop and office for the caravan park – the business aspect of the site. Then, located in the root at the south end of the caravan site, forming a wonderful root chakra, is the new 'living machine', recently installed for the ecologically sound and safe disposal of waste. Wonderful!

The other pattern that is manifesting on the site is an east-west orientated scheme. The Universal Hall is the heart centre for this pattern, just as it is the head centre for the first pattern. As you go further to the east from the hall there is an area that is not owned by the Findhorn Community (as yet, but I expect the intelligence of this place will bring that about somehow!), marking the solar plexus, with the old runway between it and the hall manifesting the diaphragm (sometimes known as the 'veil'). Further east you get to the nature area – the nature garden. Now nature places of this kind, with their nature beings, flourish extremely well in the lower chakra areas, for they provide the foundation of life. Such a place brings prosperity, in the true sense of the word. (An industrial wasteland is its antithesis.) To acknowledge the 'fairy' nature beings (as distinct from the angelic) in the sacral and root chakras is a wonderful thing to do: so it is a great thing that is happening there. Also appropriate are the offices, workshops and studios situated in this area. The root chakra with its experimental ecological houses (Bag End and the Barrel houses) and its forest, and its access to the beach, is a very important area.

To the west of the Universal Hall is Cullerne House and gardens, in the throat chakra area, whilst across the road at the west end of the whole energy pattern is Minton House and gardens, with its grand and meditative open view across the bay, marking the head of this evolving landscape scheme.

It is very important to recognise, to mark in some way and to respect every polarity – each pole of the landscape – because all manifestation depends on that polarity. The heart is the other primary focal point which should be well respected, which of course it is here at Findhorn – both in the Universal Hall and in the original site of the first Caddy caravan.

A lovely pattern is emerging. I don't think it was deliberately or consciously done, but from what I know it was done through careful attunement and guidance, and this is the wonder of what can happen when we allow that guidance to come into our lives.

There are other examples of these things that I'd like to perhaps mention. Mediaeval towns in Europe have grown up intuitively, instinctively, but also with guidance and knowledge. The monks and the nuns were guided to build their churches on certain sites and sometimes they did it with knowledge (especially in the early days of the Church), because this knowledge has been passed down. True knowledge comes when you begin with your intuition, your loving, sensitive guidance, and then you work it out in your mind and see what it all means, and then put it into practice. Because you've done it, you see how it works, give thanks, and then you have real knowledge, real enlightenment, as a result of the experience. That's what I usually refer to when I talk about knowledge.

There are a lot of examples of mediaeval towns where it is possible to see this pattern, this chakra system manifested, as also the polarities of left and right and what that means. It is a great science; but modern cities and modern societies unfortunately make it very difficult to be intuitive any more and to find the right place to build things; a situation which results in the world having the most terrible city sprawls and ugly environments imaginable. Such horrors arise from absolutely no appreciation of the landscape. This pollutes the landscape psychologically as well as physically and makes this world a sick place in which to live.

There have been places that have grown up by means of a mixture of intuition and knowledge, and also places that have a great amount of knowledge in them. One such is on Iona. Iona this beautiful island on the west coast of Scotland that is so sacred and made famous largely because of St. Columba. But it was a holy island even before St. Columba went there, and it has its own energy pattern of chakras in the landscape. It also has a double pattern, not unlike Findhorn but not the same either.

St. Columba built his community of Celtic monks on one of the major chakras of the Iona landscape temple. After Columba others came, the Roman Catholic Benedictines and the Augustinians, and built a monastery and a nunnery on the island. A village grew up as a result, and a road was built through the centre. When kings and other people died, and the population wanted to honour them, their bodies were taken to Iona and carried along this road, called the Road of the Dead. The boats used to land in Martyrs Bay and then the mourners would process along the Road of the Dead, from the sandy bay all the way up to a small, isolated and rocky hillock, called the Hill of the Dead, located within Columba's original foundation. The bodies of the dead would then be placed on the hill for a few days before they were buried near the abbey at the side of the road.

There was a whole ceremony of rites for the dead. It was thought to help the souls of those who had died to get released from the physical body and go as far as possible up into what we call the heavenly realms. This is what they believed. I think it is absolutely true and I believe I have seen it happen myself many times. One of the functions of temples is to facilitate this process, so that we don't get a lot of earthbound souls lying around this planet. These rites were to help those souls reach heaven to get out of the pull of this world – to reach heaven and to go on in their evolution, and the atmosphere of Iona gave special help to those thought worthy of such help or honour.

St. Columba, recognising the Hill of the Dead as a crown chakra in a local landscape temple stretching from Martyr's Bay to the Hill of the dead, then used that crown energy and set up a brow chakra for himself, like a bishop in a cathedral or abbot in an abbey, to see and command what was going on. His abbot's seat was on another rocky hillock, to the south of the Hill of the Dead and to the side of what later became the Road of the Dead. On this rocky eminence he built his cell. The rest of his community made a circle of cells in front of him, to the east, with the church probably in the centre. Later the site of the Celtic church was developed into the great abbey of the Augustinian monks, which still exists today in its restored state.

A hundred yards or so to the south of St. Columba's eminence is another rocky hillock, creating a natural marker for the throat chakra of the landscape temple. To the east of this was built St. Oran's chapel, the earliest building still existing. St. Oran's chapel, restored this century, is nowadays like it used to be – wonderful for singing in, as befits a throat centre. Round it is the graveyard.

The Celtic monks built huge earth embankments around these head and throat chakras, forming an enclosure. The entrance to the enclosure, in the south, marked the heart chakra, where now stands St. Columba's Hotel. (This is extraordinary. We've found this to be a wonderful heart centre of this whole area: so it's a good place to stay.)

Down in the solar plexus of this local landscape temple, whose spine is marked by the Road of the Dead, there is the church for the main community – those who have not committed themselves through vows to such a serious, disciplined life as the monks. It is here that the village starts. The solar plexus is where the majority of people prefer to be (they find heart energy or energy of the brow and head usually too strong to cope with when they are just wanting to be free and easy).

The nunnery was built in the sacral area. This follows a very ancient pattern of design which you can find throughout the world in different cultures, where the priests would go to the throat or brow, and the priestesses would go to the sacral area. From these two polarities they would try to relate and work with each other in a creative way.

So there we have a plan and structure laid out by human beings, utilising the landscape features to manifest the chakras and create a local landscape temple on the east side of the island of Iona. Obviously the people who started it knew what they were doing and were trying to make something that would help them a lot. Iona was the capital for a powerful religious endeavour for quite a time – a lot of the Celtic church influence spread from there.

Edinburgh, as a mediaeval town, also uses energies of the landscape in ways which enhance the landscape and its purpose – and those energies also enhance the purpose of the city. That is probably a good reason why it became the capital of Scotland, rather than another place. The castle itself, on the castle rock, not only marks the crown and brow chakras of the Edinburgh landscape temple, but is also a major focal point in a much bigger landscape pattern. It marks the brow chakra in the greater landscape, and it is this quality of energy which is utilised in the castle in the same way that the Normans captured the brow chakras in England.

On the top of the castle rock, crowning it, is St. Margaret's Chapel. If you go there you can obtain a wonderful crowning expansion of consciousness. It is a beautiful place, and dearly loved. It is both loved and protected by the military guard there, and by people who visit the chapel as pilgrims. The only military purpose of the fortress now is to guard the sacred relics (crown jewels) of Scotland and St. Margaret's Chapel. It's a lovely function.

Immediately below the castle walls, which wind like a labyrinth around the summit of the volcanic hill, outside the castle entrance on the south side, is an open space from which a grand view can be obtained all over Edinburgh. Forming the brow chakra of Edinburgh it is possible see the Pentland hills to the south, the sea and coast of Fife to the north, the castle to the west and the mediaeval town to the east. It is a wonderful view point, and even has an observatory there, as a fitting symbol of this brow chakra.

Descending the hill along the spinal road of mediaeval Edinburgh's Royal Mile you come to the throat area, a chakra which provides very good energy for cultural things to emerge. So it is very interesting that in Edinburgh what you have here is the Art Gallery, the Theatre and the Library – all within that throat energy. They are drawing on that energy, helping those functions to take place and to maintain themselves. At the same time the functions that we create are helping the landscape.

Further down the Royal Mile you come to the heart area which is built around St. Giles Cathedral. Here also is the Parliament House. It's rather good having the Parliament in the heart, rather than up in the brow, so that the rulership of the people comes from the heart, the seat of divinity. Outside St. Giles Cathedral there is even a heart made of stones set in the pavement. It's called the Heart of Midlothian. So it's actually got a physical heart you can stand on.

After this, descending the road further to the east, you find all the main shops and hotels in the solar plexus area, where most people congregate. It is a busy area of the town. Down in the sacral area old Edinburgh used to have its 'red light' district. It's been cleaned up now, but that was a manifestation of one of the sacral functions. In the root chakra was once the main gate (Canon Gate) to the city, through which the canons from Holyrood Abbey used to process, guarded by Canon Gate Kirk.

Right at the base of the root chakra and foot of the hill there is Holyrood Palace, that was built following a dream and guidance given to David I of Scotland. He was married to the patron saint of Scotland, St. Margaret, whose chapel crowns the crown chakra of Edinburgh. David founded the Abbey right by a sacred spring in Holyrood Park, also dedicated to St. Margaret.

Thus in this landscape temple there is the geomantic symbolism (and reality) of a source of water in the root chakra, which is itself at the foot of an ancient volcanic hill. Polarising this is the summit of the lava core of the fiery volcano, high in the air and bathed in the fire or light of the sun. Edinburgh is stretched out on the slope of the hill between the two – a fabulous temple in the landscape.

To summarise: in terms of our relationship to the environment, there are certain things which are important to remember and to do. First, to attune to the spirit of the place and its purpose. Secondly, to feel how the place relates to the rest of the country and then to the whole world, so that we don't live in isolation, in a bubble. We can feel our relation to the rest of humanity and the rest of the planet, and at the same time know that we are important, that we play a vital function in a vital place for the planet, as part of the whole. Thirdly, if we can, to recognise the chakras, to mark them and to enhance them in the best and most appropriate ways possible, especially the heart centres and the two polarities of crown and root; and then to ensure that the landscape energy flows freely through those chakras, through those areas, in a creative and joyful way.

Often there can be blockages in the flow, not only in landscapes and cityscapes, but also, for instance, in a house. Houses have their own chakras too. You usually get the kitchen in the sacral area, the work-place; the eating place – the dining room or area – in the solar plexus. The place where the family like to meet for comfort, relaxation and so on, forms the heart area. The throat is often part of that main family area, but if it is separate it often manifests as a quiet room for study or music. You often get bedrooms in the brow chakra, with the chakra system winding upstairs to the upper floor; but if you have a big house you might have a library or an office manifesting the brow chakra on the ground floor. In the crown chakra, if you are lucky to have the space, you can set up a sanctuary for meditation; but often a wall space or niche is all that is available and can be perfectly adequate. The root chakra is where storage and waste and so on are dealt with.

Houses have this natural pattern, and we make it instinctively because things work well in that way. You could say it is common sense; but that is because it arises out of a universal and basic law. However, if you get those chakras or their functions out of place – for instance, if you have to go from the dining room to the kitchen through a bedroom – you get a problem. What is actually happening at an energy level is that the energy of the house, associated with our movement and use of the building, is getting blocked or tied in knots: its not flowing properly from one chakra to another. It doesn't have to flow in a straight line – it can be in curves or circles – but the important thing is that it flows freely through the chakras in the right order. As we move through these places, we move the energy with us.

Then the last thing to note especially is to treat your house, your village, your environment, like a temple. This is important. Treat it as a holy place, a holy country, a holy land. If we can make it true that nature is our friend and we are nature's friend, as well as each other's friend, we'd have a wonderful world. With all the other ecological creativity we are discovering and doing at the moment, and our community lives that we are building up, we could have a paradise on earth. That is my hope and dream.

Reconnecting with the Earth

by Maddy Harland

Photo: Don Wood

Maddy Harland is an author and editor of *Permaculture Magazine – Solutions for Sustainable Living* and a director of Permanent Publications, a publishing company specialising in permaculture and other approaches to sustainable living. She is also on the editorial board of *The Organic Way*, the magazine of the Henry Doubleday Research Association. She lives and gardens in Hampshire with her husband Tim and their two young children, Hayley and Gail.

Address:
Permanent Publications
The Sustainability Centre
East Meon
Hampshire
GU32 1HR
England
Tel: +44 (0) 1730 823311
Fax: +44 (0) 1730 823322
Email: maddy@permaculture.co.uk
WWW: www.permaculture.co.uk

There has been a massive, fundamental change in how we live together, provide for our material needs and relate to the world. Our early ancestors hunted and gathered in forests, dependent on skills in foraging and the chase. Then came the discovery of basic agriculture; selecting seeds, propagation, sowing crops and harvesting. This harnessing of nature's inherent abundance created our own cultural abundance, allowing the time and energy to develop arts, crafts, science, religions.

Traditional agriculture, which removed the wildwoods and replaced them with pasture and arable fields, could only work in the context of small rural communities and a few cities. It required physical toil from farm labourers and was not productive enough to support large urban populations. As the discoveries of the industrial revolution changed the face of manufacture from small craft-based production to mass-production, how we lived, worked and sustained ourselves had to change. Employment, or at least the dream of 'easy' work, drew and still draws thousands to the cities. Cheap labour and technological innovation made possible large-scale systems – industrial manufacturing, monocultural chemical-based food production, off-the-shelf pharmaceutical medicines and now, genetically modified organisms.

DISASSOCIATION & ANGST

As cities and their suburbs have sprawled out, countryside and wilderness areas have shrunk and our gardens have increasingly reflected a cultural artificiality. Gardens have become collecting grounds for more and more hybridised and exotic plants which depend, like monocultural food production, on imports of chemicals, fossil fuels and dwindling natural resources to sustain them. Our attempts to hold dominion over nature are often fought most passionately on the immaculate, suburban lawn!

Advertising entices us to dream a consuming dream of comfort and leisure. In grasping at this dream, it has become necessary to deny the state of the earth and the predicament of many of our fellow human beings. This act of disassociation creates colossal angst – whether conscious or unconscious – which is at the core of our psychological and social conflicts.

We live in a world where the many challenges life throws at us are often the stuff of conflict rather than of harmony. For example, the majority of people in the North of the world now live in urban environments yet yearn for wide open spaces and the quiet solitude of the wilderness. As the Australian social activist Glen Ochre puts it, instead of belonging to the land, the land now 'belongs' only to a privileged few. Many people are disempowered by this monopoly of ownership and are consequently separated from the land and nature. At the same time, there are thousands of hectares of derelict urban land lying neglected (owned, of course, but fenced in and unused). In Britain alone, there are around 10,000 derelict sites totalling 40,000 hectares.

Symptomatic of our alienation from nature and disconnection from the land is our dysfunctional relationship with food and the way that we produce it. The British saga of Bovine Spongiform Encephalopathy (BSE) – mad cow disease – is a cogent example of this dysfunction. So distant is the food on our tables from the reality of how it is produced, that we allowed animal offal, innocuously marked as 'protein', to be fed to other livestock. This resulted in BSE in cows and Creutzfeldt Jakob disease (CJD) in humans.

Using genetically modified organisms in our seed banks is an even more dangerous example of our alienation from nature. No one knows the impact of 'Terminator Technology', the GMO which prevents the seeds of a special crop (sold as being disease resistant or high yielding) from germinating the following year. Worse than an F1 hybrid, this is a 'once only' hit designed to maximise seed company profit. We know why this technology has been developed – to make more money – but like the genetically engineered rape which unexpectedly cross breeds with wild mustard, we have no idea what effect GMOs will cause to our global environment. What we do know is that it will decrease seed saving of indigenous seeds and lessen biodiversity giving us less choice in the future. The engineering of genetic crops is an example of alienation from the natural world and the pursuit of wealth that has become a form of slow ecological suicide.

Personal & Planetary Healing

In the face of these cultural trends, it is easy to feel powerless and afraid and experience sickness and despair. To deal with this we can either hold on to a very controlled and edited view of the world, or seek ways in which to heal ourselves. 'Natural' medicine and wanting to eat organic foods are positive responses to this need to heal ourselves without pharmaceuticals and feed ourselves with the products of industrial agriculture. As more and more people look at their own health holistically, the boundaries between personal and planetary health begin to dissolve. It becomes harder to separate the well-being of ourselves from the well-being of the earth which nurtures us.

But it is not enough to have healthy bodies, good intentions and harmonious thoughts. The need to truly reconnect with the natural world and stop destroying it has never been so pressing. We have to learn to live harmoniously with all creation, not only on a spiritual level, but also in our physical environment. To do this we must also learn to live with each other.

To move forward out of this dark and painful predicament requires making fundamental changes. It is clear that the people of the affluent, 'developed' world cannot go on plundering the earth to feed and shelter ourselves at the expense of the two thirds 'undeveloped' world, who are understandably knocking on the door of material comfort wanting to come in and share Western standards of living. The West has wealth, material goods, technology, and is geared to fulfil the consumer's dream. But the industrialisation necessary to produce this standard of living has cost the West as well. Extended families have disintegrated, community support systems have collapsed and the great god 'Time' has enslaved us. 'West' is not necessarily 'best' and the repercussions of thinking that have ricocheted throughout all of the world, undermining the wisdom and values of more traditional cultures have promoted an unsustainable materialistic culture. Limited resources will eventually force us beyond this empty materialism. To do this, we need a change in our culture and to find ways of repairing the earth which are open to ordinary people, not just scientists and experts. We need to reconnect with the natural world which nurtures our psyche and of which we are a part.

Permaculture – Repairing Ecological Damage

One approach to repairing ecological damage is by using permaculture. Permaculture is not a dogma or a religion but an ecological design system. Writer, Emma Chapman, defines it thus:

> *"Permaculture, originally 'Permanent Agriculture', is often viewed as a set of gardening techniques, but it has in fact developed into a whole design philosophy, and for some people a philosophy for life. Its central theme is the creation of human systems which provide for human needs, by using many natural elements and drawing inspiration from natural ecosystems. Its goals and priorities coincide with what many people see as the core requirements for sustainability."*
>
> Permaculture Magazine

Permaculture tackles how to grow food, build houses, and create communities and minimise environmental impact at the same time. It does not advocate a return to peasant agriculture, which is labour intensive, nor an increase in conventional organic agriculture, which still depends on machinery and a transport infrastructure. Organic agriculture, though preferable to chemical agriculture, consumes more energy than it produces and does not provide a sustainable solution to the problem of producing food without irrevocably damaging the environment. Instead permaculture offers a low energy input alternative. Its principles are being constantly developed and refined by people all over the world in different climates and cultures.

A forest garden is a good example of permaculture design. Imagine a natural forest. It has a high canopy of trees, lower layers of small trees, large and small shrubs, and herb and ground layer plants, including plants which are mainly below ground and climbers which occupy all these layers. The production of plant material is mind-boggling compared to a wheat field which is only a single layer of plants occupying about half a metre of vertical space.

The trouble is, we cannot eat much of what grows in a natural forest. Instead, we can take the principles of the multi-layered forest and select wild and cultivated plants which yield food, fibre, biomass for building and heating, plants to increase soil fertility and species to support wildlife. We can also create clearings and vertical 'edges', places where the sun can penetrate to ripen fruit and vegetables. We can't grow the ingredients of a loaf of bread here, but you can grow many perennial and self-seeding plants which either crop or store throughout the year. What we are creating is a system which is relatively self-sufficient in energy terms and does not require many resources to be imported from far away.

We can complement a forest garden with grain growing systems, by using Masanoba Fukuoka's system of natural farming or by developing the work of pioneers such as Wes Jackson, an agriculturist who is part of a movement to discover and select perennial grains and grow them in a permanent pasture.

Growing food with low inputs is one example of permaculture design but the principles of permaculture are incredibly versatile and are not limited to the production of food in a home garden or perennial pasture. They can be applied to the design of any human systems, from an average household to architecture, town planning, water supply and purification, and even to commercial and financial systems.

Permaculture draws upon both traditional methods and modern innovation. It also draws upon the skills and needs of individuals. Permaculture uses nature as a model for consciously designing sustainable systems to suit individual circumstances. The aim is to use the power of the human brain, applied to design, to replace human brawn or fossil fuel energy and the pollution that goes with it. It is a system of both earth repair and people care and is a practical way of creating personal and planetary harmony.

The Need For Research

Permaculture is, however, an evolving discipline and is barely beyond its adolescence. Like other new models, it needs research. We need to test these fledgling ideas to find out their potential and quantify the yields produced in alternative ways of growing food and see exactly how efficient ecological designs and techniques for buildings are. We need to research methods of renewable energy generation, work out the embodied energy costs of manufacturing devices and find out which are appropriate for individual circumstances. In short, we need to find ways of building co-operative partnerships between all kinds of people and groups, technologists, manufacturers and end users.

It is for this reason that I have become involved in a project in Hampshire, England which is converting 20 hectares of a former military base into a centre which will demonstrate ecological building, sustainable land use, nature conservation, traditional woodland management and its accompanying tasks and crafts, encourage eco-tourism and provide a local focus for green businesses. The centre plans to provide training courses and research facilities plus education for specialists and the general public, young and old, formal and informal.

The long-term vision is that this regional centre will be one of many throughout Britain and beyond, and will be the foundation of new research and development into ecologically sound ways of living. The co-operating partners in this project come from diverse backgrounds and include local people, local government, further education colleges, and even the Ministry of Defence. Here the British Army and Navy have pledged practical support as conservation volunteers. Who knows, this may be a precursor of the eco-village, a concept which is currently such an anathema to British planning law. I hope that projects of this type will encourage more research and experimentation in sustainable technology and land-use, inspiring people new to these subjects to come and have a look at the alternatives being explored on the ground.

The Personal Effects of Permaculture

What happens when we start practising permaculture? Firstly, we begin to look at the impact we have on the earth and try to lighten the load. An easy way to begin is to start with growing our own food. Replacing externally produced resources with home grown resources is important. There are many simple ways to do this, including composting all organic matter; using composted and recycled materials to mulch and build soil fertility; using recycled materials for construction; joining a Local Exchange Trading Scheme to find skills and materials within the local community; joining a local permaculture group to share information, tools, practical tasks, seeds and plants; getting involved in projects which benefit the local community and its environment, and so on...

In the garden, we can discover a whole new world of interesting foods: perennial and self-seeding salad plants and delicious varieties of fruit that you will never find in the supermarket. Our diets change, the food we eat is seasonally based and gardening makes us more aware of the rhythms of nature.

Permaculture actively encourages wildlife into the garden, using techniques like companion planting, mixing herbs, trees, bushes and vegetables with flowers which attract beneficial insects. Habitat creation is also important. Ponds, however tiny, attract frogs and toads, log piles attract hedgehogs and these creatures in turn prey upon slugs and snails. The aim is to control pests by creating a stable ecology with a diversity of species. Stability and diversity help create an environment with healthier plants which can resist disease. As well as the satisfaction of feeding ourselves fresh, organic food, the gardener welcomes frogs, toads, hedgehogs and all manner of insects and native birds into the garden. On balance, it is a better way to garden than using slug pellets which not only poison their intended victims but also visiting birds like song thrushes.

For me, Spring is connected to vibrant shoots of winter hardy greens; Summer to the fragrant perfume of greengages; Autumn to the abundance of plums, pears, apples, blackberries, sloes...; and Winter for rest and consolidation, whilst we gorge our way through home-grown stores until early Spring comes round again. Co-operating with the patterns of nature year after year creates a deep inner awakening. This contact with the soil reminds us that we are an integral part of nature, rather than feeling shut out and excluded.

Permaculture can design more than houses, gardens or farms. It can also design community structures. For example, at the core of our publishing company are key permaculture principles. People not goods are the key local resource. All employees live within a five mile radius of each other. This engenders a greater sense of community and also minimises car use by allowing lift sharing. We swap plants, share our food surpluses, lend tools, equipment and other resources, help each other out and have an interest in each other's families. The downside is that if we fall out with each other we can't avoid meeting in the village! But this closer connection requires that conflicts are resolved for the sake of that community and not just ignored, as they can be in more impersonal working environments. Resourcing our needs locally is also very important. First we try to trade with local suppliers. This reduces fuel consumption, contributes to the local economy and creates many useful networks.

Diversity is as important as resourcing locally. There is no human stereotype found here. Among us are a teenager, student placements, parents (single and 'nuclear') and grandparents. This range in age is matched by a diversity of life skills and backgrounds, adding to the richness and challenge of learning to work together. Other permaculture principles such as 'each important function is supported by many elements', 'energy cycling' and 'edge effects' are also incorporated into the design of the company as they not only make the organisation more efficient but they also help us to achieve our aims – to make available useful information for empowering individuals to create a better environment for people and our planet. And yes, we do reuse and recycle our waste wherever possible and we don't have a weekly waste collection!

SPIRITUAL RECONNECTION

This is a spiritual reconnection as well as an ecological strategy. The scientist, James Lovelock, theorises that the earth is an interconnected living organism, Gaia, which has the ability to self-regulate. This theory is based on Lovelock's scientific observations but many people regard it as a breakthrough which echoes the experience of mystics all over the world since time immemorial. In states of enlightenment, the mystic realises the timeless interconnection of all things. Instead of experiencing beginnings and endings and fragments of time and space, consciousness exists in a seamless web of life, flowing in and out of cycles yet always existing as a whole beyond them.

To find this state in meditation and other spiritual practices is a great gift. Yet it is so hard to translate the mystical experience into ordinary life. It is hard to contact the unity of all things whilst hurrying to work, bringing up children, nursing dying loved ones and carrying out the duties and responsibilities that are a consequence of human life. It is easy to lose the vision of the divine whilst being focused on the temporal and particular. Yet in the subconscious of all of us is this knowledge of connection and we reflect the yearning for it by always trying to become 'whole'.

The simple acts of growing and eating our own food; recreating habitats in which nature's diversity thrives, and taking steps to live more simply are practical ways of living which connect us to an awareness of the seamless whole. As we begin to heal the earth, we inevitably begin to heal ourselves and to harmonise our relationships. This is a powerful form of conflict resolution – the resolution of the distress caused by our current unsustainable presence on this earth.

REFERENCES

Bell, G., 1995. The *Permaculture Garden*. London: HarperCollins.

Mollison, B., 1996. *Permaculture: A Designers' Manual*. Australia: Tagari.

Morrow, R., *Earth User's Guide to Permaculture*. Kangaroo Press:

Permaculture Magazine – Ecological Solutions for Everyday Living. Hampshire: Permanent Publications.

Whitefield, P., 1998. *How To Make A Forest Garden*. Hampshire: Permanent Publications.

Whitefield, P., 1997. *Permaculture In A Nutshell*. Hampshire: Permanent Publications.

For more information on publications and information on permaculture and related subjects, please request a free copy of *The Earth Repair Catalogue*, from the address given at the start of this contribution.

EVOLUTIONARY CIRCLES
A New Process for Personal and Planetary Transformation
by Barbara Marx Hubbard

Barbara Marx Hubbard is an author, futurist, social architect and public speaker. She is dedicated to connecting, communicating and strengthening humanity's capacities for a positive future. Her books include *The Revelation: A Message of Hope for the New Millennium*, *The Hunger of Eve* and *The Evolutionary Journey*.

Her latest book is *Conscious Evolution: Awakening the Power of Our Social Potential*. She is the President of the Foundation for Conscious Evolution and a founding board member of The World Future Society.

In 1984, Hubbard's name was placed in nomination for the Vice Presidency of the United States with her Campaign for a Positive Future.

She has designed a Master's Degree Program in Conscious Evolution to establish this new meta-discipline to assist us in becoming responsible for the ethical guidance of evolution on a planetary scale.

Address:
The Foundation for Conscious Evolution
PO Box 6397
San Rafael
CA 94903–0397
USA
Tel: +1 415 454 8191
Fax: +1 415 454 8805
Email: fce@peaceroom.org
WWW: www.cocreation.org

INTRODUCTION

When we view our predicament on earth and ask: What is wrong here? What is the problem? There will be many responses but all would stem from one fundamental root cause. It is the illusion that we are separate from each other, from nature and from spirit. Our nervous systems are so designed that we suffer from this illusion. It is the tragedy of the human race. It has caused all the cruelty we have wreaked upon one another as well as upon nature and other species.

Our lack of empathy has reached an almost fatal point for we have gained the power to destroy our world. The separated mind has given us the tools of destruction through science and technology. It has brought us to the point of possible annihilation of our life support system. It has produced weapons that can destroy life on Earth.

Yet at the same time, many people from every culture, tradition and discipline seem to be awakening to oneness, to attunement and to the passionate desire to harmonise with the whole of which each of us is a part. The problems we face are evolutionary drivers, stimulating us to seek new means of conflict resolution, new forms of social co-operation, and deeper ways of communion with one another and all being. We might assume that in response to the social, ecological predicament, there is emerging on planet Earth a new humanity, a universal humanity, ordinary men and women overcoming this illusion of separation within ourselves, personally, in our families, workplaces, communities and world.

The difficulty is that our social systems and customs do not facilitate that aspect of ourselves which seeks greater harmony. In most cases we are trained to compete, to win, to gain supremacy over one another in a win-lose world.

What can we do to reinforce the growing human tendency for harmony, for healing the wounds of separation? The answer that is emerging everywhere is the ancient, yet ever new form of the circle of peers, the core group, the council, the support group. This 'social architecture' fosters love and truth, it encourages mutual support, sensitivity and harmony.

In my own work at the Foundation for Conscious Evolution we have developed a unique kind of circle designed specifically to nurture in ourselves the emerging 'universal human' in harmony with all being. We call them Evolutionary Circles.

Evolutionary Circles

Evolutionary Circles are created when a small number of community members meet regularly on a weekly basis for a specified period of time. These Circles are seed beds for a human ecology of harmony and inner guidance that can form the foundation for eco-villages. The enduring basis of an eco-village must be sustainable consciousness. At this stage of our evolution, so many of us have had experiences of higher states of awareness, flashes of unitive consciousness, peak experiences of oneness, yet these moments are still unstable within us. They flicker on and off. The Evolutionary Circles are a way of stabilising our universal consciousness and keeping us connected with both our inner guidance and our awareness of the larger processes of creation that we are a part of. They could be used by an eco-village as a way of creating and maintaining harmony in the group, and of finding the way forward together. Through the 'resonance' fostered in the Circles, inspiration comes from the divine and not from the ego-level. Circles could become the 'glue' for a community to stick together.

The speciality of the Evolutionary Circle is to combine the inner work of spiritual growth with the outer work of learning the larger story of the evolution of our species, to help us fulfil our life purpose as conscious participants in the co-creation of our world.

Evolutionary circles consist of at least two, and up to twelve members. Seven is an optimum number to aim for. Meetings take approximately two and a half hours, and include three elements.

The Inner Work takes place during the first part of the meeting. After introductions and brief sharing of the news of our lives, a sacred space is established. Guides are rotated. A meditation to open the heart is given. A declaration of purpose is stated, such as:

> "We are gathered here together as a deep communion of pioneering souls from every culture and tradition to give birth within ourselves to the universal human, the co-creator of new worlds.
>
> "We accept assistance from beloved teachers and masters, knowing that it is now our turn to be the universal human ourselves..."

Then speaking from within, listening actively to one another, each person does a spiritual check-in, responding to this question: Where am I in my spiritual journey in this moment?

Then follows 'shadow work' and confession: Where am I off the mark? Where do I need forgiveness or to forgive? Do I experience any fear in this moment? What is the sacred gift underneath the fear?

Finally we affirm those qualities in ourselves which we require to become our full potential self. We ask ourselves: What qualities of myself as a universal human do I now affirm? What guidance do I receive as to my next step in embodying the qualities I choose? Each person affirms the chosen qualities and receives support from the group. During the week a journal is kept, noting the actual progress made toward the realisation of the desired characteristics.

The key to the inner work key is resonance, resounding, echoing back to one another the higher qualities which we affirm. Resonance creates a field of love which calls forth the emerging self. It feels exciting and affirming, encouraging us to express ourselves more deeply and truly than ever before. Resonance creates a harmony that amplifies our inner self and unites us with the inner self of other members of the group. Where two or more are gathered in a resonant field, the indwelling spirit of each is amplified. Through the cultivation of resonance, knots of conflict, ego struggles and fears often are dissolved rather than resolved. Our relationship to one another, to nature, to spirit is reinforced, attuned, until at last we become a community of self-aware humans. Our intuitive knowing, our wisdom of the heart becomes a continual guidance to action.

Our evolutionary vocations and untapped creativity tend to emerge naturally in the loving field. That emergent aspect of ourselves is fragile, delicate, and needs tenderness and appreciation to come forth. It seems as though the separated mind and the isolated individual have gone as far as possible. It is time for the attuned human, the group mind, the bonded resonant partnerships, the communities of conscious evolution to take us the next step. The Evolutionary Circle helps us create this field of resonance in the first hour.

Then in the second part, the Outer Work begins. Members listen to audio tapes while remaining in the resonant state, so that integration between the left brain and right brain occurs. The intuitive mind fuses with the rational intellect, stimulating the wisdom of the heart. These tapes, accompanied by the gentle music of James Owen Mathews, evoke from participants their own inner knowing. Our 'memories of the future' are awakened. We find that when we are in resonance we 'know' what to do. Each tape offers insights into a major theme of co-creation and conscious evolution, from our new spirituality, our new personhood, our co-creative relationships, and our work, to the formation of co-creative communities and society as a whole, with steps we might take to achieve a world equal to our potentials.

In this highly charged space of consciousness, participants cultivate a deeper form of conversation. 'Co-creative dialogue' follows. Each of us has within a 'still small voice' of intuitive knowing that is often obscured by the chatter of the mind. Co-creative dialogue occurs when we allow our inner voices to speak with one another, bypassing the critical analytical mind, drawing forth our innate vision. We tap into a deeper field of knowing accessed by the group mind in the field of resonance. From time to time, participants develop inspired insights which transcend the limits of the self-centred mind. We learn to listen with our heart for the essence of what is being communicated. We maintain a sacred silence until the inner voice prompts us to speak. Then we communicate spontaneously, without self-editing and judging others, without telling stories of the past, or philosophising, but expressing the truth we feel in the moment.

This process was highly developed in the Findhorn community. Peter Caddy taught me their process, which was based on small groups, and the evoking of attunement and higher guidance as essential to decision-making. I believe that out of this work together there will emerge the next stage of human self-government. It will not be world government. It will be self-government. Higher self-government. Eco-villages are a vital arena for the experimentation with the next stage of democracy. It might be called 'synocracy', for synergistic democracy. It is the government of ourselves as members of the whole, wherein each member is called forth to actualize his or her unique potential through participation in vital functions within the whole.

In Circle, we learn to use our differences as an opportunity to evolve. Upsets are not examples of the Circle not working, but they are the work of the Circle! We must learn to overcome our differences without attack if we are to survive and grow. Instead of reacting to disagreement, we commit to listen, understand and incorporate other points of view into a more inclusive synthesis. Yet Circles are not designed for therapy. While acknowledging the struggles and challenges of our lives, seeking to cast light upon the blocks and pains, their primary focus is upon the positive growth potential of each member and their contribution in the world. This activates the creative genius of the person, and has a healing effect.

A booklet, four audio tapes and one video tape setting the context are offered in each Circle album. Soon each Circle develops its own style, rituals and rhythms. The Circles become small self-organising schools for conscious evolution. They are 21st century seminaries for the future human to teach and learn the processes of self and social evolution. A reading list is provided for each theme. Journaling, discussion, projects and creative artistic expression are encouraged.

Circle members, wherever they are, (and Circles are now replicating throughout the world) might conceive of themselves as 'imaginal cells', bringing to life the new person, the new communities (eco-villages) and eventually, a new society of universal humans in harmony with one another, with nature and with the processes of creation. In some sense, we are engaged in a process of metamorphosis from the self-centred *Homo sapiens* to the whole-centred *Homo universalis*. When a caterpillar builds its cocoon, its old substance disintegrates and turns into a fertile and mysterious mush. At this time, imaginal cells appear that hold the image of the yet invisible butterfly. At first the caterpillar perceives these cells as foreign. Its immune system seeks to destroy them. But gradually, so many imaginal cells appear that the immune system of the caterpillar is overwhelmed. It surrenders to the imaginal cells which replicate and connect rapidly in a new pattern. They transform the body of the caterpillar into the butterfly.

We can see Evolutionary Circles as imaginal cells in the social body, part of a rapidly growing 'critical mass' that holds pictures of the emerging human in community. Since the special function of Evolutionary Circles is to grow the seed of the new person in the evolving community, they play an organic and vital part in the accelerated process of transformation now occurring on the planetary scale. They are seeds of metamorphosis in the global brain, members of the social body whose function is to awaken the whole system to its potential for life ever-evolving.

Evolutionary Circles, by whatever name they are called, are now seeding the 'morphogenetic field' of Earth with the thought that we are all members of one body, created by the same Source and activated by the same creative power to express our divine potentiality for the good of the whole. When the time is ripe, we can expect a 'planetary birth experience'. What has been foreseen by the great mystics of the world may be experienced simultaneously by enough of us, to shift the consciousness field of Earth.

We invite you to join with us in this great journey into the unknown, as pioneers in the next stage of human evolution.

> *"If you bring forth what is within you, what you bring forth will save you. If you do not bring forth what is within you, what you do not bring forth will destroy you."*
> The Gospel according to Thomas

EVOLVING TOGETHER

The Emergence of a New Form of Evolutionary Group

by Monica Bryant BSc. (Hons)

Monica Bryant's business, Evolutionary Concepts, offers Evolutionary Consulting and Coaching. Monica's approach is transdisciplinary, focusing on the emerging unified worldview and its application in the fields of science, medicine and business. Her work is process oriented and explores the deeper patterns, cycles and organising principles found at all levels of life. This integrated approach deals with both inner and outer evolution, and can be applied at the biological, personal, group or community level.

Monica has over 20 years of experience in the field of human potential development and complementary medicine. She is trained in Transpersonal and Archetypal Psychology. Monica is also an international lecturer who trains natural health practitioners on pleomorphism and the Enderleinian biological remedies. Earlier Monica was director of Symbiogenesis Ltd. and was founder of The International Institute of Symbiotic Studies promoting probiotic approaches to microbiology. Her writing is widely published.

Address:
Kestrels, Burwash
East Sussex TN19 7JP
England
Tel: +44 (0) 1435 883640
Fax: +44 (0) 1435 883642
Email: monica@evolutionary.co.uk

INTRODUCING AN EVOLUTIONARY GROUP

Evolution is an ongoing process which happens through holons. A holon is a whole/part. Every part belongs to a whole and every whole is in turn a part of another whole, which is within another whole and so on. For example, a cell exists within an organ, which is within a body. Life is comprised of holons embedded one within another like a series of nested concentric circles. A holon can also be described as a living system or complex adaptive system and is the unit through which evolution takes place. This could be almost anything; a microbe, tree, person or group. The term holon was first named by Arthur Koestler and more recently has been elaborated fully by Ken Wilber[1] to describe the evolutionary process from a perspective of the perennial philosophy.

Evolution happens in and around us all of the time so it is possible to include many forms of group meetings as evolutionary even if in the most minimal way. An evolutionary group could be defined in many ways. However, I would describe a group as evolutionary if it includes the following essential elements:

Becomes a Defined and Integrated Whole (a Holon)

Like an organism or living system an evolutionary group becomes a defined unit or a morphic field. It is difficult to determine exactly when a group becomes a true whole, however certain factors do clearly contribute to the creation of a group as a holon. Most importantly an evolutionary group is clearly *born* into being as compared to simply being a gathering of people. The more a group becomes integrated as a whole, the more rapid the shared learning, responsiveness and adaptability of the group.

The group is very aware of the individuals (parts) within the whole group and also has an awareness of the greater whole to which the group is a part. It is also conscious of its interconnectedness with the environment and holographic and non-linear dynamics. The whole is naturally greater than the sum of its parts thereby enabling creativity and novelty to be expressed.

Allows Creative Emergence

An evolutionary group creates a space for what 'wants to happen' to happen in the moment. This process of manifesting something from the invisible realm of nothingness is in itself an act of birthing into being whatever has the most energy in the now. For emergence to occur freely, there is a need for minimal or no fixed leadership, structures or techniques, and a strong process orientation in order to move with the forces of self-organisation. This also allows spontaneity, creativity and group intelligence to emerge and a high level of flow-state and consequent feelings of happiness. The observation of phenomena and valuing of direct experience are useful ways of accounting for what may be unfolding.

Values the Transpersonal Dimension

It is essential for an evolutionary group to foster an environment for transpersonal dimensions of consciousness to be experienced and appreciated. This includes a high degree of self-reflection and self-awareness, a contemplative mode, archetypal awareness and much openness of heart and mind. In particular, the group provides a very high quality of listening on many levels, embraces symbolic insights and creates shared meaning. An evolutionary group works to bring as much as possible into conscious awareness including who and what its true self-identity is.

Consciousness evolves and the most significant evolutionary step for humanity at this time is the shift from the ego level of functioning to a transpersonal or soul level. Each shift in consciousness can be seen as a move from one holon of consciousness to a more expanded and inclusive holon.

In this case a shift is needed from the limited reality of the personality or ego to a transpersonal perspective, whilst still honouring the role of the ego for healthy functioning.

Undergoes Transformation in Form and Consciousness

Evolution is the constant transformation of one form to another and this also applies to evolution in group situations. As an evolutionary group becomes a whole unit it will begin a developmental process undergoing organic metamorphoses, which can be gentle or profoundly transformative where a death-rebirth experience is often involved. The self-generating capacity of living systems enables a shift from one holonic level to another. It transcends and includes that which went before. So an evolutionary group:

- Enables its parts to evolve.
- Evolves itself as a whole.
- Contributes to the evolving of the whole to which it is a part.

Transcends Polarities

Creating a safe container and environment enables the transcendence of conflicting opposites. By not repressing the chaos which occurs with polarisation, new higher-level order can emerge. This ability to keep transcending and moving on is central to the evolutionary process. Learning to recognise the unique role of each individual in and for the group can also help overcome conflicts and lead to a celebration of diversity in the group as a source of strength and joy.

As a result of being part of such an evolutionary group, the participants are often left with an experience of having reached a greater level of wholeness where they are able to be more fully and authentically true to the Self and able to relate to others in deep friendship. This form of group process can be distinguished from other personal growth workshops or psychotherapy groups as they do not aim to be educational or therapeutic. However, as a result of creating this particular quality of group space much soulfulness, insight, empowerment and deep healing are enabled.

The Emergence of an Evolutionary Group

To explore further, some of the qualities of an Evolutionary Group, I have used my experience of having been part of a unique small group called the 'Surprise Being'. These summarising reflections on the Surprise Being as being an evolutionary group are my own and may be shared by others, but are not a representative expression of the group as a whole.

The Surprise Being developed out of the International Business Network in 1984 and its name evolved by observing what happened when the participants were together. Out of a focus of *being* rather than *doing* the only constant that would emerge was surprise. The Surprise Being was an international community which maintained a core group of about twelve participants, aged from the twenties to sixties, representing ten different countries. They were primarily organisational consultants, who met every six months for up to a week in various countries throughout Europe until 1994 when the group decided that its life cycle was complete. For several years the group process was continued by publishing a 'Surprise Scanner' newsletter between meetings, which enabled a sharing of emerging trends in our lives and intensified the sense of community despite living apart.

The individuals involved were all experienced in personal development work and therefore started out with a certain self-awareness and self-responsibility. This enabled a common foundation from which the group embarked upon the voyage, an adventure into the unknown, which was utterly unpredictable and endlessly creative. The process of being together oscillated between being frustrating, filled with impossibility, darkness and confusion, and then peak experiences, blissful states of unity and communion. This created a deep intimacy which was at the same time impersonal.

As a group of explorers we created an atmosphere of discovery together, spending much time at the soul level, which also enhanced our individual evolution. There was no fixed agenda, defined purpose or leader and the only rule was no rules. A strong focus was placed on the process, commitment and maintaining a spirit of play which enabled its evolutionary unfoldment.

As we did not have an apparent external reason for existing, we spent a lot of time with an inner focus including reflection on the meaning of our meeting together and the nature of the internal dynamics of our group. The sense of learning something together and the creation of shared meaning was essential, as there was, for the most part, no other task or goal to bring us together or to justify the amount of time, international flights and expense involved.

The Surprise Being provided an intensive experimental laboratory for a study of consciousness and group dynamics. Much of what we learnt could be usefully applied to any other group, organisation, conference, company or community. Our experience and learning is related to the above key evolutionary principles as follows:

Becoming a Whole – Creating the Holon or 'Container'

A container 'holds' something; thus, as a group consciously creates a container for itself, this becomes the 'holding energy field' or morphic field (as described by Rupert Sheldrake[2]) in which all processes of change occur. There are many factors which contribute to the creating of a container for a group meeting, which are equally applicable to small and large numbers of people. Although some of these factors may appear to be very obvious, even common sense, they are worth mentioning because observing these thresholds with respect is a key to successful and more sacred meetings.

The first factor to consider is the nature of the commitment of being together for a certain time. We spent much time discussing our levels of commitment to the Surprise Being. Commitment is not just an attitude towards the group but is what determines whether we actually attend the meetings or not. This fundamental agreement to be present does seem to affect the possible potential for the group. Although each meeting becomes a whole in its own right, we also found a noticeable difference in the energy level when everyone was present. In fact, if any one was absent we always spent some time reflecting on the absence of that person. This did not mean we were unable to 'go with the flow' in terms of attendance, but overall we valued every one being present. There is a resemblance here to a psychotherapy session which can only be effective if there is a clear agreement and a clear time boundary. Paradoxically for true freedom and fluidity to happen there also has to be structure in the form of the container.

In alchemy a hermetically sealed container or flask is the essential prerequisite before the process of transformation can begin. Once committed, a group of people will experience the intensification as the 'heat' in the flask increases, spurring on the alchemic changes. This intense pressure which powers transformation will be experienced in any situation where there is a binding commitment, be it a marriage, a family or group of people bound by a need to endure a certain time and place together.

Secondly, there is the physical level such as the location itself, more specifically the meeting room and the clear boundary indicated by the closing of the door. Consistency of attendance adds a seriousness to being 'there' for each other, as does punctuality, which demarcates the container in time. In the Surprise Being, we always sat in a circle. This was, in fact, one of the only fixed forms we had. A circle represents equality and mutuality. It also holds the symbolic imagery of a feminine receptive vehicle and is the form long used by other cultures.

In defining a container it is useful to make a distinction between inner and outer, although ultimately there is no such division in the greater unity of life. There are many influences on a group as a holon. On a larger and more subtle level a container must also be considered in the light of the spirit of the place and time. Each community will be affected by its location and the specific issues emerging from the collective unconscious.

The third factor is how a group is started and ended, which helps demarcate the container and to influence the environment in the container. In the Surprise Being, the most simple and powerful way was with silence. Silence embodies different qualities each time and enables an emptying of busy thoughts and a grounding into a deeper place of being and nothingness. From this deep space of silence we found that the energy builds up to a point where a person began to talk spontaneously. What often happens in groups is that the space becomes filled with the strongest personalities. We found that if each person spoke only when they are genuinely *moved* to speak then the energy level stayed higher and far more was possible. This demanded awareness of why one should need to say something at a particular moment. Did it improve on the silence? We experienced a silence emerging of itself as much more potent than a proposed silence.

Rituals can be used as a way of defining the beginning and ending of a meeting, the closing and opening of the container, clarifying when it is a sacred place in which the true meeting can begin. This can take the form of an attunement, a circle 'check', a song, chanting or a short story. What is important with a ritual is that it is something which is an authentic expression for all of the participants, otherwise it becomes an imposed 'form', which is carried out without meaning and therefore does not actually 'make a difference'. In the Surprise being we tended not to adopt any of these usual group-forming rituals.

Another factor to consider is the consciousness of the whole group itself. For example, a shared vision acts as a binding force and on an energetic level acts like a container. Being as aware as possible of what is contained in the seed stage of a vision says a lot about the context and therefore the potential for the unfoldment of that group. Once a vision has been created it also needs to be recreated time and time again in order that it stays alive and true. This is essential as it is the vision which seems to create an organising field which provides the environment for all that manifests within it. The intention of the participants and their degree of commitment plays an essential role in building the containing trust and safety that enables deeper work.

Becoming an Integrated Whole System

Over time this container or morphic field seems to take on a life of its own. It could be considered the soul of a group; a particular presence of qualities or unique essence that can be sensed by any one who is familiar with the group. As the energy field of the container strengthens with time and as the level of attunement increases, the group can then take on the life of an organism in its own right, fully differentiated and with its own identity. When this occurs individuals or sub-groups 'become' the various aspects of a living system such as the head, heart and belly. In all groups there is a balancing between thinking and feeling functions and often certain individuals will 'carry' one aspect on behalf of the whole group. This is when an awareness of what is transpersonal and what is personal is very valuable. As the intensity in the Surprise Being increased as we became closer, the more we needed to be aware of an individual reaction being a symptom for the group as a whole rather than it being 'just a personal issue'. Although there may certainly be a link to personal material, a person's extreme emotional reaction may in fact be an expression for the whole of the group. This whole system approach can support great healing especially for the person who is the supposed 'symptom'.

When there is a strong group alignment the transpersonal dimension becomes apparent as individuals express particular behaviours which may be seen as archetypal, such as, parent figure, child or court jester. This is when a person can move beyond the small 'I' to become a conduit for universal qualities which are expressed through them. In the Surprise Being we found it to be healthiest when these archetypal roles changed among us so that one person, according to their propensity, was not stuck holding one role in the group all the time.

Time that is spent together in an evolutionary way increases resonance and alignment, helping a group to become more efficient when applied to practical tasks or decision making, which can be swift and elegant. What from a linear time perspective may appear as 'wasted' time is an investment in future growth. As in nature's cyclic laws of economy, the hours of group time that can pass, which may not appear to have had value in terms of usefulness, create the necessary, fertile compost for future growth.

Allowing Creative Emergence

Out of nothingness comes the unfolding of the multitude of phenomena of life. There is a power in the art of 'naming' what the quality of the moment is, in the here-and-now. Speaking the truth with total honesty has a profound effect and increases the experience of immediacy and the level of energy, which is a useful barometer for how the group is progressing.

Sometimes there can be the feeling that something is 'wanting to happen' and when the group focus goes in this direction there is more energy than when attention goes elsewhere. This ability of really tasting the moment helps in dealing with things at the appropriate time. Using the measure of energy and flow present in the group as a guideline can alert one to when another issue is needing priority. This is not always easy when several processes and levels of communication are all happening at once. However, when the 'right' issue is addressed most members experience a sense of fulfilling what is needed. Perhaps this is the honouring of a deeper evolutionary impulse.

In the Surprise Being emergence happened in the form of creating music together, dancing or other spontaneous activities which simply emerged out of the group, not as a result of a decision making process. Occasionally someone would make a suggestion to do something. This was often received as an imposition onto the group and therefore rejected regardless of how pleasant the proposal. We seemed to operate mainly from this place of emergence and therefore what we did do or share felt genuinely authentic and had a sense of immediacy to it. Any group decisions that were made often involved quite lengthy discussions, whether it was to plan a sightseeing trip or decide where to have dinner. This was because we tuned in to all the variables and options to feel what was truly 'right' and emergent there and then.

One of the very touching aspects of the Surprise Being was our ability to provide an atmosphere of listening which enabled us to express for the first time what was emerging out of our deepest selves. It was a very safe and loving space to give birth to our new selves.

Embracing the Transpersonal Dimension

Reality is multi-dimensional and multi-layered and it is possible to place many lenses on what emerges. There are many modes of knowing and much misunderstanding can be generated if there is not clarity about which level of consciousness the group is operating at. This involves the question of self identity, life's dance between the co-evolving personal and the transpersonal.

Cultivating self-reflective awareness is essential for learning to take place and is of primary importance for an evolutionary group. As there are many modes of consciousness and perceptual positions, there are therefore many ways in which one can reflect on a group process at any one time. Increasing the witnessing observer function is the essential step for a group to move from reactive responses to a more detached awareness, which enables more clarity of perception. However, there is a fine line here between transcendence, denial and dissociated states.

In delving into the depths of a mutual enquiry it is important to not disconnect from one's body. The art of listening to others, as well as to the self, is best when combined with body listening. Also, to recognise that what may appear to be a personal bodily symptom may also be an expression on behalf of the group. This awareness in the group can help us also in our own integration as a psychophysical whole.

Through others and our relationships with them, a group provides a multi-faceted mirror with which to increase self knowing. Deliberately slowing down the speed of communication is like taking a magnifying glass to the group process which enables far greater insight and adds to the practice of group mindfulness. Bringing a more meditative awareness to the phenomenological observations can support the emergence of a shared intuitive knowing. The group can then become a sounding board for learning to trust one's own intuitive insights. Developing the group mind through co-operative enquiry enables far greater intelligence and wisdom than the sum of individuals involved.

The symbolic use of imagery, metaphor and analogy are valuable tools for integrating our inner life ecology with the outer ecology. Interestingly, in the Surprise Being the issues we were concerned about at a practical or outer level were a rich source for insight into what needed to be addressed at the inner level. Building these bridges between inner and outer gave greater meaning and integration, liberated energy and made many activities clearer and more purposeful.

From the transpersonal perspective the archetypal realm is another level of awareness to develop. For example, as the holding energy field or container becomes more established the group takes on the archetypal role of mother. Our mother is the first place where we experience being contained, firstly in the womb and then in the arms and love of our mother. A warm and intimate group can recreate this containing experience and therefore reactivate childhood material. Also, on an archetypal level there is the opportunity to experience the dark and life giving aspects of the feminine.

The group as container can be viewed as a birth canal through which individuals and the group itself can be born, created and recreated. Extremely painful conflicts can be linked to what is personal but may at the same time be an archetypal process in motion, such as the intensity of a death-birth initiation. The very primal nature and extremely confrontational feelings associated with birth makes it more understandable as to why so many groups break up once deeper thresholds of intimacy are reached. To stay with these intense human feelings takes great courage and patience. Being in an evolutionary group is not a soft option!

A Whole Transforming in Form and Consciousness

The Surprise Being took on the qualities of various types of group such as a meditation retreat group, a psychotherapeutic group, a professional support group, a dream group, a family therapy group and a conscious dying group. It contained elements of all of these and more yet at the same time was none of these. This very freedom of being so eclectic and transdisciplinary made our group refreshing and unique. Any attempt to 'pin it down' to one reality did not work or resulted in diminished flow and energy as if a homeostatic function was at play behind these various expressions. This shifting of quality and form could be seen as a relatively gentle metamorphosis compared to the more extreme and tumultuous transformations we also experienced. These profound transformations were experienced as a death-rebirth taking us from one evolutionary holon to the next holon. We really felt that we experienced the dynamics from within, of being a far-from-equilibrium living system, living at the edge of chaos.

The number of death and rebirth experiences shared together is the core of group evolution and adds *depth* to the group in a holarchic sense. That is, each time a holon existing at one level of consciousness is transcended it is born to a more inclusive new level of existence. This was very much the case in the Surprise Being, especially because there was nothing else for it to hang on to in terms of external structures. Sharing this experience of holonic deepening (death-rebirth) may explain why the closest bonding still exists among the most long term members who have gone through this cycle more times together. This depth of a group or holon can be visualised like the circles in the trunk of an oak tree. The greater the number of rings, the greater the age, depth and wisdom.

This death-rebirth theme also became apparent to us with the integration of new members, each of whom seemed to undergo their own death-rebirth process into the group (this is without there being anything 'done' to the individual by the group.) Similarly if someone missed a session although they were part of the next group meeting there would be a sense of discontinuity in experience having missed the prior session.

As a group we certainly became a transforming whole and went through some momentous changes yet at the same time maintained a unique essence. This almost soul-like presence is a quality to which we can still attune or re-experience on meeting another member of the Surprise Being.

In terms of the Surprise Being making a contribution more overtly to the greater whole, as we matured as a group we became more conscious of the effect we had on our immediate environment whether this was a restaurant or the places we stayed. When we held our group within a larger conference it seemed that we became a sub-holon or core container, which processed shadow material on an inner level not just for ourselves but also on behalf of the wider group. Our transformational shifts seemed to have a noticeable effect on whichever community setting we were in. It was as if we created a ripple effect enabling the rest of the grouping we were surrounded by to proceed with greater ease. This holographic reflection, from a microcosmic small group to the macrocosmic whole, is also apparent with conference-organising groups, company boards of directors and committees. The extent to which they are evolutionary, or not, will influence the potential of a whole conference, company or organisation.

Transcending Polarities

In this container, sooner or later, tensions and conflicts will emerge. These polarities seem to be inevitable and are central to the process of group chaos. Some of the typical polarities include those wishing to 'ascend' into spiritual life /'descend' into the earthly realm, doing/being and masculine/feminine, which then give rise to a myriad of different types of conflict and arguments. These apparently irreconcilable oppositions generate an atmosphere where individuals tend to cling defensively to their positions, beliefs and opinions. To maintain the group it is necessary to reorganise at another level which is more inclusive than the level where the conflict was generated. This involves a group experience of death where ego beliefs are let go of and surrendered in order for this emergence to happen. This stage is essential and not an easy or comfortable experience. If avoided, then true community does not seem to happen. In our society where there is much denial of death or these death-like experiences much of the fullness of life can be missed.

Conflict and opposition is something which is often avoided since it is seen as undesirable. Any such suppression or denial of the oppositions between people in a group is a major way of blocking the evolutionary process. The ability to hold and maintain the 'creative tension' in a group is the key which enables the group to transcend polarities and move forward as a whole. This is a step which seems to go beyond compromise, tolerance or consensus. In the Surprise Being we excelled at sitting through long periods of extreme tension. As a result possibilities and solutions always emerged and we came to trust the vitalistic, self-healing capacity within our group.

The nature of the ego is to split reality and project the shadow self on to others. By knowing and owning one's shadow material, there is a greater integration of internal intrapsychic oppositions and thus less likelihood of acting these out in group situations. This inner reclaiming of shadow parts of the psyche is evolutionary work. Similarly moving beyond duality is one of the key steps in psychospiritual development and in any community there is plenty of opportunity to practise this. Shifting from a world of either/or to a both/and approach is the only way through. No longer splitting black from white, right from wrong and thus embracing paradox.

In the way that yin and yang are complementary forces, so there needs to be in a group this ebb and flow from one polarity to the other and back again. In this way we can see how a group, like an individual, is striving for balance and wholeness through self-regulation. Taking a whole system perspective, a conflict between two individuals or sub-groups is an expression of a deeper imbalance being expressed through them, which has not yet been integrated. Every such polarity could be viewed as the necessary potential and opportunity for an evolutionary shift to take place in the group as a whole. Carl Jung described the psyche as made up of processes whose energy spring from the equilibration of all kinds of opposites and that the unification of opposites is to experience God[3].

The Self versus Other Polarity

There are differing needs for boundaries according to one's developmental process, especially if dysfunctional childhood and co-dependency issues are involved. The balancing between inner and outer needs such as 'saving the world' versus the need to 'save' oneself is also true at the group level. So often our needs can be projected onto others or onto environmental issues rather than healing them within. This is a difficult balance to find when there are so many real, urgent, outer issues to deal with, which in turn are also having an impact on any ability to experience true well being. There is an important transition which takes place when the belief that one ought or should be 'doing good' is replaced by living life in alignment with one's soul purpose. Where there is the simultaneous effect of being of service, any polarity between the individual and group or world is transcended. A fusion of seeming inner and outer. This is also a more sustainable way of functioning which enables us to flourish in our unique expression whilst also contributing to the needs of the greater whole.

An important 'self and other' issue is that of abuse which, seen at its most basic level, is the overstepping of another's boundary; whether this be physical, sexual or emotional. The spectrum of what might be termed abuse is very broad and in a group setting it is something which requires attention as there are so many ways in which people can be over-ridden or communications can violate another person through lack of sensitivity. In the Surprise Being we increased our awareness of the more subtle ways we abuse ourselves and each other. This process of honouring each other as sacred became a constant area for increased awareness.

The common form of abuse in a group is scapegoating. This is when one person carries an aspect of the group shadow (unconscious negative emotions or unactualised potential) and is then rejected by the group for this role. Although this is a hazard which is recognised in many groups, it still needs to be watched for, as scapegoating can happen in increasingly insidious, unconscious and subtle ways. Sometimes the person who may appear to be a source of irritation, if embraced, can hold the key to a group insight or transformation.

Another popular self/other conflict or part/whole tension is between personal time and group time especially as there are many needs and there never seems to be enough time. Building the solid foundations of relationship for creating community does demand a lot of time and energy. When a group is attuned, the polarity of personal needs versus those of the group simply seem to dissolve and everyone feels their needs are met.

Honouring Diversity

How do we celebrate the diversity of individual uniqueness, while at the same time staying connected to an underlying unity? In any group, the strengths, weaknesses and qualities of each individual become known over time. Each member becomes like a sub-personality at the group level. Any symbolic system or matrix, which can help us to see a greater pattern or myth thereby enables us to take a detached view of the qualities and dynamics involved and helps us find appropriate balances between them. Examples of these systems include the four functions of Jung, the four elements, the astrological map, the five elements of Chinese medicine, the enneagram, the *I Ching*, the Kabbalistic Tree of Life, the chakras and so on. These maps of reality are useful, however we found in the Surprise Being, it was most powerful when we found our own meaningful images.

In any group there is always movement and the dynamic interplay between various qualities which forms an ongoing dance, continually self-organising into new constellations, although patterns of self-similarity reoccur. Behind all of life are the universal ordering patterns, shown through systems of knowledge and sacred geometry. Each group has its own particular mandala or note which is itself a unique part in the macrocosmic whole. Evolving together we create a kaleidoscope of cycles within cycles, ever-changing and transforming yet sustaining the dynamic harmony essential to the evolution of all life.

Other Emerging Evolutionary Groups

There seems to be a number of new forms of group which, from my experience, could in various ways be described as evolutionary. These independent groups and communities have differing styles of meeting, with their own origins, terminology and culture, but have in common, in varying degrees, one or most of the elements of an evolutionary group. A few brief examples of such groups include:

Dialogue

Initiated by David Bohm, first held in 1984 and documented in the book *Unfolding Meaning*[4] by Don Factor. Bohm, a physicist, terms the process of emergence as the unfolding out of the invisible implicate order. This manifest explicate order is then enfolded back again into the implicate order. Dialogue is generally for groups sized from twenty to forty. It has continued to grow worldwide in various ways according to the influences of the people who have chosen to continue and develop this style of meeting. (See 'Suggested Reading' at the end of this chapter for a list of references on dialogue.)

Process Oriented Psychology

The work of Arnold Mindell described in *Sitting in the Fire – Large Group Transformation using Conflict and Diversity*[5]. Mindell shows how attention to power, rank, revenge and abuse helps build lively and sustainable communities. As a group facilitator he values the ability to stay centered while sitting in the fire of conflict and diversity to enable further development of the group.

Community Building

Developed by Scott Peck since 1984 documented in his book *The Different Drum – The Creation of True Community – The first Step to World Peace*[6]. Peck describes four stages in community building – pseudocommunity, chaos, emptiness and community. This model is very useful for identifying what could also be seen as a cycle of group death and rebirth. It is an efficient way to move a group from conflictual chaos to reconciliation and true community.

Open Space

A technology developed by Harrison Owen and described in *Open Space Technology – A User's Guide*[7]. It is a way of organising meetings sized from five up to several hundred participants. It is a simple yet profound way of allowing what needs to happen in the moment and has been applied in large conferences for businesses and organisational consultants.

Evolutionary Circles

Developed by Barbara Marx Hubbard. (*See pages 55-60.*)

Life Science Seminars

Based on the observation work of W Goethe and developed by Margaret Colquhoun. (*See pages 27-34.*)

There are undoubtedly many other groups and communities that could also be included here as being considered evolutionary. What is significant is the fact that both these groups and the Surprise Being developed independently of each other yet during a parallel time of the 1980s, with little, if any, knowledge of each other. This may indicate that a broader evolutionary process or morphic field is gathering, hopefully moving towards a critical mass, which will benefit meeting styles, conference formats and group cultures in the future. If enough groups of an evolutionary nature happen globally this may enable a holonic shift, the essential step needed for humanity to evolve together in greater harmony.

References

1 Wilber, K., 1995. *Sex, Ecology and Spirituality – The Spirit of Evolution*, Shambhala.

2 Sheldrake, R., 1988. *The Presence of the Past.* London: Collins.

3 Jung, C.G., 1960. *The structure and dynamics of the psyche – The Collected Works, Volume Eight.* London: Routledge and Kegan Paul.

4 Factor, D., 1985. *Unfolding Meaning – A weekend dialogue with David Bohm.* Foundation House Publications.

5 Mindell, A., 1995. *Sitting in the Fire – Large group transformation using conflict and diversity.* Lao Tse Press.

6 Scott Peck, M., 1988. *The Different Drum – The creation of true community – the first step to world peace.* London: Arrow Books.

7 Owen, H., 1992. *Open Space Technology – A User's Guide.* Abbott Publishing.

ACKNOWLEDGEMENT

I would like to thank all the individuals who participated in creating the Surprise Being and in particular Rainer, Andrea and Peter for their editorial comments.

SUGGESTED READING

Dialogue References

Bohm, D., 1980. *Wholeness and the Implicate Order*. London: Ark Paperbacks.
Bohm, D., 1992. *Thought as a system*. London: Routledge.
Bohm, D., 1992. On Dialogue. *Noetic Sciences Review*. Autumn 1992.
Bohm, D., and Peat, D., 1987. *Science, Order and Creativity*. London: Routledge.
Bohm, D., and Edwards, M., 1991. *Changing Consciousness – The Hidden Challenge of Humanity*. Harper and Roe.
Bohm, D., and Hiley, B. J., 1993. *The Undivided Universe*; London: Routledge.
Briggs, J., 1989. Quantum Leap. *New Age Journal*. September/October 1989.
de Maré, P., 1991. *Koinonia: From Hate through Dialogue to Culture in the Large Group*. London: Karnac Books.
Factor, D., ed., 1985. *Unfolding Meaning – a weekend of dialogue with David Bohm*. Foundation House publications.
Factor, D., A Pool of Common Meaning. *Resurgence* No. 161
Keepin, W., 1994. David Bohm: A life of Dialogue between Science and Spirit. *Noetic Sciences Review*. Summer 1994.
Keepin, W., Lifework of David Bohm – River of Truth. *ReVision*. Vol. 16 No. 1.
Krishnamurti, J. and Bohm, D., 1985. *The Ending of Time*. Victor Gollanz.
Olausson, I., 1996. *Dialog!*. Svenska Dagbladet. (Swedish).
Zohar, D., and Marshall, I., 1993. *The Quantum Society*. London: Bloomsbury.

Part II

CONFLICT SOLVING

Lessons from Communities All Over the World

Lessons from the Villages of Ladakh

by Helena Norberg-Hodge

Author, futurist, activist, Helena Norberg-Hodge speaks seven languages and has studied numerous cultures at varying degrees of industrialisation. In addition to twenty years in Ladakh, she has observed the impact of economic development on Bhutan, rural France and Spain (over 10 years) as well as Sweden, UK, USA and Germany. In reaction to the changes occurring in Ladakh, she helped to found the local Ladakh Ecological Development Group (LEDeG) which seeks to adapt changes to Ladakh's decentralised community structures without sacrificing cultural values or ecological stability. Today LEDeG, with 130 full time staff, is the most influential NGO in the region running an extensive programme in public education, appropriate technology, sustainable agriculture and crafts.

Helena is also founder and director of the International Society for Ecology and Culture. Based in the US and UK with subsidiaries in Sweden, Germany and India, ISEC's primary goal is to promote a discussion of the social and environmental impact of economic development and globalisation, while promoting more localised end equitable patterns of living in both North and South. She is co-director of the International Forum on Globalisation and also a member of GEN, the Global Eco-village Network.

Address:
Apple Barn
Week
Dartington
Devon
TQ9 6JP
England
Tel: +44 (0)1803 868650
Fax: +44 (0)1803 868651

Also:
850 Talbot Avenue
Albany
CA 94706
USA
Tel/Fax: +1 510 527 3873

A central problem for all seeking fundamental social change is the disconcerting fact that much of the existing social order, much of what we would like to reform, are actually entrenched deep within ourselves. Having been socialised within, and educated by, a consumer society we are often unwitting inheritors of a whole range of ideas, values, ways of looking at the world, that naturally work against change.

If our attempts at real change are not to be undermined by this 'social order within' we need to become conscious of our common sense presumptions and beliefs. Invaluable in this effort is exposure to assumptions and values deemed common sense, by cultures far removed from our own.

Through twenty years of working with the people of Ladakh I have been blessed with a continuous series of epiphanies which have revealed to me truths about human nature, community and the possibilities for human happiness. Above all, I have been constantly amazed by the tremendous, and in the West largely unknown, possibilities for harmonious, peaceful, even blissful, co-operation between people. What initially seemed to me to be a bizarre pretence of constant happiness and wellbeing among Ladhakhis, has grown into an understanding, that it was my preconceptions that were absurd, and that it really is possible to build happiness, solidarity and community in a way that far transcends our normal understanding of these words.

The West sometimes seems obsessed by the hope that some alien race will one day descend from the skies to teach us how to live, to return to us what we sense has been lost from our lives and society. My experience in Ladakh has taught me that such alien races do exist; not in the skies perhaps, but in the mountains and high plains of Northern India and in many other places – with humility we can re-learn their lessons and bring their very earthly healing home.

This does not mean that we should romanticise traditional cultures: they are human, which is to say that they are not perfect. Not everything traditional is better. On the other hand we should not dismiss respect for traditional cultures as mere 'noble savage' idealism. What has for so long appeared to Westerners as merely 'primitive' turns out, on careful inspection, to be simply appropriate to the real needs of people. By comparison, progress – however dazzling and powerful – very often involves movement away from the satisfaction of real to artificial needs. No wonder then that Westeners, for all their gadgets and widgets, are far less satisfied than traditional peoples who have nothing – except what they really need.

What initially amazed me so much in Ladakh was the extraordinary lack of aggression in the culture. The arguments, squabbles and fights that so often bedevil co-operative efforts in the West are almost unknown in Ladakh. If asked when there has last been a fight, the average Ladakhi will simply laugh at you, or make a joke: they will likely not know what you mean. Why should we argue, they respond "We just live together, that's all". This peaceableness is protected by tried and tested social mechanisms designed to ensure a minimum of social conflict.

In this traditional culture the status of women is very high. Modernisation, on the other hand, has served to marginalise women and remove them from the centre of the economy. Photo: John Page

Agricultural work in Ladakh is founded in co-operation. Labour and draught animals are routinely shared. Photo: John Page

One such mechanism is what I have called the 'spontaneous intermediary'. As soon as any sort of difference arises between two parties, a third party steps in to act as an intermediary. Whatever the circumstance, whoever is involved, whoever appears to not be involved, an intermediary always appears to be on hand. It happens automatically, without any prompting; the intermediary is not consciously sought and can be anyone who happens to be around; it might be an older sister, or a neighbour, or just a passing stranger. I have seen the process function even with young children. I remember watching a five-year-old settling a squabble between two of his friends in this way. They listened to him willingly. The feeling that peace is preferable to conflict is so deeply ingrained that people turn automatically to a third party. This mechanism prevents problems from arising in the first place.

The spontaneous intermediary, it seems, is always around in any context that might possibly lead to conflict. If two people are involved in trade, for example, they can be sure that someone will be there to help them strike a deal. This way the possibility of direct confrontation is avoided. In most situations, the parties already know one another. But if someone unknown to the others intervenes, it is not seen as meddling. The help will be welcomed.

Of course some matters have to be decided on a village level. The village council meets periodically throughout the year and is presided over by the *goba*, or village head. The goba is usually appointed by rotation. If the whole village wants to keep him on, he may hold his position for many years, but otherwise, after a year or so, the job will pass on to another householder. One of the goba's jobs is to act as adjudicator. Though arguments are unusual, from time to time some differences of opinion arise that need settling.

Beyond such social mechanisms, the peaceableness is deeply-rooted in their value systems, particularly in the Buddhist devotion to compassion, forgiveness and the understanding that all is essentially one. There is a world of difference between the Western notion that compassion aids those who suffer and the Ladakhi understanding that compassion aids the compassionate as well as those who suffer; in which case, why not be as compassionate and kind as often as possible with as many people as possible? What could make more sense!

Emotionally Healthy and Secure as the Ladhakis

An important factor in their emotional health is undoubtedly the fact that Ladhakis belong to their place on earth. They are bonded to that place through intimate daily contact, through a knowledge about their immediate environment with its changing seasons, needs, and limitations. For them 'the environment' is not some alien, problematic sphere of human concern, it is where they are. They are aware of the living context in which they find themselves. The movement of the stars, the sun, and moon are familiar rhythms that influence their daily activities.

The understanding that is gained through a life rooted in the natural world seems to create a sense of kinship with plants and animals that nurtures a profound respect, and even love, for the humble creatures that share the world of the Ladhakis. Children and adults who witness the birth, rearing, mating and death of the animals around them seem unable to view those animals as merely a natural resource to be plundered.

My experience of life with the Ladhaki people taught me that human happiness and co-operation are not just a matter for dreamy optimism but are facts. More remarkably I learned that this happiness can, and perhaps can only, be won in a situation where there are no winners and losers, just winners. Happiness is possible, not through aggressive individualism and the struggle for betterment over others, but through simple compassion and kindness for others. Somehow I knew this all along; perhaps we all do – it comes as no surprise that kindness leads to the happiness of all, while selfishness leads to the impoverishment of some and the weary, but empty, bitterness of others. If it is true that the mark of the divine is that it is like 'having your cake and eating it', then there was certainly something divine about Ladakh – everyone gained from the desire that no one should suffer.

It is deeply tragic, then, that our mainstream culture led by government and industry moves relentlessly toward continued economic growth and technological development empowered by the belief that satisfying selfish individualism, greed and pride will somehow lead to the sort of happiness and peaceable co-operation so noticeable in societies in which such traits are notable by their absence. Meanwhile real human needs and the real needs of a collapsing environmental order are all but ignored.

The changes we need to make can greatly enrich our lives. Yet they are often treated, even within the environmental movement, as sacrifices. The emphasis is on giving things up and making do with less, rather than recognising how much we stand to gain. We forget that the price for never-ending economic growth and material prosperity has been spiritual and social impoverishment, psychological insecurity, and the loss of cultural vitality. We think of ourselves as 'having everything', and are surprised when young people turn to drugs or gurus to fill what is actually a void in their lives.

At the moment, the emerging local economy and the growing domination of science and technology are not only severing our connection to nature and to one another but also breaking down natural and cultural diversity. In so doing, we are threatening our very existence. In a modern setting it is easy to believe that economic development has increased diversity. Efficient transportation and communication bring together a vast array of foods and products from different cultures. However, the very system that facilitates these multicultural experiences is helping to erase them and to eliminate local cultural differences throughout the world.

The best antidote to the growing globalisation of the economy is decentralisation. This would involve a succession of changes in the whole socio-economic system. The need to belong to a group is in itself an important reason for human-scale social units. Here we can learn directly from Ladakh, where families are large, but communities small. Children are nurtured by people of different generations, benefiting particularly from the special bond with their grandparents. Though the relationships in this larger family are close, they are not so intense as those of the nuclear family. Each individual is supported in a web of intimate relationships, and no one relationship has to bear too much weight. In Ladakh, I have never observed anything approaching the needy attachment or the guilt and rejection that are so characteristic of the nuclear family. All the signs tell us that the nuclear family is not working. The divorce rate, the alienation of adolescents from their parents, the shocking extent of domestic violence and sexual abuse within the family are examples of this breakdown.

If decentralisation is vital for the rekindling of family life, it is also vital for the creation of communities in western society. Mobility erodes community, but as we put down roots and feel attachment to places our human relationships deepen, become more secure, and – as they continue over time – more reliable. We tend to believe that a person should be completely self-sufficient, that he or she should not need anybody else. Yet the close-knit relationships in Ladakh seem liberating rather than oppressive. Inner security springing from familial and community support breeds tolerance and an acceptance of others rooted in a sense of personal security that is the wellspring of true freedom.

The move to smaller scale communities does not mean small-mindedness. Eco-villages should link up around the world in the understanding that we need widescale examples of small scale development. Eco-villages can restore the sense of place and belonging to the land and can build communities on ecological principles. These communities can relearn much of the art of co-operation and conflict resolution from traditional cultures.

Above all, perhaps, they can learn the vital part played by compassion. No community can flourish solely on a desire to reject consumer societies or on a desire to protect the environment. A real alternative to modern alienation will be provided only by a community based on compassion for people and the living world around us. That is to say: by a community that satisfies the real, as opposed to the artificial, needs of people. Where this happens a genuinely compelling challenge will have been raised to our powerful, but in the end humanly impotent, society based on organised lovelessness.

Eco-villages can also add a subversive element to the tide of propaganda sweeping the South that persuades traditional peoples that something must be good because ‘it’s done in the North’. The fact that what is now being ‘done in the North’ closely resembles what has long been done in the South should add some timely confusion to the debate on what actually constitutes progress.

Tolerance and Solidarity in Everyday Experience

Experiences with Conflict Resolution in the Sarvodaya Movement on Sri Lanka

by Dr A T Ariyaratne

Dr A T Ariyaratne initiated the Sarvodaya Shramadana Movement in 1958. Sarvodaya (universal awakening) is a people's movement which is non-profit, non-sectarian and non-political. It is a practical model for empowering individuals and communities to build their own future. Sinhales and Tamils have been fighting for 40 years and Sarvodaya has been a continuous effort to bring them together. Current programs cover 10,000 villages (out of a total of 23,000) with the participation of hundreds of thousands of volunteers and trained workers. Special programs cover: legal services, early childhood development, women's education, banking and income generation, environmental initiatives, alternative energy projects and training in conflict resolution.

By integrating ethical, cultural and social dimensions with modern science and technology, Dr Ariyaratne has formulated a universal development model applicable to individuals, families, communities, nations and ultimately global societies.

Publications include 6 volumes of Collected Works and numerous articles covering Sarvodaya's philosophy, global peace, education and the challenges facing the human race in the decades ahead.

In 1996 he was awarded the Ghandi Peace Prize by the government of India.

Address:
Dr A T Ariyaratne
Lanka Jathika Sarvodaya Shramadana Saangamaya Inc.
100 Rawathawatte Road
Moratuwa
Sri Lanka
Tel: +94 1 64 71 59 / 64 52 55
Fax: +94 1 64 70 84 / 64 65 12
Email: arisar@sri.lanka.net

Let me begin with some real life experiences I had in trying to practise the Sarvodaya methods in the fields of education, people's participatory development and peace building.

About five months before the 1971 JVP uprising, the Principal of a senior school not far from Colombo came to Nalanda to meet me. He was a highly qualified and an efficient Principal and a well known teacher. He related to me the pathetic story of a group of students who had deliberately broken down the discipline of the school community completely and are now systematically destroying the buildings, equipment and even the science laboratory. He requested me to come and do something. He said that the Department of Education itself was indifferent and helpless.

I asked him whether he could bring the senior students together to the school hall the following day, so that I could go and speak to the children. He said he would try and cautioned me that they would even physically harass and hurt me. I consoled him by saying I would take the risk and went with some senior students from Nalanda. Students were gathered in the hall and the Principal and a couple of teachers tried their very best to silence them and give me the opportunity to speak. I asked the Principal to sit down and I got up and faced the students. For nearly another half an hour I was standing on the stage before the students, facing a continuous round of hooting, ridicule and abuse. I never lost my temper but took all that in great humour and with a smile and waited.

When there was silence I started speaking and told them that they had had their say and now they should give me a chance. Within a few minutes the students were responsive. After almost one and a half hours of gentle persuasion, a sane dialogue started. All the students except a few hard-core ones came round and agreed to my suggestion that over a three months period they would work in the afternoons and weekends, along with fifty Nalanda students I promised to bring, to repair all the damage, whitewash and paint all the buildings, redo the garden beautifully and convert the school to be a model educational institution in all respects.

We fixed the dates and immediately started work. The parents, teachers and the community all gave a helping hand and in less than three months we achieved our target.

The Principal was so happy that he invited a senior member of the Education Ministry to be the Chief Guest at a special Mahatma Gandhi Centenary Exhibition organised jointly with the Sarvodaya Shramadana Movement at the school. All guests were seated on mats spread on the ground on the stage. Among the invitees were the Principals of Royal, Nalanda and Wesley. The Chief Guest arrived and when we all welcomed him, he looked at me and said, "Ah, the shramadana man".

In essence, what he said was, "Children in those big houses must be attending big schools in Colombo like Ananda, Nalanda and Royal... Those from the poorer houses must be attending this school... All disparities are due to the class structure of our society... We should get together and destroy the existing system..." All of us were shocked at his irresponsible words and most people gathered there including the parents looked at me.

It was a text book example of ignorance of the reality of the place he was in and the people he was addressing. The barrage of words he used was a typical example of intolerance using the spoken language.

It is so important that even so called educated people find out the historical background to a situation and the kind of audience one is addressing, (even more so in public speaking), before making sweeping statements and demonstrating one's knowledge and administrative or political authority.

My generation of Sinhalese has had many opportunities to learn, to teach, to play and work with human beings belonging to other races, religions and even nationalities. There was no feeling of discrimination and inequality at all in our associations. Very often I brought home my fellow students, teachers or friends and my mother always called them '*putha*' (son) or '*duwa*' (daughter). When we organised the first Shramadana Camp in Neervaly – Kaithadi in Jaffna in 1960 to cut a road, my mother was among the thousand other volunteers who went to Jaffna. She stayed in the camp for seven days and physically worked. In us there wasn't the faintest feeling of communalism. When we left Jaffna hundreds of Tamil people gathered at the railway station to bid us goodbye and asked us to come back. Tears fell from the eyes of both the Sinhalese and Tamils when we parted.

In that camp at the very first meeting we had (what we call a family gathering) a highly respected and reputed Tamil scholar for whom I too had a deep affection asked me a question at the open forum. He asked whether we were for 'Sinhala Only' or for parity between Sinhala and Tamil languages. We were all taken by surprise at this unnecessary question, but I had to give an answer. I asked him what answer he expected from us. If I had said Sinhala Only, all of them would chase us away from Jaffna and that would be the end of the Amity Camp. On the other hand, if I said we were for parity the moment we returned to Medawachchiya or Anuradhapura the Sinhala extremists would deal with us and that would be the end of our efforts to bring the Sinhala and Tamil people together for a better understanding of one another.

I said, as people believing in non-violent conflict resolution, our first objective was to bring people physically together in a friendly and tolerant psychological and social environment. It was much easier to solve difficult problems under such circumstances. That was why during the ensuing seven days we should forget about the Sinhala and Tamil languages and strive to talk the language of love which was superior to all man-made languages. I stressed the importance of overcoming what some now call 'tablomania' (sitting at a table to resolve problems) and giving an opportunity for direct dialogue among the affected populations.

We held a seven-day Shramadana camp on the very spot where the first Sinhalese, one Mr Seneviratne, was killed in 1956 and which led to the first communal riots. The name of the place was Wantharamullai and the year was 1959. About 300 Sinhala and Tamil youths were working in the camp digging wells and building irrigation canals when suddenly a stately looking Tamil lady suddenly drove up to the camp office and started reprimanding me for bringing Sinhala youths to Batticaloa.

She said, “British imperialism has been replaced by Sinhala dictatorship on the Tamil people,” and asked us to leave. I think she was the sister of the then Federal Party leader. I didn’t take offence but quietly said, “Madam, shall we go to the village where they are working and then decide what we should do?” She agreed and I took her to the work sites. What she saw was several hundred people, young and old, working together, with their soiled hands and feet. It was very difficult for her to see the Sinhalese separately from Tamils. The Sinhalese were talking broken Tamil, while the Tamils were talking broken Sinhalese. She wanted me to call everybody together at lunch time, promising to come back and meet them personally. She did come back, bringing a lorry load of rice and other food requirements which were sufficient till the end of the camp. She made a very fine speech, complemented us and wanted us come back with more people, promising to feed us all. She admitted publicly that what we were doing was a people’s solution to a problem created by politicians. She further said, “Of course your approach will take a long time”. She was right and we are still continuing after 40 years!

In the sixties we had groups of Tamil and Sinhala volunteers camping in such places as Bulathsinhala and Nedalagamuwa in the South and in Kilinochchi, Pungudutiu and many other places in the North and East. In the seventies onwards, individual volunteers were placed for longer periods from three months to one year as a part of our long term volunteer exchange programme where Sinhala youths lived with Tamil families and the vice versa. Whenever Tamil youths came to the south for various exchange programmes they were always accommodated at Ananda or Nalanda Colleges, which were the two leading Sinhala Buddhist schools in Colombo.

In the 1960s in Jaffna Peninsula itself, we took the initiative and constructed 10 school buildings for the Tamil Buddhist communities. One young boy just out of Wesley College and myself were the only two Sinhala people who were in Jaffna supervising the construction. While he was permanently stationed there, I paid occasional visits. The funds were contributed by a number of philanthropists in Colombo led by Mrs Somi Meegama and Mr Ananda Semage, two well known Sinhala Buddhist leaders. The people of Jaffna gave their full co-operation to this project.

All this work was done in a very friendly spirit and the word ethnicity was not uttered by anybody. It was Tamil people who suggested that the schools should be named after Sinhala Buddhist leaders in the south. For example, the schools were given names such as Amunugama Sri Vipassi Vidyalayam, Sri Madihe Pannasiha Vidyalayam, L H Metthananda Vidyalayam, Ananda Semage Vidyalayam and so on.

The ten mile road to the ancient seat of Buddhist learning, Vilgam Viharayain at Trincomalee was constructed in the 1960s by a one-week Shramadana camp we organised. While about 500 Sinhala people from the south joined this Shramadana camp almost double that number of Tamils joined us in constructing this road. When we started the cleanup campaign at Girihanduseya, north of Trincomalee, all three communities of people from all religions participated in this venture.

When a terrible tidal wave struck the Mannar district, the Sarvodaya movement rushed there and with over 300 volunteers from the South reconstructed the houses and services. I personally led the campaign, staying there for three months. The government assistance was directed through Sarvodaya. When a similar tragedy occurred in the Eastern province a few years later, it was Sarvodaya that led the Relief and Rehabilitation campaign in over 200 villages. The local Sinhala and Muslim people liberally contributed to help their Tamil brethren.

We cannot think of one single cause that disrupted the solidarity, tolerance and unity that prevailed among the common Sinhala, Tamil and Muslim people in our country. Multifarious factors contributed to the series of communal riots which culminated in the worst of all – that black Friday in July 1983 – which I personally believe was the beginning of a new era in our history.

Having tried every possible way to prevent this catastrophe, once it happened there was no alternative but to do our utmost to repair the damage. We did this first in the form of immediate relief to the victims of communal riots. Sarvodaya started the first camp in Ratmalana Airport to which Tamils were brought amidst all threats from extremist Sinhalese. The Sarvodaya volunteers manned this camp and provided temporary shelter, first aid, food and other immediate relief. Several other camps were started by the government and we gave help to those also.

Having set up the camp and organised relief work with assistance from certain committed government administrators and political leaders, we rushed to all the districts in the south, north central, Sabaragamuwa and Uva provinces addressing large gatherings with the help of the police and the army to bring back sanity to our people. Meetings were held in Kalutara, Ratnapura, Kandy, Badulla, Hatton, Anuradhapura and Vavuniya. Amidst a lot of advice from my own colleagues not to make the trip, I drove up to Jaffna during the first week of August itself.

On the way I met a lot of Sinhala people leaving the North and security personnel who advised me not to go. When I reached Jaffna Kachcheri even the government agent was surprised that I was there. I called the then MP for Jaffna who came to the Kachcheri and the first words he uttered were, "It is all over now. The bridge is broken and we can never live together. Please go back." I consoled him and told him that I had come to start rebuilding the bridge. He and the agent accompanied me to go to Kankasanturai where the refugees were brought in by ship. There I met the TULF leader and the President who exercised tolerance towards me. Through our Jaffna Sarvodaya District Centre and the staff, I organised the maximum I could do for relief.

I went to meet a number of groups and addressed meetings in schools even in the Jaffna Nursing School. In spite of what had happened all were cordial to me. The members of the Jaffna Municipal Council received me and all I could do was to make a symbolic donation of Rs10,000 to start a Library Reconstruction Fund. I paid courtesy calls to religious dignitaries, who listened to and agreed with me, that we should work together to build reconciliation. Only one elderly high Christian religious dignitary kept me standing at his house and reprimanded me for over one hour for coming to the Tamil Eelam to bring about reconciliation. He even asked my Tamil friend, our Jaffna Sarvodaya Co-ordinator, what he was doing with a Sinhalese. This was the only instance my solidarity mission for non-violence and peace failed!

On the third day, one of the service clubs in Jaffna invited me to meet young separatist leaders. They severely scolded me and shouted at me for all the faults of the Sinhalese in the past. They branded me as an agent of the Sinhala chauvinists. Having had the experience of being branded as a communist, then a capitalist stooge and finally a CIA agent. This was not a new experience. The only new thing was the terrible violent conflict that could be felt hanging in the air. Most of the young men who took up arms to fight for a separate state were there.

Maybe unlike some in the south, they were not jealous of me, they were not afraid that I would be a political threat to them. Perhaps with my track record from the mid-fifties and from what they had heard from their parents and elders about me, they never questioned the genuine effort I was making after almost four hours of discussion. When I left they wished me good luck and said they were ready for both an alternative just solution or an armed struggle to win their just rights.

At this point I got a call from a Ministerial Secretary to the President from Colombo who said that the President had heard I had come to Jaffna and inquired whether I was safe. I replied positively, and courteously told him that I did not need any special security from the government. My security is the common people whether they were there in Jaffna or in my home town Galle. Anyway he told me that the President wished me to see him as soon as I returned.

Even before I went home on my return from Jaffna I dropped in at the President's residence and appraised him of the very tense situation and the importance of preventing our country plunging into a bloody civil war. I met several other government and opposition leaders to whom I had easy access and also pleaded with them not to treat this situation lightly. I knew among most leaders personal power and political interests were stronger than national interests and feeling for human lives, and the only alternative was to do whatever we could within our limitations, as citizens of this country.

The following month in September 1983, I went back to Jaffna to invite participants for the first ever National Conference on Peace and Reconciliation which was held at the BMICH (Bandaranaike Memorial International Conference Hall) on the 1st and 2nd of October 1983. On this trip I also got the consent of a cross section of people in Jaffna, Pungudutiv, Nagadipa, Point Pedro, Kilinochchi, Vavuniya, Medawachchiya and Anuradhapura to participate in a massive meditational march from Kataragama to Nagadipa.

Over 1,200 delegates, including leading members of the Maha Sangha, dignitaries representing all other religions, races and interests adopted unanimously A People's Declaration for National Reconciliation and Peace.

Based on this declaration we initiated the follow-up programmes such as the Sarvodaya 5R Programme – Relief, Rehabilitation, Reconstruction, Reconciliation and Reawakening – which is continuing to this day. Under reconciliation, seventeen national large peace meditational walks where a minimum of 50,000 to a maximum of 100,000 participated, peace rallies, peace seminars and *Shanti Sena* (peace) Camps were held.

Before the first meditational peace march started from Kirivehera in Kataragama to Nagadipa in Jaffna on the 4th of December 1983 we organized religious ceremonies on the 2nd and 3rd at respective shrines of different faiths. Buddhists, Hindus and Muslims have their places of religious worship in Kataragama. Christians don't have one. So after several thousand peace pilgrims participated in religious ceremonies of all faiths, except the Christians, I suggested to Buddhist monks and the Basnayake Nilame that we should allow Christians of all the different denominations to conduct a special service in front of the Kataragama Kovil.

There were several hundred Buddhist monks and among them were many leading Nayaka Theros. To my surprise, they unanimously agreed to my suggestion and a colourful Christian service was conducted.

It was an inspiring sight to see hundreds of Buddhist monks in their saffron robes, Hindu priests and Muslim mullahs encircling and watching in silence hundreds of Christian priests and nuns performing their religious

Dr A T Ariyaratne guiding a mass meditation for conflict resolution.

rites at Kataragama for the first time in our history. It was a true expression of solidarity of all religions for reconciliation and peace.

When the Peace Walk started at an auspicious time on the morning of December 4th with over 25,000 peace pilgrims and reached Tissamaharama by noon amidst thousands of common people lining up on either side of the road and expressing their solidarity, we had no doubt that People's Power would triumph over violence and bring peace and justice to our people. Our hopes were short lived. How this peace effort was aborted by small minds close to the seats of power is an altogether different story.

At the time that Sarvodaya organised these activities, there were no other similar efforts known to us which were launched by the government or others. They all cooperated with us and therefore we could keep our efforts away from petty power politics and narrow selfish objectives and contribute to lasting peace and reconciliation even in a small way.

There were no peacemakers from outside the country who worked on their own with their own agendas drawn up outside our shores. There were no organisation who was doing relief or rehabilitation comparable to the scale that Sarvodaya was doing these programmes. Even if they did, they used the Sarvodaya network.

When I visited Jaffna last year before the peace talks started and the war was still going on, several people thanked Sarvodaya for feeding several thousand people for two weeks in 1987 when the IPKF forces were in control.

Happily, during the last few years several organisations have taken up these activities. We were, however, very disturbed when between 1988 and 1993, a series of mock peace marches etc. were staged by the then President where one could see in the media uniformed personnel carrying peace banners. So Sarvodaya operated with a low profile during this period though it never stopped its activities.

The Relief and Rehabilitation Programme is an excellent area to release reconciliation processes. Sarvodaya being a non-religious, non-racial and non-sectarian organisation always sent a mixed team to the affected communities for this work.

For example, when a Muslim village or Sinhala village was attacked by Tamil terrorists and a Sarvodaya team rushed there with relief, the affected people were surprised when the Sarvodaya team had Tamil persons in it serving the Muslims or the Sinhalese. Similarly, when R and R services were carried out in the Tamil communities Sarvodaya teams consisted of members of all three communities. This was an eye-opener and an example to the people which had a tremendous psychological effect.

There was another distinct advantage in our approach. It was easy to get the co-operation of the government administrators and the Army as well as the LTTE and other militant groups for our humanitarian work.

Certain international aid organisations deliberately sabotaged this programme. They went on the presumption that Sarvodaya was predominantly Sinhala and Buddhist and therefore should confine its work only to the

Sinhala areas. They openly said this at a Donor Consortium meeting. They pretended ignorance on Sarvodaya's track record of working for almost four decades with all communities and each area was manned by workers from that area whether they were Sinhala, Tamil or Muslim. They interfered in appointments of staff members to the Sarvodaya 5R section and even started laying down conditions as to where bank accounts should be kept and with what amount of advances. Finally, they withdrew all aid to the 5R section.

In non-violent resolution of conflicts we have to persevere and keep going with patience years on end and exercise a lot of tolerance, not only when confronted with conflicting parties, but also when confronted with hypocrisy and make-believe campaigns for peace and reconciliation. We also have to deal with some expatriate organisations with hidden agendas.

In the words of Professor Johan Galtung, "Violence is irreversible; that should not serve as a model. Non-violence is always reversible, substituting for one act of non-violence another, in a great chain of non-violence." This is exactly what we are doing.

The commonly used words such as solidarity, tolerance, peace and reconciliation lose their relevance and usefulness unless these are practised in our personal life in everyday relationships. The relationships we have with our parents, siblings, wife and children, grandparents and grandchildren, relations, neighbours, friends, superiors and subordinates in the work place, school or higher educational institution and those strangers we meet in everyday life are fundamental for us to develop inner peace as well as to contribute to social harmony. When we are estranged from our closest family members at home it is ridiculous to think of building solidarity with others who are not even known to us.

I am not a believer in Sinhala solidarity or Tamil solidarity. Neither do I believe in Buddhist, Hindu, Islamic or Christian solidarity. The dictionary meaning of solidarity is a state of unity resulting from common interests, feelings or sympathies. In practice this kind of partial solidarity polarises the existing differences between human groups creating greater potential to try to resolve differences with coercion and violence. Even within these groups complete solidarity cannot be achieved. Israeli Prime Minister Yitshak Rabin was killed by a Jew and he was one of the foremost leaders who worked for Jewish solidarity. Mahatma Gandhi was killed by a fellow Hindu, but he strived to build solidarity among all human beings. I strongly believe in solidarity with the living world, with humanity as whole. I believe in solidarity with universal spiritual values which can be drawn from all religions and not merely of solidarity with one religion or with all religions.

The foundation of true solidarity, Peace, Tolerance and Reconciliation is BOUNDLESS COMPASSION. We have a beautiful word to express this, namely, *Metta*. "Mettanca Sabba Lokasmin, Manasan Bhavaye Aparimanan – Have boundless compassion towards all humanity and all that is living." This may appear as an ever receding ideal for the practitioner but what is indispensable for greater peace and harmony is an incessant striving to reach this ideal in our everyday life.

During the last thirty eight years the Sarvodaya Shramadana Movement has organised 47,690 camps and put in 45,470,444 days of gift labour for village infra-structural activities, according to the records we have maintained in the Sarvodaya central office. While I do not underestimate the economic benefits accrued by the poorest of the poor by this non-monetised capital contribution to the development of our country, I must mention that we were equally or more concerned with awakening the individual, family and community personality of our people along certain universal value systems. National Reawakening can only become a reality if we can have enough human beings, families and village and urban communities to tread a path to self-awakening.

Having participated in hundreds of these camps and other projects in all parts of our country and with different communities, I have gathered unforgettable experiences. I am one of those helpless individuals who witnessed at a distance from the seats of power how a people's value system was torn apart by vested interests be they party- politicians, bureaucrats or technocrats, religious dignitaries, Marxist ideologists and activists, proponents of capitalism and centralisation of political and economic power. What we were doing never fitted into their set theories and aspirations and therefore were not tolerated.

They gave their own interpretations to what we were doing. To this day this is still happening. Of course I must admit that among all these categories there was a good number of persons who personally and privately admired and assisted this work, but very few had the courage to openly come out and support this process of building broad-based solidarity and tolerance by non-violent direct constructive action leading to lasting peace.

Metta is the first universal value a critical proportion of the population should cultivate. Every human being should strive to inculcate in his or her life METTA or RESPECT FOR ALL LIFE. This is not easy but can be achieved. *Metta* will not become an integral part of one's consciousness unless it is carefully cultivated and translated into KARUNA or COMPASSIONATE ACTION. What we attempted to do in the form of about 80 programmes we developed pertaining to welfare, development and peace-building and so on were the external manifestation of Karuna or Compassionate action.

If correctly practised this kind of humanitarian action results in the development of a unique kind of joy in the participants' consciousness which is a form of MUDITHA or IMPERSONAL JOY – a kind of joy one gets from a selfless and non-egoistic act.

Most elites in a society that is drifting aimlessly, with most of its leadership engaged in power-seeking, money-making and publicity-hunting will hardly understand the deeper meaning behind the Sarvodaya Shramadana action.

The communication media, that generally subserve these elites will more often than not give misinformation which is more sensational than the deeper truthful information. They insult the average readers by assuming that they cannot grasp non-sensational truths.

George Simson the founder and director of the Center for Biographical Research and the journal, Biography, in a recent afterword to a book titled *Hawaii's Journeys in Non-violence* (a publication of the Matsunaga Institute for Peace), has written the following interesting passage:

> *"The great bold premise in recent times conjoining verification, validation and non-violence is the 'Seville Statement on Violence' promulgated by a group of natural and social scientists (but unfortunately no humanists) in 1986 and endorsed by the American Anthropological Association. It asserts five basic propositions:*
>
> *"IT IS SCIENTIFICALLY INCORRECT TO SAY:*
>
> - *That we have inherited a tendency to make war from our animal ancestors.*
> - *That war or any other violent behaviour is genetically programmed into our human nature.*
> - *That in the course of human evolution there has been a selection for aggressive behaviour more than for any other kind of behaviour.*
> - *That humans have a violent brain.*
> - *That war is caused by instinct or any single motivation...*
>
> *The same species who invented war is capable of inventing peace.*
>
> *"Here we see that the validating principle is the scientific proposition, 'it is scientifically incorrect'. One may object that the validation is only scientific validation, not religious or cultural, as is the case with most of the essays in this collection.*
>
> *"But one can then object to the objection by arguing, that if the most carefully disciplined of the validating routines, the 'sciences', can be this bold, it is equally possible for the more imaginative routines of the spirit and heart to find a way for the last proposition quoted here: that we can learn to be violent or non-violent. As violence has failed, we should try non-violence."*

We tried the 'more imaginative routines of the spirit and the heart' to find a non-violent way – cultivation of *Metta*, *Karuna* and *Muditha* in social action. We were treated with indifference, ridicule, abuse and oppression by those who wielded power as well as those who aspired to wield power, while the poor and the powerless accepted us with respect and affection.

In essence there was hardly any difference in the way a non-violent constructive social transformation movement was treated from that of a subversive violent one. In fact those who take to violence and then transform themselves for whatever reason get better treatment and are listened to more than those who never resorted to violence. Why this is so I still fail to understand.

In the Cakkavattisihanada sutta Lord Buddha says, within everyone of us there are five communities – Brahmana community, Samana community, Khastriya community, Gahapati community and Migapakkhi (beast) community. Within our personalities we have to develop a proper balance between the forces symbolising the first four and build solidarity if we are to defeat evil represented by the beast community. Then only can we raise the *Dhamma Dhajo* – Flag of Justice.

Maybe in the subconscious of most of those who are powerful there is more respect, recognition and adoration for violence than for non-violence. This is the Migapakkhi element. It may even be a fear in their subconscious to recognise a moral force which they themselves do not possess in sufficient measure. This is the weakness in aspects pertaining to Right Understanding, Detachment, Principles of Justice and Reality pertaining to the household life. We can even assume that the nature of our political, economic and other social structures are basically violent and, therefore those who temporarily control them lose their confidence in non-violent and moral alternatives. However those of us who have a life-long commitment to non-violence have to accept this reality with compassion and continue to go on our path accepting both praise and blame, loss and gain, comfort and pain, with the same detached mind.

In other words we have to cultivate a fourth quality to awaken our personality, namely, UPPEKHA – Equanimity. All our actions should end up with mental joy. "You do it. You are happy. You are mentally peaceful. You then keep quiet." That is equanimity. In the words of the Buddha: Nibbana Manasa Naro – Man's actions should always end up with mental peace.

At the personal level, it is my experience that, what Buddha called the Four Sublime Abodes (*Satara Brahma Viharana*) are very effective principles in generally inculcating qualities of solidarity, tolerance, reconciliation and peace in our relationships with our fellow human beings. With the exception of a negligible few who live a secluded life and practice higher meditation and try to acquire these sublime qualities, the common citizen needs to be provided with organised and systematic opportunities to cultivate these qualities. These have to be learnt.

That opportunity is provided by the Sarvodaya Shramadana Movement in the form of Shramadana Camps where a physical, psychological and social environment is provided for such practice. This is followed up by an integrated development programme to build up a new society.

When it comes to social action certain principles, namely, Sharing, Pleasant Language, Constructive Action and Equality in Association are given pride of place and practised by us. These are traditionally known as *Satara Sangraha Vastu* or Four Principles of Social Conduct. The place where this form of conduct can be ideally practised is the family. If it could be extended to the extended family and to the broader community life to that extent there will be social progress and harmony.

This is what we have been attempting to do through Sarvodaya Community Awakening Programmes (called *Gramodaya-Grama Swarajya* and *Nagarodaya*, when we work in cities).

However spiritual, moral, cultural and social development alone would not sufficiently influence people to have harmonious and peaceful relationships. The economic and political transformations are also of critical importance. Therefore, as Sarvodaya progressed over the years and faced numerous challenges, it became necessary for us to develop creative, innovative and non-violent programmes as an alternative approach to influence the economic and political life of the people. We were aware that we were getting into more difficulties as we expanded to these fields. We knew that in addition to individual harassments we have faced thus far, now we would be facing organised and structural opposition.

Starting with 100 villages (1967), and then expanding to 1,000 (1975) and 5,000 villages (1980) and now to 10,000 villages (1995) Sarvodaya has progressively extended this Village Awakening Programme. Sarvodaya is committed to empower these communities in three integrated sectors: social, economic and technological.

There are over 80 different categories of activities Sarvodaya is engaged in, which come under these three sectors. Sarvodaya activities range from early childhood development programmes to Insight Meditation.

When implementing these programmes it is a daily occurrence that we have to contend with those who lack understanding of what we are doing or pretend not to know. We have to live and work in a society where such people live, and move with great patience and understanding of human nature, even though we have to waste a lot of time on these trivialities, so distant from our ideals.

Today, as I am writing this paper, I was disturbed by two incidents, which needed my intervention. I am relating here only one of these.

I got a telephone call from a distant city. A twelve year old child was taken to the Police Station and remanded yesterday. Today he will be produced before the magistrate. Along with other children, this child was playing in the playground of the Sarvodaya centre. The ball had fallen into the next garden which belonged to a guest house. The child had gone near the wall and seeing a gentleman on the other side called him and said, "Uncle, can you please pick up the ball and throw it back". The gentleman got angry and asked the boy whether he knew who he was. The child got scared and ran away. The gentleman who happened to be the magistrate living at the guest house called the police.

The police came and took him to the police station. He had to stay overnight like other suspects at the police station. The complainant was the Magistrate himself and today he will also be the judge. The offence was a child calling an adult 'uncle'.

When I heard of this incident what came to my mind were several past incidents like this including the one about the angry educational bureaucrat. Lord Buddha cautioned us about the danger of thinking too big about ourselves. I quote from the Karaniya Metta Sutta.

"Nathi mannetha kaththa cinan khanthi, byarosana patigha Sanna Annamannassa Duhhan Ichcheyya": If one thinks that one is a big person one gets heated up and angry and one wants to make the other person suffer even if the person concerned is a child. Intolerance is sometimes the result of self-importance and self-righteousness on the part of some people.

I was told that the police headquarters gets reports on an average of about 1,000 complaints a month from the provinces about violence on children or child abuse. A child in our law is any person below 18 years of age. But how many of us realise the damage that will be caused to child's psyche even when the child is in the mother's womb, or an infant or a teenager by our ill-treating them? (I was told that good sense prevailed and the child was released after a learned lecture by that judicial official. But who can assess the seed of disrespect and mistrust about the institution of law and order sown in the mind of such a child by that experience?)

Intolerance and violence are acquired evil habits. It is my understanding that if, from the conception of a child in the mother's womb up to the end of teenage, proper care is taken by the family and the society to ensure normal physical and psychosocial development both intolerance and violence can be successfully prevented.

For this education of adults in nutrition, health care and psychosocial development of human personality needs to be placed on the top of the social development agenda.

In Sarvodaya community development programmes we give a special place to the mother and child. A pre-school children's group (ages 2 to 5) and a mothers' group are organised in every village we work. The content of training, education and activities are similar in all villages with necessary adjustments pertaining to their geographical, cultural and religious differences. So when this programme operates in Sinhala, Tamil and Muslim areas, the natural outcome is generations of young people who grow up respecting one another's linguistic, religious and cultural differences.

This early childhood development programme is supplemented by other social, economic and technological programmes which give people a vision of self-development towards a no-poverty, no-conflict society, the realisation of which they are participating in.

If we don't get into dogmas and learn to see things clearly with a disciplined mind which can overcome intolerance, that I think is the first step to build solidarity, reconciliation and peace. Building highly devolved social, political, economic and structural networks giving every human group full freedom to express themselves culturally both at local and national levels has to be done simultaneously. Sinhalese, Tamils and Muslims in this country are living around one another in a high level of mix. Territorial separation will be, as Johan Galtung said at a recent meeting in Sri Lanka, 'an invitation to engage in ethnic cleansing.' Cannot we think of something original and creative?

Embracing The Fire

by Dr Rashmi Mayur

Rashmi Mayur is an ecologist and director of the International Institute of Sustainable Future, Bombay, India. He is a longtime environmentalist, dedicated speaker and advisor to UN and 15 countries in the South. He is a member of GEN (the Global Eco-village Network) working to improve traditional villages north of Bombay to make them more sustainable. He is an unfolding poet.

Address:
Dr Rashmi Mayur
73A Mittal Tower
Narriman Point
Bombay 400 021
India
Tel: +91 22 204 57 58
Fax: +91 22 287 12 50
Email: iisfb@gias bom01.vsnl.net.in.

The procession was
pompous and elegant.
I glimpsed at you
in your embellished attire
accompanied by your
young and charming
wife.
You were just so
majestic
that you seized
my heart.
When the procession
left,
I was bewildered and
forlorn.

How does a person
of your stature
succumb to such
an absurd blunder?
How can you be so
imprudent?
I laughed in
anguish and
felt pity for you.

To day I have come
to proffer myself
to you –
my heart, body, and spirits.
I just want to be
yours – forever.
I want you to
consume me.
Then all the
pleasures will be
yours eternally.

Married. I also am –
arranged by my elders.
That is our custom.
I have a child.
I am young and
beautiful.
I am carnal.
Even wine becomes
intoxicated
beholding me.

I am from the tropical
Africa, but my husband
is from the South Pole.
The Sun is too
cold for my body.
He adores the Moon.
He is too sterile
to fulfil me.
He knows about love
as much as the
penguins know about
the desert.

Glory to love!
Let the Sun,
the Moon and
the Earth be frozen
by the snow.
Let there be only
tropical Africa.

I am love
I am special.
No one knows about
the mysteries of love
as I do.
The stars shine
because of me.
I am lightening –
million times
more fiery
than the sun.
It can incarcerate
every woman
on Earth.
I need your
devouring touch
to quench my
uncontrolled desires.

My love
will take you
to heaven –
where we belong.
The Earth is for
the barren earthlings.
Only impotents
live here.
In paradise exists
only love.
Time, space and
the mortal existence
cease.
There, we shall love
forever.
Even Gods will be
vanquished by
jealousy.

Now I am
violently passionate
I cannot wait
even for a moment.
You must hurry.
Remember, patience is
the betrayer of time.

I am wild in fury.
You will die
of my curse
if you fail
to embrace me –
now.
And I will burn
along with you
in my own
fire.

Living in Auroville

Community Conflict Resolution

by Marti Mueller

Marti Mueller has divided her time between Auroville and Paris since 1983. In Auroville, she has worked in environmental education, spiritual philosophy, youth and cultural programmes. She was one of the Aurovillians who represented the community at the Earth Summit in Rio de Janeiro in 1992 and at the Global Forum in Moscow in 1990. She is dedicated to stewarding our planet and safeguarding the earth and ancient wisdom.

Address:
Marti Mueller
81 Rue de Temple
Paris 75003
France

Also:
Shanta
Success Road
Via Abri
Auroville
Tamil Nadu 605101
India

How we live in harmony and resolve our differences in a diverse multicultural community such as Auroville is a major concern. No matter how sincere our intentions, when we live and work together on a daily basis, some disagreement and conflict are inevitable. This is perhaps one of the most interesting and challenging aspects of community living.

Auroville – A Brief History

The international community of Auroville was founded by the Mother in 1968 near Pondicherry in South India. It was founded on the principle of 'unity through diversity' and was to be a 'living laboratory for human evolution'. Auroville is just that. It is a crossroads for people from all cultures and socio-economic backgrounds to come together to work and live together in human unity. It is a place for pioneering in all fields from education and spiritual research to reafforestation, renewable energy and computer software.

Auroville is based in rural India. There are more than a dozen villages in Auroville's immediate vicinity with a population of more than 30,000 people. Auroville's relationships with nearby villages offer a difficult challenge: how to be a viable replicable model for the developing world where new technology and ancient customs can exist harmoniously side by side.

Auroville is an international forum for exploring new visions of life, culture, spirituality, evolution of consciousness and unending education. It is often called 'the city the earth needs' because its aim is to be a living laboratory for evolution towards human unity and sustainability in a world where urbanization and alienation are a major force.

Auroville does not meet up to its goals in every respect, but the charter of Auroville (*see opposite*) touches the heart of Auroville's purpose and serves as a grounding and aspiring force for Auroville's development.

Auroville is situated on a previously barren plateau on the southeast coast of India near Pondicherry. About 2,500 acres of what was once heavily eroded land have been almost entirely reafforested. More than 2 million trees have been planted and water catchment areas have been established throughout the bioregion. Auroville has been slowly acquiring the land it needs through donations. The community comprises about 1,500 people from nearly 40 countries throughout the world. It is an incredible melange of people from different races, cultures and socio-economic backgrounds. One of its primarily challenges is to achieve unity through diversity. And ironically, its diversity was the initial limitation that has become its eventual strength.

There are nearly 80 settlements within Auroville varying in size from single family dwellings to settlements of 40 to 50 people who eat and live together in the same geographical area. Auroville is divided into four zones: international, cultural, residential and industrial. The *Matrimandir*, a place for silence and concentration, is located in the center of what is to be a spiralling galaxy of residential, cultural, and service areas with corridors leading into a greenbelt of farms, parks and forests.

Auroville has been endorsed by UNESCO and the Government of India. The community is recognised internationally as an experimental base for many diverse projects ranging from traditional agriculture and medicinal use of plants, to renewable energy (wind, solar, biogas), handicrafts, health, experimental education, philosophy and spiritual research, appropriate architecture (compressed mud, natural building materials, traditional and modern design), the arts (music, dance, painting, sculpture, etc.), and appropriate rural development.

At present there is an International Advisory Council of prominent world citizens (such as the Secretary General of UNESCO). These individuals advise Auroville on its general development. Under the Auroville Foundation (established by an Indian Act of Parliament), there is a Governing Board of prominent Indian citizens who advise Auroville on specific issues concerning India. Auroville also has a Residents' Assembly, and an Executive Council of local residents to handle internal day to day affairs. There is also a Working Committee to do liaison work with the Government of India and

international bodies. Auroville International Centers (AVI's) also exist in different parts of the world (France, Germany, US, Spain, etc.) to disseminate information about Auroville.

Auroville's economy is based on a collective fund. In principle, there is to be no money exchange between Aurovilians, and each member or family in the community has an account at Pour Tous, the local resource and food distribution center. Pour Tous offers Auroville-grown food and local market foods in areas where Auroville is not yet self-sufficient. Aurovilians are expected to work 5 hours a day in one of the many service, educational or production units in Auroville. They receive a basic maintenance which is credited to their central account fund. While there are many differences in incomes and lifestyles, Auroville's aim is to provide a basic maintenance for everyone and to encourage a broad-based sharing of resources. Auroville was founded on principles of collective living and members are encouraged to live accordingly.

Auroville's yoga is based on karmic yoga, or action and work for the community as a whole. People are free to practise their own spiritual traditions as long as the broad and general founding principles of Sri Aurobindo and Mother are respected. There is a Tibetan Pavilion which was consecrated by His Holiness, the Dali Lama. There are martial arts classes in the Japanese tradition for aikido and karate; research into the Sufi tradition; a choral group with music largely from the Judaic Christian tradition, Indian philosophical seminar groups, etc.

The Auroville charter emphasizes that Aurovilians should be willing servitors of the divine consciousness, which can be interpreted in terms of universal principles of human unity, respect for the environment and good will.

The ideals of Auroville are beautiful; the real challenge is living up to them. Interestingly, most Aurovilians say they have not chosen to live in Auroville because of the people in the community. They say they have chosen to live there because Auroville is a spiritual path.

THE CHARTER OF AUROVILLE

- Auroville belongs to nobody in particular. Auroville belongs to humanity as a whole. But to live in Auroville one must be the willing servitor of the Divine Consciousness.
- Auroville will be the place of an unending education, of constant progress, and a youth that never ages.
- Auroville wants to be the bridge between the past and the future. Taking advantage of all discoveries from without and from within, Auroville will boldly spring towards future realizations.
- Auroville will be a site of material and spiritual researches for a living embodiment of an actual Human Unity.

The Mother, *28th February 1968*

His Holiness The Dalai Lama on one of his visits to Auroville to lay a cornerstone for the Pavilion of Tibetan culture. Auroville has strong links with all of the Tibetan communities in South India. Photo: Ireno Guerci

The great Indian yogi and philosopher Sri Aurobindo saw humans as 'transitional beings'. He said that when consciousness came down and manifested in matter, a new world would evolve. He saw India, which represents all the difficulties of modern humanity, as a place where that consciousness would develop. Sri Aurobindo described India as a 'forerunner' in her mission and service to humanity. He said that as India had been the cradle for inner spiritual life for the individual, now India's task would be to discover a new integral collective expression for the world.

Inspired by Sri Aurobindo's work, his disciple, Mirra Alfassa, whom he called, 'the Mother', founded Auroville as a place where that consciousness could manifest collectively. The focus in Auroville is on karma yoga, or evolving to achieve a higher level of consciousness through working and living together. When the Mother founded Auroville, she said:

> *"There are people who love adventure. I call them and I tell them: I invite you to the great adventure, and in this adventure you are not to repeat spiritually what others have done before us, because our adventure begins from beyond that stage. We are for a new creation, entirely new, carrying in it all the unforeseen, all risks, all hazards... It is something which has never been in the present universe and will never be in the same manner. If it interests you, well, embark. What will happen tomorrow, I do not know. You must leave behind whatever has been designed, whatever has been built up, and then march on into the unknown. Come what may."*

On an outward plane, Auroville is not necessarily any more spiritual than any other place. But all the ingredients are there to learn about ourselves in a context where people dedicate their lives to a divine purpose. And most of the people who live in Auroville say they find that evolution happens there at an accelerated rate.

We are a mirror of all that is around us. Inevitably, all the archetypal problems that exist in the world at large, exist in the microcosm of Auroville too. But what is interesting is the possibility of transforming these energy forces into divine consciousness through common projects and goals. In a community like Auroville, probably every major personality and ego type that one could find in the world exists. In some respects, whether we actually acknowledge it or not, we are all there to help each other on the path towards spiritual realisation. Each obstacle is a point of growth, or revelation. Each individual person is a helper on the journey, for each person represents a personality type that strengthens our natural capacities and reveals our weaknesses. Both of these dynamics are necessary, but it's rare that one person embodies only one or the other for us. We all have a great deal to learn from each other and Auroville is a place that we can learn about serving the divine, loving others, and developing patience, self honesty, purity and harmony of spirit. But it is more than a community where these are simply aspirations, it is a place where we are constantly challenged to live our ideals in a real way.

In Auroville, our deepest personal aspects are challenged most in the context of our ordinary lives. How we get along with each other, how we blend our personalities and visions for a common goal, how we work together on mutual projects, how we actualise our dreams – each is important in building personal change and each is important in building community too. Every community has its own unique learning process. Auroville has had its share of deep problems. What helped Auroville most in the early years was Mother's guiding hand. She was always there to help people find the right path. She said:

> *"What the new consciousness wants is: no more divisions. To be able to understand the spiritual extreme, the material extreme, and to find the meeting point, the point where that becomes a real force."*

After she left her body, the community went through difficult times. But Mother's vision and the wisdom that Sri Aurobindo left us in his teachings has always been a true inspiration and guiding force for the community.

And Auroville is evolving, too. We are slowly working to establish guidelines, tools and techniques that may help us with the practical aspects of living together. In conflict resolution in Auroville, or elsewhere, what is important to remember is that the process is often much more important than the results. It is always good to continually remind each other of this fact. There are a number of techniques that not only can help a community to resolve its conflicts, but to live more harmoniously as well. I have tried to summarise a few of them here...

A Higher Vision

Hold a higher vision. Remember that we are all part of one body, one consciousness. As the great Indian poet Rabindranath Tagore said in his Gitanjali:

> *"The same stream of life that runs through my veins night and day runs through the world..."*

When conflicts occur, ask people to remember the higher vision or collective ideals that have brought them together in the first place. (In the case of Auroville, it is, of course, Mother and Sri Aurobindo's yoga.) In a rapidly changing world, where our planet is seriously endangered and our existence as a species threatened, we humans have more reasons than ever for finding an inner harmony within ourselves, and with each other, nature and the divine. Besides, a 'win-win' situation is more fun and enriching than a context of conflict and dissension.

Conflict is Natural

Recognise disagreements and conflicts as a natural part of community living. Don't try to ignore them, push issues under the carpets or hide behind ideas of perfection. Acknowledge problems and encourage people to speak openly about them.

When conflicts arise, ask people to wait until they are emotionally in control before beginning the negotiation process. Then invite community members to sit together and ask each person to take some moments in silence for inner searching and to ask some essential questions: "How do I really feel? What is really important for me? Can I understand why the others feel as they do?" And another important question: "Do my personal desires match with what is ultimately beneficial for the community as a whole? If not, how can I strive for a rapprochement between my personal needs and what the community wants or needs?"

Web Holders

In meetings it is sometimes useful to ask a few people to sit on the outside of the circle and to form a web of unity around the others. Their task is simply to hold the energy and focus on the higher goals of the community while the others discuss the issues. Choose individuals who are not actively or emotionally charged up over the subject matter. Web-holders do not speak or participate. Their task is simply to hold the web and focus on unity. (This technique which Aurovilians brought back from Findhorn, can have a powerful effect.)

Personal Agendas

When personal agendas are a factor or at the root of community conflicts, help individuals to realise and identify them. Identify sources of power and fear. Be supportive of the person's need to change, and always create a safe space for discussion. Be inclusive not exclusive. Encourage the community to respect individual diversity as something that makes a community richer, even if life is not necessarily easier. Describe rather than judge. Identify and acknowledge everyone concerned. Work for a common goal which everyone can acknowledge as valid.

Some of us have found that in Auroville, when people are going through times of conflict, it can be useful to hold them in one's thoughts and encourage positive energy and good vibrations. When people live in communities, they are often psychically linked in any case, even if these connections are not expressed or necessarily felt on a conscious level. Psychic links become evident when people share on the dream plane, which is a common phenomenon in community contexts.

Be Prepared to Wait

Don't force decisions when individuals or the community aren't really ready. Sometimes it's good to wait on a problem until there's more clarity. In Auroville, some of our major decisions have taken years. It is important, however, to encourage individual members who oppose an issue, where possible, to express their opposition, and not to block the general community feeling. In Auroville, while we often try to reach a genuine consensus, we define our reality by what happens, not by how many people are for or against an issue. In this respect, Auroville has strong elements of what we call 'divine anarchy', which may not be so obviously relevant for other types of communities.

Impartial Arbiters

If a situation really moves into a long impasse, call in impartial arbiters to assure a safe space and to encourage co-operation between individuals or groups. Arbiters can sometimes be very useful, whether the conflicts are interpersonal or involve the larger community. Anyone brought in must be deemed impartial and be fully accepted by all of the parties concerned. Rather than serving as judge and jury, or making any decisions, an arbiter provides a neutral 'safe' space for differences to be aired and acknowledged. This person might give suggestions, which could help to clarify the issues or to move the struggle closer to a solution. Under no circumstances should arbiters lay any judgements on the situation. Their purpose is to provide a safe space for people 'to agree to disagree' because this is the first step ultimately to finding a common solution.

Auroville has a Unity Group, a team of people who have volunteered their services to help out when negotiations are necessary and people need a safe space in which to air their feelings and resolve their difficulties. Sometimes ad hoc groups are formed too. An essential requirement for such a team to work well is that both parties agree to the selection of the facilitators and that both parties actively want a solution. In some cases, it actually suits one or both of the parties to continue the debate and this should also be openly recognised.

Active Listening

Teach and encourage 'active listening'. This can be done in workshops where community members practise role playing and where they learn to listen to and acknowledge the issues of others. One person speaks. Another listens and repeats what the first one has said prefacing it with, "I heard you say that..." We need to remember that this is not the same thing as saying, "I agree..." While conflicts may not actually be resolved in such a way, learning how to listen actively is the very first step towards resolving conflicts. Listening leads to understanding and while understanding is not the same thing as agreeing, it is a recognition that we are all part of an interconnected web of life.

(Earth-stewards Danaan Parry and Jerilyn Brusseau have given us good conflict resolution techniques in the workshops they have done when visiting Auroville.)

Share Power

Communities that have a rotating power base often have less difficulties moving forward to resolve problems and to meet new needs than those where

A study group under the Banyan tree, Auroville. Photo: Ireno Guerci

the power is entrenched. Power entrenchment usually focuses around seniority aspects (those who have been there the longest); financial aspects (those who have access to the money and physical resources that the community needs to operate or realise its dreams); relational aspects (those who know or are friendly with those who have power or influence); and physical aspects (those who find the energy and time to be involved.)

This fourth aspect is a big factor in communities like Auroville, where the physical difficulties of climate, responsibilities for children, etc. are very important. Auroville presently has a working committee that changes every 1 or 2 years. This helps to provide continual new leadership and to prevent people from becoming too entrenched in specific lines of thinking. However, in Auroville, many decisions are made outside of any group that represents the collective. The real 'consensus test' is whether decisions are actually ignored or respected by the community at large on a daily basis.

Whatever the community's organisation, it is important that a wide diversity of different personality types are included in decision-making to increase a sense of involvement and enhance imaginative possibilities for the entire community.

Empower Youth

Empower youth to be part of the community decision-making process. They are less attached to the old models. Help them to become self-motivated and encourage them to make real choices. Show them how to respect themselves and each other and how to develop self-esteem. Help them to believe in their talents and encourage their creative spirit. Let them know that they are valued by all the members of the community.

Gender Issues

Encourage your community to deal consciously with gender issues. Men and women are as different as Venus and Mars, yet real magic happens when they can live together well. Many community conflicts have at their base, unspoken, subtle or explicit gender issues. Encourage men and women to acknowledge their real differences and to work toward acknowledging their complementary aspects, too.

Involve People

Before initiating new projects, brainstorm with all kinds of people in your community. Write down their ideas. Get as many suggestions as possible before working to choose the ones that might work well in the community. Invite continuous feedback to encourage group participation. Ask guests. Even though they may not know your community intimately, they may have some relevant observations and interesting suggestions. Find out how other communities do it. We all learn from each other even though our community contexts and philosophies may be very different.

Teach Patience

Living in community can be both very rewarding and frustrating. Some projects are heightened and accelerated by group participation. Others take longer. Sometimes its important to wait until the vibration is good to adopt a certain action, even if most people know it will be positive or inevitable in the long run. Remember it's how and why we do things that counts the most.

A Beautiful Place

Work to make your community environment a healthy beautiful place. This will inspire people to be more creative and productive. It will also motivate them to make that extra effort to get along because they will like their environment and want to invest their time and spirit in keeping it that way. Have places in your community where people can be alone with themselves and in nature. Trees, for example, are more than aesthetic; they are therapeutic. We shape our homes and afterwards our homes shape our lives.

Celebrate Spirit

Do fun things together. Remember other people are also on soul journeys, just as you are. Affirm those areas where we can share and all work and play together. When a community, or group of people get together, their total energy and thrust is greater than the sum of its parts. There's nothing like working on projects together to loosen up the energy and build understanding and mutual co-operative goals.

Some general individual tips for conflict resolution are: Speak in a way that everyone can hear you. Focus on how you've experienced the problem. Be brief. Describe rather than judge. Allow people time to listen and respond. Listen carefully to the other person telling their side of the story. Summarise both their feelings and the content to be sure there's mutual understanding with "I heard you say" comments.

Identify what's important. Express your main concern in only one or two sentences and ask the others to express their main concern in the same way. Identify what each person wants and why. Brainstorm possible solutions by getting ideas from all sides about possible ways to resolve the issue. Write the ideas down and get as many suggestions as possible. Evaluate solutions and choose the ones that will work for both sides. Be as specific and realistic as possible. Always affirm each other and a basic commitment to change.

Remember understanding is not the same thing as agreeing and that the perspective of others is their reality, just as your perspective is your reality. Neither perspective is the 'truth'. Truth is always relative to a point of reference. Try to keep in mind that other people are on a soul journey just as you are. In most cases, they are also trying to learn. So relate to them in a human way. We are not strangers, but fellow travellers on the path to greater awareness and awakening. There are no enemies, only people sharing with each other and evolving.

Watch where your energy goes. If you focus on your problem, you make it more real and difficult than it actually is. Focus, instead, on the solutions and remember your collective vision. If we put our energy into our vision, we help to manifest what we really want to create. This technique is used in martial arts to break wooden beams with a blow of the hand. By focusing our attention on the other side of the beam, rather than on the wood itself, we are able to cut more easily through the obstruction.

Be prepared to go back to the drawing board as many times as necessary until a harmonious solution is reached. If the negotiations do not lead to an immediate solution, remember that impasse is not defeat and that there is no such thing as forever. In the Auroville context, we try to remember that tomorrow is always another day and that nothing is ever permanent.

If you cannot reach an immediate understanding, it may be because fears on one or both sides are too great. Fear can be broken down by understanding and acknowledging the other person's right to feel different from you and by providing a safe space. Rather than hating or despising people who feel different, we need to give them our respect and love. By remembering that they suffer too, we release some of our own pain and immediately feel better and more connected. Forgiveness is often necessary. Forgiving is always an act of self-love and it activates positive feelings.

We are at a turning point in our history. We are on the verge of a new adventure in planetary consciousness. Our fragile, beautiful planet has been seriously endangered by human carelessness and greed. Our human spirit has been greatly eroded by our loss of a deep and close interconnection with the earth, nature and the divine. This has led to a deep crisis in consciousness. And to add to our difficulties, technological and environmental changes are happening at a dizzying speed. We are being pushed to re-examine our very *raison d' etre* and our bonds with the earth and the cosmos, precisely because we have forgotten our sense of unity. Today the problems that we face are truly global and the answers to our planetary dilemma can only be met with strong collective conscious action. Communities offer wonderful places to explore our potential and to live and manifest our collective being. Auroville's charter speaks of Auroville in the Mother's words, as a living laboratory of human evolution, a place of unending education, with a youth that never ages where people can become willing servitors of a divine consciousness. One of our first steps in Auroville, as elsewhere, is to learn to resolve our differences and to make a commitment to human unity and a deep planetary consciousness.

AUROVILLE
A Living Laboratory for Human Unity
by Bhaga Gabriau

Bhaga Gabriau came to Auroville in 1972. Previously a teacher in France, she has become more and more involved in research and practice of the integral Yoga developed by Sri Aurobindo and the Mother to consciously accelerate the process of evolution for those who choose to dedicate their lives to it. In 1985, she started two twin units in Auroville, in which research is done and shared about the individual aspects of the evolutionary work to be accomplished and about its collective aspect: human unity.
Address:
Repos
Auroville 605 101
Tamil Nadu, India

> *"Auroville wants to be a universal township where men and women of all countries are able to live in peace and progressive harmony, above all creeds, all politics and all nationalities. The purpose of Auroville is to realize human unity."*
> The Mother

Human unity as an ideal is not new. But it has always remained an impossible utopia, because of human nature being what it is. The uniqueness of the Auroville experiment is that it is based on an evolutionary vision of our future, as expressed by Sri Aurobindo:

> *"The changes we see in the world today are intellectual, moral, physical in their ideal and intention: the spiritual revolution waits for its hour and throws up meanwhile its waves here and there. Until it comes, the sense of the others cannot be understood and till then all interpretations of present happening and forecast of man's future are vain things. For its nature, power, event are that which determine the next cycle of our humanity."*

In this evolutionary vision, which we owe to Sri Aurobindo and his spiritual collaborator, the Mother, what we now know as 'human nature' is only a transitory phase towards a higher and truer consciousness. According to Sri Aurobindo, this consciousness will gradually transform, not only our mentality, but our whole being, down to the very cells of our body, revealing the true, spiritual nature which has been secretly growing in us since the beginning of time. That evolutionary new step has already started to take place, and will enable more and more human beings to discover their inner, spiritual oneness, and to live this 'unity in diversity', which we only dream of today. For in our new nature, 'unity in diversity' will become our spontaneous perception of things, instead of the divisive mental consciousness which is now our biggest obstacle in Auroville, just as elsewhere in the world.

In the mental way of looking at things, the 'normal' way for ordinary human beings, contradictory views are seen as irreconcilable opposites. Usually one view is seen as the 'truth', and the other as 'falsehood'. The problem is that both of the poles can equally be seen as the 'truth' and validly so, depending upon each person's psychological make up and natural tendency. Each of us is like a specific mental filter of the white light of truth. It is as if each one could perceive and express only one, or at most, several colours of the white light. Only when we put all the colours of the rainbow or the prism together, can we recompose white light. The time has come at last to move to a higher level of consciousness than the mental one; a consciousness which naturally, spontaneously, sees the truth as a whole, a living 'totality', where every point of view finds its source and has its place, however big or small, in an arrangement which furthermore rearranges itself all the time as evolution marches on, so that all aspects of the truth which are the most relevant for a certain period of time, come to the forefront, and then recede when their time of predominance has passed. But no one aspect should ever be considered as complete and absolute truth, as our minds might have us believe. The Supramental Truth which this world here is meant to manifest is a harmonious totality, a balanced whole.

So, this is Mother's purpose in Auroville, for it is the new consciousness for the manifestation of which Auroville was created. In February 1996, she wrote, "Auroville... at last a place where nothing will have the right to impose itself as the exclusive truth". Only when all of us, the Aurovilians, instead of justifying or even glorifying our confrontational attitudes, learn how to develop, or at least allow the development in ourselves of that new consciousness, only then will Auroville be truly 'the City the Earth needs', 'the City at the service of Truth'.

This is the only way that true peace, a concrete human unity, can be realised among us in Auroville, especially when we recognise at last that we are all complementary, and that we all need each other, with all our differences, for a fuller manifestation of the ONE Truth we all manifest partly.

So, in Auroville, any techniques that are useful in helping us on our way to human unity, any means of alleviating our present human state of division and disharmony, are of course, welcome, and are practised to a certain extent. But they can never be seen as the real means; the main emphasis and effort has to be put rather on the central, and radical change within us which will have human unity flow out of it as a natural consequence. This change is the gradual shift to that higher and truer consciousness which is the next step in our evolution. As it gradually happens in more and more of us, human unity too will unfold just naturally and inevitably among us.

Towards Sacred Society

The Life of Tui Community, Aotearoa/New Zealand

by Robena McCurdy

Robena McCurdy is a community development worker, teacher, permaculture designer, landworker, innovator and pioneer. As well as living and working at Tui Community, she works as a consultant for 'Village Development' in South Africa based at the Tholego Development Project, a permaculture education and demonstration centre for rural and regional self reliance.

Address:
Tui Community
Wainui Bay
RDI
Takaka
Aoteroa/New Zealand
Tel: +64 (0)3 5259654
Fax: +64 (0)3 5258659

Introduction

In this article I share from my own perspective about the character and qualities of Tui, and the forms we as a group use to deal with conflict: 'preventive' in the way of social design, and 'emergency' in the way of crises management strategies. The strongest emphasis is on preventive measures. By sharing my experience, I hope to help minimise certain negative aspects of community development by other intentional community villages. It also offers inspiration and guidance, hopefully giving new projects the confidence to begin, and flagging communities the encouragement to change and move forward. Were other members of Tui to write on the theme of this chapter, each would come up with their own quite different expression of it. The uniqueness of each individual enriches our community. In my observation a group follows the same life stages as a living being:

Conception	ideals, ideas, spiritual impulse;
Pregnancy	nurturing the vision;
Birth	launching into unknown territory, and the need for commitment via material means to sustain the newly born (e.g. money, labour, goods);

Walking	venturing forth, putting down roots, physical expression;
Childhood	unfoldment of original seed, modified by environmental influences;
Teenage years	exploration, testing models, challenging structure, rebellion against established forms;
Adulthood	re-evaluation, refinement, full responsibility, managing the initiative you have undertaken.

Adulthood has several maturing stages. I do not know how many years each stage takes. Although a cat, a dog or an elephant have similar stages of development, they all have different timing to reach maturity. In my observation, Tui has after 11 years, reached a stage of adulthood. We have stumbled our way through these stages, and learned so much along the way about how to live with each other with caring, honour, honesty and respect. Often our learning was painful, taking us down to granite bedrock and through molten fire. The outcome of our commitment to 'stay with the process' has meant that Tui has evolved into a healthy community organism respecting individual freedom; to nurturing relationships, maximising co-operation and minimising conflict.

Origins

Tui Community is situated in Wainui Bay, adjacent to Abel Tasman National Park, in Golden Bay, Nelson Province, Aotearoa/New Zealand. This coastal land totals 150 acres, with a mix of rolling hills and flat arable land; clear, year-round streams of drinking water quality; and a valley of regenerating native forest. In 1996, Tui consisted of 22 adults and 18 children, from 6 nationalities. Tui arose out of an holistic gathering in Nelson province in 1984, when a few of the 300 people present committed to continue the spirit of the gathering by forming an intentional community. A year from conception, and after three major meetings, several people rented a large farmhouse and moved housetrucks, housebuses and caravans onto the surrounding land. There we lived for a 'trial time' together, discussing community ideals, experimenting with financial systems, co-operative business ventures and collective childcare.

'Tui Land Trust', our legal entity, was formed during this phase. We used a specific participatory process to create and consolidate the aims and management method, which constitutes our legal commitment. Tui Land Trust is legally classified as a charitable trust for the broad purposes of landcare, holistic education and healing. The land is held in perpetuity for the purposes stated in the Trust deed, for future generations. There are no shares that can be bought and sold, and no individual land titles. This system of legal ownership and governance has saved us many times from the kinds of conflict we have seen arise in other communities which have a co-operative or a company legal entity. Such things as the fierce debating of the price of shares for new members, or having to quickly raise money at a high interest rate to pay out a member, can jeopardise the survival of a community. 'Unit Title', at the other end of the ownership scale, does not encounter this problem.

After nine months, when we felt ready to purchase land together and build a permanent community, we went through a visioning and commitment process, making written pledges of how much money each of us would personally contribute towards land purchase, and defining our requirements for quality and characteristics of land by drawing up a group mandala of essential and preferred features. We then wrote up our requirements, together with potential available purchase amount, and 'cast the net' for land within the Tasman Bays area. Three months later we had purchased land which met our criteria, and moved our mobile accommodations on.

SETTLEMENT AND LAND

Soon afterwards we drew up a broad zoning of the land for house sites, waterlines, waste disposal, food gardens and forest preserve, and submitted a 'Specified Landuse Departure' planning application to the local council for multiple dwelling status, within our District Scheme. During this time we launched a deliberate public relations campaign with local residents and business people to make ourselves known and visible, with the intention of countering any unsubstantiated resistance and alleviating phantom fears. Our first practical steps were to begin a large communal vegetable garden and to establish a kindergarten for our young children.

At this stage there was a lack of support from within the community for a holistic and integrated design of the land. Had we attempted a collective permaculture design, using participatory methodology, the very different underlying values held by members of our group with regard to land use, would have become glaringly obvious. Instead they surfaced in emotionally clouded ways through tasks and issues as they arose through time. We were in the roles of guardians and developers of this remarkable property, and we discovered that we had fundamentally different approaches to land management.

This varied from 'let the land take care of itself', from those whose motive was to live less stressfully in a beautiful natural environment, to 'let's plan a long term land management strategy', from those who were committed to actively manage the land for the purposes of food and timber self sufficiency. These issues had not arisen before we actually moved on to the land. The outcome of this division was a strong tendency towards an anarchistic style of land management, typified by someone planting trees in places that would in the long term block sunlight from future house sites, and other people transplanting them; some people pulling out wildling pine seedlings because they were viewed as a weed encroaching on native forest, and some people banding together as a 'save the pine tree' group.

My perception is that at the core of the value conflict was 'my value system is right and yours is wrong'. The 'land managers' were considered synonymous with land developers = land rapers. The 'conservationists purists' were considered as unrealistic dreamers, who could hold their 'leave nature unto itself' philosophy because they had the privilege of shopping at the supermarket and purchasing building timber from the timber merchants. This was in the early days, when we had little experience with conflict resolution and we were struggling to find our way together. Yet we sensed that unless we got down to the 'root', we could not manage to carry on living together. You could feel the fear. A few of us had experienced a form of open, honest and reflective group communication used by the Maori (indigenous people of Aotearoa/New Zealand) called *whaikorero*, which makes it possible for people with even vehemently opposing points of view to hear and accept each other to love and forgive. We decided to adapt this sacred protocol to our emerging Tui culture, and the 'Tuki' (outlined further on) was born.

We held a 'Tuki' around the issue of landuse and relationship with the land, and soon got down to the deep, underlying emotional issues. One of the issues I strongly remember coming up was the feeling of guilt and responsibility some carried from their colonial forefathers who basically stole land, branded it 'my property', then exploited and raped it. This, together with the contemporary image of the typical subdivision land developer who scapes off flora and fauna, then reshapes natural terrain into characterless soulless landscape, all for the goal of money. People expressed abhorrence to these attitudes to the land, and their current caretaking responsibility to do it right, to play a tiny part in redressing the balance, weighed heavily. Models were few and far between, and it was inevitable that we would become a model ourselves.

I share this detail as a caution not to judge too harshly nor to react too fast – to take the care and time to discover what underlies people's attitudes. What I have described is the kind of typical polarisation that a group of people, particularly from very diverse backgrounds might strike. It is wise to address attitudes to land use before purchasing land together. Although most of us have now spent eleven years on the land, to a much lesser degree, this difference still lives with us at Tui today. We came from predominantly city backgrounds, and many of our members were relatively new settlers from other countries. Consequently, our collective experience in farming, and particularly within the ecological conditions of this country, was very limited.

We managed to work within the initial zonings we planned for our council application, and adapted as we learned more about microclimates and other environmental behaviour patterns. We have made mistakes aplenty, and learned a lot through time, from living and working closely with the land. We are now reasonably attuned. Commonly managed land is now the responsibility of the 'land group' to administer.

This group is composed of people who are actively engaged in specific areas of land management – such as shelter belts, woodlot, nursery, stream and sea wall maintenance, roads and tracks, lease arrangements and farm machinery. They are autonomous, but guided by community policy, and require community consensus for major developments. Individual households are responsible for designing and implementing of the 'caretaking areas' around their own homes.

Two of the owner-built energy efficient houses at Tui.

View of Tui's vegetable garden.

INFRASTRUCTURE

Currently there are 16 permanent owner-designed-and-built dwellings and 2 mobile homes. Other major structures on the land are: a multipurpose community house, a craft workshop, barn, tool and implement sheds, two visitors' accommodations, a small counselling retreat and massage hut, and a community cultural/spiritual/education centre.

Energy sources are a combination of mains electricity, primarily for communal buildings and heavy machinery, and some solar energy for lighting, water heating and light appliances. The Tui Stream is our source for domestic water supply and gardens irrigation. Sewerage is taken care of via a centralised settling pond with wind, sun and micro-organisms as catalysts to break down the sludge. The liquid nutrient is sprayed onto a coppicing woodlot in a nearby field. It functions well, though some would prefer composting toilets, complemented with a reedbed greywater system, but too little was known or officially documented about these systems at the time of our sewerage application, and so they were not acceptable to our council health inspectors.

SOME PHYSICAL INFRASTRUCTURE KEYS

I uphold that for a community to become close socially, it is essential to have a reasonably central community house and a real plus to have communal washing facilities. In the Western world, if you want to retain individuality, I would caution against living in a communal housing setup – even sleepouts with shared facilities such as kitchen and washroom, are likely to engage people in a lot of group process.

Another area of caution, from our experience at Tui, is communal ownership of tools and machinery. People have such different standards of use and maintenance, and different attitudes and knowledge about machinery. A co-ordinator who sets and monitors the standards is essential if you are going to do this. A special caution is chainsaws and vehicles. These are best to be personally owned, unless they are consistently checked and maintained by an experienced person, and the users have to pass a test to show that they are competent.

SOCIAL ORGANISATION

Tui has a steady stream of visitors, coming to experience community life for a short period of time. Most people are primarily interested in the social aspects of community living.

Of all the questions asked, by far the most common are around issues of human relationships within a close living context. As a reflection of 'Western' society today, people are most concerned about individual versus communal – rights, freedoms and responsibilities, and communication, conflict resolution, decision-making and leadership. Behind these concerns is the fear of losing ones individuality within the group, coupled with the realisation that group interaction and involvement is important for personal wellbeing.

These issues are at the forefront of our lives at Tui. We have worked continually on them over the years, both philosophically, and in experimenting with appropriate structures and guidelines to facilitate quality relating. I believe this area of endeavour to be Tui's greatest strength. The Tui Community Mission Statement, written in 1991, captures the essence of why we choose to live in community, "As a community living together, we are seeking wholeness through fulfilling relationships with ourselves, others and our planet."

MEMBERSHIP

In order to assume full rights and responsibilities for living at Tui, one needs to become a member of the Tui Land Trust, requiring a trial period as a resident in the Tui Community. Membership follows the following steps: short term visitor (up to 1 month); long term visitor (6 months); prospective member (up to 18 months); full member (after official election, for the duration of living on the land). Each applicant requires individual consideration. The procedure is common for all, but the conditions are flexible in order to meet individual needs. When a person applies to become a prospective member, they choose a 'facilitator', who guides them through the more formal aspects of living at Tui, whilst providing personal support where needed.

The staged membership process provides a way whereby members and non members have time to find out if living together works for them. Non members have the opportunity to discover if the culture, customs and philosophy of Tui are sufficiently aligned with their own, in order to invest their future with that group of people. Tui has specific requirements for moving through the various stages towards membership.

LEADERSHIP

Tui's leadership is non hierarchical, and there is no specific leader, neither political nor spiritual. Overall there is a respect for each other's skills and personal qualities, as we entrust each other with guiding the group in particular arenas of decision-making and action plans. As we encourage development of the whole person and mobility of roles, each person takes a turn at meeting facilitation, and people are encouraged to change roles of responsibility at least once a year. There is an overlap period for training of skills and learning of systems, as one person phases out and another phases in.

In recent years the role of the Trust Chairperson has expanded to include keeping an overview of the community wellbeing and Trust affairs on a regular basis, and bringing attention to any areas which are neglected, not respected, nor followed up. This has been an important development. It has noticeably improved Tui's functioning and inter-relationships and generally the community runs more smoothly.

For those of us being raised in the 'Western World', our conditioning towards fending for ourselves as individuals has been so strong, that it needs vigilance to counter that conditioning if one chooses a co-operative lifestyle. Unless it is implanted through upbringing, the pull to be separate and competitive can be so persuasive and unconscious, that it can destroy even the most well-intentioned of communities. I have seen many communities who began as idealistic co-operatives, gradually 'degenerate' into subdivision style nuclear households, where it has become difficult to live as neighbours because of unresolved differences causing bitterness.

LABOUR

In the early days there was more informal labour pooling for communal tasks. We were at an excited, idealist, pioneering stage, and the economic support system gave many of us the time to put our energies into building up Tui. We were living in temporary accommodations, and the children were still very young. Input was based on trust and collective dedication of 'the pioneers', with individual choice as to how much time you put in. The style was fairly anarchistic. In the longer term, this approach led to a wide difference in labour input. This became a contentious community issue, which gave rise to a 'Tuki' on the theme of labour input and community organisation.

As a result of this, we established a fairly efficiently organised system of specific roles and tasks needed to keep the place running smoothly, with teams or individuals for all areas of community and land maintenance. Now each person gives a similar amount of time input per week, a minimum of one day.

Each area has a job description put together by those workers and endorsed by the community. Jobs are: land maintenance, machinery maintenance, orchard, vegetable garden, food/kitchen/shop, services (water, power etc.), visitor co-ordinator, house co-ordinator/maintenance, other community buildings, administration (finance, secretarial), Tui T'mala building, sewerage pond and spray-field woodlot area. All teams are empowered by the rest of the community to make decisions, act, and run their finances as they see fit in the interests of us all. Freedom with responsibility and accountability is the keynote.

Development projects are done by everyone, working-bee style, under a co-ordinator. Additionally, we each take our turn at cooking the daily community meal, via a cooking roster, (one's turn comes around about one every three weeks). Each person has a specific house-cleaning job, which rotates every few months.

With our individual and group income earning activities, housebuilding or maintaining of caretaking area, plus family and personal interests, this is about all we can manage to give voluntarily to the community.

FINANCES

I believe that the greatest test of a community's spiritual alignment is how they deal with the financial realm. In my experiences of community work and life, this is where the most energy gets stuck, and the atmosphere in which a discussion takes place can easily become 'leaden'.

Already Tui had come far along the track to consensus around financial matters by deciding to purchase land under a Trust rather than Company structure, and declaring that the amount a person pledged to the Trust for land purchase be voluntary. This later changed to a guideline amount and proportion of an incoming members assets. Individual circumstances are taken into account when the incoming member meets with the finance group to discuss their contribution.

On a daily level, income earning is an individual's responsibility. Each month we all contribute a small amount to community and land management overheads and development, as well as for bulk food such as grains, which we do not grow on the land. Members earn their income in a diversity of ways, including outside wage-working, small businesses, government benefits, consultancies and products.

Our only business co-operative is 'The Tui Bee Balme Co-operative', a very successful community business which makes natural skin care and healing products, sold by mail order and direct marketing throughout the country. By lifestyle choice, most Tui people devote only half of the week to income earning. This allows time for family, community work and other pursuits. This is made possible by Tui members having lower financial overheads than individual property owners, primarily because the cost of land is shared, as well as facilities, machinery, rates, county services, and bulk food. Labour is voluntarily provided by community residents, and food is primarily home grown.

It is my opinion that for a community to function holistically on all levels, an essential ingredient is to have a form of income earning that ties people together. Of necessity this keeps people having to move forward as a group, as their 'food source' is bound in with evolving sustainable relationships.

Management and Meeting

Each week we hold a two hour business and sharing meeting. It has rotating facilitation (generally one person will facilitate four to six meetings), and decision-making is by consensus. Diverse and creative methods are used as appropriate, to arrive at decisions efficiently and yet sensitively.

If a block to decision-making happens, the facilitator may call a time of silent reflection, or challenge the person or people who are holding on the agreement to share in depth what is behind their decision, and after that there may be further discussion as new information is brought to light, or the person may be asked if they are prepared to stand aside so that the matter can be actioned, although they may not agree with the decision. At times it is obvious that it is too premature to make a decision, in which case items are brought forward to a future meeting, allowing more time for digestion and/or further research. Items passed are recorded and usually empowered with a "ho!".

Similarly, if a person assumes a new position of responsibility they are actively empowered. At times we have used a specific technique: people rub together their palms, then hold up their hands, with palms facing towards the person to be empowered. This little ritual, which consciously focuses positive energy towards the one taking on the responsibility, is powerful, unifying and actively felt by the person. I believe that this act anchors the memory of support in all concerned if the going gets rough.

Small management groups are also empowered in a similar manner. Empowerment means that the person or group is actively given the trust to make decisions and act on behalf of the community. Only people practically involved in that area of work on behalf of the community, serve on these management groups. The groups are: finance, land, garden, technical development, building, community facilities, festivities. Before a group needs to work on an issue, broad policy has already been formed and endorsed by the community as a body. If it is an entirely new area, the group will bring it forward to the community for a policy decision, often with a proposal already formulated for discussion. Since we have adopted the small group and empowerment system, our community meetings are less unwieldy, less frustrating, not overloaded, more efficient, lighter and more fun.

Meetings typically begin with a circle of silence for 'getting ourselves present', at times taking the form of a brief guided meditation, followed by acknowledging each other's presence. Meetings traditionally end with a circle of silence, for reflection, completion, and possibly a song which often captures the mood of the meeting. Each meeting reserves a personal 'sharing spot', which is booked in advance on the agenda sheet. This is a space for a person to openly share about things that are happening for them which they want the whole community to know about, often to do with a shift in life direction. Usually there is no decision-making component, rather an atmosphere of support. Sharing topics cover such themes as children, relationships, work, health, finances. A person may request, or be offered, support outside the meeting time in a particular way. This can either take the form of quiet 'in principle' support from the community for a major life direction shift, or input/suggestions as to how to tackle a problem they aren't able to manage alone (such as a difficulty arising with parenting).

Once a month a part of the meeting is devoted to issues which concern Tui children, and all children, from the youngest to the oldest, are present. This is an opportunity for children or adults to bring forward proposals or problems which need total community input, or to report on particular progress or events. Typical items would be outings, funding for a children's item, serious behavioural difficulties, community sports events. At times it can be overwhelming for children to speak out in a big group. In these instances one or two adults of the children's choice would meet separately with the group of children, and report back to the meeting.

We have formally elected officers of the Land Trust, but as all members of Tui are Trustees, our Trust meetings happen within our community meetings, one precedes the other, and separate minutes are kept. It is easy to determine which is Trust and which is community business, although this was not the case in the early days. Our only separate Trust meeting these days is an SGM to elect a new member, or an AGM to do financial review and planning, and to elect officers. The AGM is also a celebration of the completion of another year together.

Conflict Resolution

Conflict resolution per se is a process needed 'at the end of the line'. Conflict does and will happen in any group, so learning ways to deal with it is vital to the life of a group. It arises because of lack of honesty, differences in habits, lifestyle and values, projections and reflections, and inappropriate structures to meet the needs of a particular group. Providing ways to deal with these areas significantly minimises conflict. If the group does not have agreed mechanisms to deal with conflict, the tension that builds up, spoken or unspoken, inevitably brings about distancing. The imploded energy created by denial is likely to destroy the group eventually.

In my observations and experience, groups which have not upheld personal growth as a prerequisite for group growth and prosperity, have ultimately destroyed themselves. Conversely, if the group's members have a self-centred approach to personal growth, the group's growth will be seriously stunted, although it may have the illusion of appearing healthy upon initial contact.

There is a strong caution here for the New Age movement, where the right jargon can make it look as if people are being accepting, understanding, adaptable and responsible, whereas underneath another personal agenda is going on. e.g. making 'I' own/accept statements when the underlying tone is 'you' are to blame. The privileged society has become so sophisticated at using the communication styles learned through higher education and transpersonal workshops, that these 'underground streams' are often unconscious. At Tui we are not absolved from this tendency. Our collective commitment to giving feedback and 'speaking our truth', helps to minimise the exercising of this somersault psychology.

Personal growth is an important aim of all of us at Tui, and because of this, the approaches outlined here work for us. If personal growth is not one of your group's common aims, you may need quite different approaches. For instance, ones which deal with issues purely at a structural level in order to function. However, with singularly structural approaches, the issues will still be there – instead they can be side-stepped and repressed, and may fester then take another form. If your group is determined to avoid intimacy (getting below the surface), the 'structural solution' will probably be your approach. The result will tend to be a hierarchical, inflexible power structure, and rigidly defined roles.

All prospective members and members of Tui make a commitment not to walk away from conflict. If requested, a member, small group, or, if necessary, the whole community, can be supportive in conflict resolution. We have learnt, and continue to learn useful communication skills to help us move and grow through these times. We expect children, as well as adults, to deal with conflict constructively.

The following is our agreement around conflict:

> *"If a major conflict arises between two members, or between one member and the rest of the community, and they are unwilling or unable to resolve it, the situation is unacceptable to Tui. A community meeting shall be called by any resident member in order to work towards resolution. It is required that both members attend. More than one meeting may be necessary. If no satisfactory progress is made, an outside facilitator, acceptable to the members in conflict, will be invited, and a further attempt made."*

Common Agreements for Daily Living

At the beginning of our time on Tui land, after a year of our experiences of living together, the Common Agreements document was drawn up. Although it is useful as a reference, as a community we generally felt that the discussion and decision-making about the issues raised is more vital than the document itself. However, I would strongly recommend for any group coming together to get clear on boundaries around behaviours which affect their daily lives. It is surprising how different seemingly insignificant personal attitudes and behaviours can have a major impact on people who share territory. It is useful to have these things out in the open early on, to avoid 'battles' or imploded resentments. It is also a useful guideline as to whether or not you can live together.

Common Agreement themes are different to those which appear in a legal document for land ownership or caretaker-ship, although some may overlap. The following headings constitute our Common Agreements document: meetings (procedures and rules), organisational and administrative responsibilities, personal growth and relationships, work (community workload, gender roles in work), visitors, children, employment, religion, medicine/healing, trees, animals, tools and machinery, vehicles, media (radio, hi-fi, television), noise level, food, drugs, chemical sprays, nudity, violence, conflict resolution. A few diverse examples are:

Religion	the community provides for freedom of choice of religion or spiritual path.
Vehicles	are to be kept in allocated vehicle parking areas. Internal roads to be used for utility purposes only (i.e. to drop off and pick up goods).
Gender Roles in Work	we encourage the sharing and teaching of work skills not previously learned because of our backgrounds of role stereotypes and gender inequality in the workplace. Note: In reality this transference has mostly been one way – with the men teaching the women skills such as building and tractor driving.

Consecrating the land around the spiritual centre of the community with flower essences.

Carrot weeding in the community garden – a great way to share stories!

At Tui, new agreements are made and written up as issues arise which need some clear and committed position from the group. These common agreements set a standard for members. They govern communal areas only, where they are taken seriously, honoured, and strictly adhered to. It is important to note that these rules are not 'top-down' dictated, they are decided and agreed upon by all of us, for the sake of minimising stress and optimising harmony. Nowadays it seems that protocol is sufficiently established in Tui daily life for visitors and intending members to pick it up by observation and osmosis. Tui is not about oppressing individual freedom, depriving people of their needs, or forcing personal growth. People's homes are their own domain where they freely determine their own standards. Generally, there seems to be little variance between individual standards and communal standards.

Emotional Management

Tui's mode tended towards crisis management before we faced the fact that, as individuals and as a community, we needed to do something major about taking responsibility for our own realities. This has meant learning to own our mental attitudes and emotional states of being rather than attributing cause or blame to others. Ultimately it amounts to taking 100% responsibility for our inner and outer worlds – creations and reflections, responses and reactions. There is a lot to say on this, and I would refer anyone wanting to investigate deeper, to search in personal growth and healing literature.

When, through various teachers and workshops, we increasingly began to take full responsibility for our belief systems and strengthened commitment to actively bring about change, the way we related to each other and dealt with differences, shifted remarkably. Instead of arguing, backbiting, repressing, 'putting each other down', or 'dumping' on each other, we listened, considered and valued each other's perspective. This was not and is not always so. Taking full responsibility requires vigilance and constant practice and behoves feedback to keep on track. The more support and positive feedback from life itself there is, the less effort it takes, and this way of seeing the world and relating with others becomes natural. The learning never stops.

In my experience, as I unravel the immediate and gross level makeup of my belief system, space is created for the more subtle beliefs to come to light. These seem to be carried intergenerationally and are culturally embedded. In an international community, these culturally ingrained unconscious attitudes will play into how we interact with each other, and will colour our viewpoints.

The introduction of Domain Shift philosophy and technologies to some of our members (via workshops) had a significant influence on our community's growth. Domain Shift is about quantum leaps rather than incremental change, and aims for nothing less than personal and societal transformation – the creation of Sacred Society – bringing sacredness into the most profane activities and the most superficial relationships.

Whereas many transpersonal psychotherapies focus on the mental and spiritual levels, or depend on other people to stimulate and support an individual in the process of change, Domain Shift focuses on the physical and emotional, through to the mental and spiritual. It begins with the information that our neurology hold the keys to our makeup, and one needs to 'rewire' unbeneficial connections, initially by creating a lot of energetic space through movement and emotional release. Space is then opened up for looking clearly at belief systems which cripple us in activating our potential as humans, and changing these into beneficial beliefs through an affirmation process. I have stated the approach of Domain Shift simplistically and in my own understanding. There are many strings to its bow, resulting from intensive research into, and integration of the best of personal growth tools, backed by the evidence of contemporary psychology and science.

By individuals in their own right practising the techniques for emotional management and transformation, it has become acceptable and supported as a part of everyday life, for people at Tui generally to release an 'emotional charge' they may have around an issue, in open space with minimum effect on others. No-one need ever know what it was about or become involved in that person's process at all. This makes our relating so much freer, and opens up space for quality, rather than being bogged down with each other's dramas.

A couple at Tui now teach this technology, and have added to it a process they call 'Quality Circle', a more still and reflective process of training to become fully present in the moment. Tui has greatly benefited from Quality Circle also. More recently, Tantra has been introduced to most people at Tui, and three people now run workshops in this throughout the country. Although the expression of Tantra which is the transmutation of sexual to spiritual energy, thus far happens within monogamous partnerships at Tui, I experience the personal growth that has occurred through Tantra, enhancing the quality of intimacy between all of us, in a sacred and respectful way.

Tools and Techniques for Group Clarity Within a Meeting

Hand Gauging

The use of the hand as an indicator, on a gradient of one to ten, about where a person stands on an issue. People stay where they are, and the facilitator asks for a hand gauge, with 0 being the ground level and 10 being as far as the arm can stretch. People can also indicate with their hands where they are on a feeling level around an issue, by showing a steady hand for firm and clear, to a wobbly hand for unsure. Hand gauging gives an instant readout of where a group is at. It shortcuts a lot of discussion or guides the discussion in the necessary direction. It is a useful tool for us.

Sociogram

A sociogram is a more sophisticated version of hand gauging. It is useful to find out about the range of behaviours, values and attitudes within a group. The facilitator lays out written or verbally indicated numbers from 1 to 10 along the floor in a straight line. People then assemble themselves along that line, depending on where they stand on a particular issue. For example, on an issue of diet, vegans might stand at one end, and carnivores at another, with others placing themselves along the continuum. From then on there are a lot of options – for everyone simply to note the pattern, for people at various places along the continuum to talk with each other about their position etc. A most interesting aspect is the finding of one's position, by finding out where and why others have placed themselves where they have. Again, the position of the group is made clear, and areas in need of discussion become focused.

Role Reversal

If two people are attached to their different points of view, and their attitudes are holding the group up from moving forward, the facilitator may suggest that they come into the centre of the circle and reverse roles several times, to 'stand in the other person's shoes' and have a better understanding of their position. In our experience this frees people up from being locked in their standpoint, and enables people to shift, usually closer to each other.

Contemplation

Going into introspective silence is an appropriate thing to do when there is an issue which is at a deadlock, or when a debate has become sufficiently heated that the group can no longer function effectively. After the silence, usually for only a few minutes, people will share any insights they have with the group, and they are taken as an important contribution. Silence for this purpose has always proved invaluable to us at Tui. It is not uncommon for people to have similar or complementary insights, which are a completely different angle on what has been discussed beforehand, and for a decision to arise clearly and swiftly after a contemplative silence.

Visual Aids

Specially charts and graphs are invaluable for keeping track of a meeting, recording the thread and thrust or simply group decisions. The forms they can take are only limited by the imagination, and can be designed to meet the need of the particular issue. We use all sorts, from straight recording on large newsprint paper in mindmap or list form, to bar graphs done on computer, to coloured counters placed on the ground, as indicators of group progress.

Biographies

A biography is a life story of key people and events which have influenced who a person is today. It is, to me, a very important technique in bringing about intimacy. Learning about people's backgrounds helps us to understand why we have such individual differences. A common outcome of biography sharings is acceptance and appreciation. They require time, genuine interest and listening patience of a group to make the commitment worthwhile. At Tui we have begun to use this tool, but did not follow through, because we were unable to honour the time it took to be of high value. In Anthroposophical (Rudolf Steiner) initiatives, biographies are considered an important tool as a forerunner for staff to begin working together. They have a particular approach, and I would recommend getting a facilitator from this movement to at least start a group off with biography sessions.

Tuki

Tuki stands for Tui Community Integration – a word coined by a Tui wordsmith. A 'Tuki' is an oratory 'heart sharing circle' process, which we have adopted and adapted from the Maori whaikorero and American Indian tribal council. Its purpose for us is to go deeper into the family, cultural and historical conditioning and values which underlie emotional and attitudinal blocks, to us as a group, making aligned decisions and defining collective direction. It also serves to renew inspiration and therefore commitment. Tuki are usually held when we get stuck in a way which hinders our positive progress as a group. This is when mistrust and misunderstandings build, when differences create separation, when we loose sight of loving over divisive community issues.

Tuki often facilitate major structural and organisational changes, which realistically reflect and update where we are at as a group. The result is that the structure serves us, rather than us being servants of the structure. To me Tuki is a fundamental cornerstone of Tui's social system. Without them we could be living with a lot of misunderstandings, mistrust and alienation. Tuki is one of the most powerful methods of conflict resolution. This tends to happens indirectly, within the Tuki process, and as an outcome of it. A Tuki can take place with any size group. Limiting factors to be aware of, are the audibility of people's voices, and how long people can sit without going for a pee!

At Tui, our Tukis centre around a theme or issue which is 'up' for us, sometimes stated as a question. We are aware of the theme for several weeks in advance, and we have time to reflect about it, take it into our dreams, research it, talk about it with others. A Tuki generally happens for two days, including the evening in between. It can happen for longer, but it is inadvisable to plan for shorter, because there is insufficient time to reach and sustain the depth as a whole group. In the 'old times', when the children were small, we used to all bring our sleeping bags and sleep overnight in one room. The children still fondly remember those times when they were bathed in the essence of community.

It is important that everyone is present, as it is almost unavoidable that the group will have a 'paradigm shift', and it is difficult for a person being left behind to be integrated later. A consequence is that the absent person may be holding on to old stuff and be thinking in outmoded ways, that no longer fit with the evolved group.

A Tuki works like this: two facilitators, usually one male and one female, guide the process, and 'hold' and monitor the group energy as it proceeds. They are like pillars of a building, who uphold the physical and energetic structure to provide a space for sacred ritual. There is a 'talking stick' which is picked up from and returns to the centre of the circle by the person who speaks. A person only speaks once, and everyone is strongly encouraged to speak.

If time has been created for it, there may be a second 'round'. People are free to communicate in their own way, so long as they respect the circle, and do not 'dump' on another person, or respond directly to another. This is a time for sharing what matters to you personally, however it may come. This may include few words and a span of silence, vocally expressing emotions, sharing gems of spiritual wisdom, or addressing the 'nuts and bolts' of an issue.

The Tuki offers us spiritual inspiration and a strong sense of the pulse of the whole community around an issue, at the deepest level. It is important not to leave it there. To bring what we have learned into the realm of active change, we use a different process. It requires prepared facilitation and a rational, clear thinking mind. At the completion of the Tuki, the facilitators may get together and, based on what they have heard and felt, formulate a proposal, strategy or items, to take through a formal consensus style community meeting. This is done reasonably close to the completion of the Tuki, so as not to lose momentum. The focus is on action plan, followed by implementation.

This approach has never failed us. It has brought about monumental changes at Tui, always for the good of the whole. For example, our labour and financial structures at Tui have radically changed as the result of a Tuki, and now reflect our 1996 group composition rather than adhering to structures which did not serve the majority of current members.

Note: It is not appropriate for other groups to use the word 'Tuki', as it is specifically coined for the needs of our group. The international generic form, as used in 'Heart Politics' gatherings, is called a 'Heart Sharing Circle'. I would advise other groups to modify the form according to their culture and customs.

Some Social Keys

Amongst many of the major areas to discuss openly and honestly in order to form community policy and practice on, I believe that the most important are: financial input, labour for communal projects, collective income earning, population growth, childraising, diet and communal cooking, sexuality, and the use of social drugs and alcohol. Of course, the reality is often different from the theory, and one's stance today can change tomorrow, but it is important to have accord initially, to know that it is worth investing in living together. (Check other categories under 'Common Agreements for Daily Living'.)

Clarity is also needed to determine how intimately your group wants to live and become intertwined. The goal-setting process mentioned in the following section covers this. Basically there are a cross-section of village models, globally, ranging from kibbutzim (most communal) to strata title or company subdivision-style (least communal). It entirely depends on how the village is designed physically and socially. The need to communicate and co-operate can be built in or not in the way the village functions. For example, it is possible to have a land manager paid by the village, so that people do not need to work together on the land but this choice will inevitable have its own effect on the local environment and the community who lives there. Materially, choice will primarily depend upon the level of financial involvement, and style of land and home ownership that people want, and the size of land each household desires.

Were I to begin afresh with what I know now from experience, I would do four things as a group before committing to land purchase:

1. A training in conflict resolution, meeting facilitation and consensus decision-making.

2. Holistic participatory goal setting (*see below*).

3. A course in permaculture design – to provide common principles and methodology from which to observe, and subsequently design, the land in order to meet group needs, with sensitivity to the local environment.

4. A trial project (such as the creation of a permaculture design supported by the local council and its implementation of school or hospital grounds) in which no one in the group had a vested interest. This would be for the purpose of testing, in microcosm and telescoped time, how the group works together, involving such things as leadership hierarchy, group decision-making ability, financial management and the practical application of ideals.

Participatory Goal Setting

Through our experiences of working with permaculture in Africa, a colleague and myself have developed a simple participatory process of group decision-making, inspired by a process called 'Holistic Goal Setting', an aspect of 'Holistic Resource Management' researched and taught by Alan Savory. Our approach also draws from Participatory Rural (or Rapid) Appraisal. I only want to mention it briefly here, because it is a step by step process in its own right, and it is not yet something we have used at Tui.

This process begins with values. It offers an effective way of guiding and recording group processes and focuses on what members of a group have in common, yet differences quickly show up. It has the potential for lots of fun and is strongly action oriented. If we had had tools like this available to us in our initial stages at Tui, I believe that we would have shortcut our unwieldy development or maybe we would have split or some people would have left? Another member's viewpoint is that a group can only set goals when it has worked through its 'stuff' to become aligned.

Parenting

To me, growing up in an extended family is the biggest plus of all aspects of community life. The children are surrounded by many role models and styles of parenting. At Tui a child is ultimately under the care of his or her blood parents in all respects, and yet every single adult in the community develops their own form of relationship with each child, including discipline and guidance. They form natural affinities with different adults besides their parents, to whom they go to for nurturing and support. The importance of this is evident at Tui as our children enter teenage years. Children grow up with others of all ages, who become like brothers and sisters, just as in a bloodline extended family.

Community life is extremely supportive of parents. They are not isolated in the home; the environment is safe for small children to roam and explore without supervision; there is the emotional and physical support of other parents. There is the opportunity to work co-operatively with other adults, pursue your interests, and still be in close contact with your children. As is the case at Tui, community living provides scope for parents whose relationships change, and who choose to part ways, to live separately on the same property and co-parent – with a minimum impact on the child emotionally or physically.

I want to outline what for me is a healthy progression from dependence to independence of children to their parents. This true scenario is made possible because of the unique nature of community life. Kaj and Zora are twins who live at Tui. They came to live at Tui when they were three years old. Their parents had already separated, but decided to live on the same land for the sake of the children, and because they wanted to keep in contact and desired the same lifestyle. When the twins were young they lived with their mother, and saw their father every day. At primary school age, they spent three months living in each parent's house. At early teens they each had a caravan, and lived nearby their parents houses, one girl near each parent. Every three months, they swapped location with each other, the tractor towing their caravans from one location to the other. Now they are in their mid teens, their caravans are close together, near the community house, and away from their parents. They are autonomous in every sense, managing their own budget, cooking and washing for themselves. They have amiable relationships and plenty of contact for both parents. I consider them to be reasonably well adjusted teenagers.

Seasonal Celebrations and Rituals

As we live close with the land and choose to deepen our relationship with nature, we come together to celebrate and honour the change of the seasons, at solstice and equinox. A few people prepare an appropriate ritual, with inclusion of the children where appropriate. We customarily begin our gardening working bees with some form of attunement and thanksgiving to the land. Our daily community meal begins with a circle and blessing song.

Men's and Women's Gatherings

The women (regularly) and the men (occasionally) meet in their own groups separately to share in sacred ways on the full moons. We hold men's and women's gatherings concurrently as a national event during the summer. These take various forms, and are held for the purpose of sharing and support

Autumn Equinox and Harvest Festival.

for each other in ways which we simply can not get from members of the opposite sex. I can only really speak for the women. Our gatherings range in nature from cultural events, to sharing life stories, to honouring life stages, to sharing about sexuality, to participating in a Goddess-focused ritual, to opening the space for emotional support, to massaging each others feet. To me they are a very important aspect of life at Tui. The bonding with my sisters is precious to me.

A core group of men and a core group of women, host men's and women's national gatherings annually, for around 35 people per group for up to one week. They are held at the same time, on Tui and neighbouring land. There is a 'runner' from the men's and from the women's core group to update daily about intended programme locations, so that the groups do not intersect. We view this as important, as we do not want the growth process we are experiencing as men and women, to be distracted by chance encounters with the opposite sex. We are embarking on a deep healing and sacred journey into knowing ourselves as men and as women, of having the support of those of the same sex to look at, process and resolve issues that are unique to each sex, and what it means to relate to each other beyond all the conditioned facades, pseudo-self and games that we have learnt in order to avoid intimacy and being real.

On the last two days we come together as men and women, in what we warmly call, 'the merge'. During these two days we spend times together and apart as one group, yet always staying at our own camps. We initially come together in silence, showing each other who we are in our vulnerability while at the same time in our power. The first meeting has been a very sacred moment, and an honouring of the universal man and the universal woman.

The oratory *waikorero* (essence of heart circle sharing process) that follows is insightful for both sexes to understand, appreciate and accept each other on a new level.

I believe that these gatherings play their small part in creating a new paradigm of men and women to relate with each other, and I believe that the healing is inter-generational. I have been beneficially changed by them and it is a deep and lasting change. It is worthwhile to write an entire chapter, maybe book, on these gatherings! I hope that some day someone will. The healing of relationships between men and women is essential for world peace.

Spiritual Basis

It is difficult to define our spiritual basis because it is so interwoven in how we live our lives, our relationships with each other, the land we are guardians for, and our planet generally. The closest names may be Deep Ecology or Earth-Centred Spirituality. We do not adhere to any dogma or religion. We embody New Age, but could not be defined as that, as we acknowledge all chakras as sacred and valid, not just the 'higher' ones.

We bring spirituality into physicality in a tangible way through our relationship with each other, the earth, and our work. We encourage humour,

Co-operative games: 'Crossing the river without setting foot in the water'.

Women's gathering: A craft-making session.

passion for life, and dropping addictions, both substance and behavioural. As a community we encourage a vegetarian diet, and strongly discourage drugs. A vital part of our spiritual growth is that we commit to clear, honest communication and feedback, and taking responsibility for our emotional energy (e.g. anger) rather than 'dumping' on each other.

We are by no means holier than those who have not made conscious choices to do these things in their lives. It is just that by choice we are willing to heal our wounds and become more whole. Collectively, we believe that this is fundamental to the creation of a sustainable society, and we want no less. Community life accelerates this opportunity many-fold.

Be honest with yourself about whether you are ready for this challenge before you embark on any community venture! Well known author, Scott Peck, has defined that to get in touch with true community we go through the stages of pseudo-community and then chaos. We at Tui have surely done that – and we are richly rewarded. I encourage you to hang in there should you take the plunge!

Philosophical Reflection

Personally I find living in community fulfilling and stimulating, sustaining. I have sometimes heard intentional community referred to as 'a social experiment'. Yet for me it is 'the norm', with the current Western-lifestyle norm of the socially isolated nuclear family being the social experiment! Through life at Tui I am rediscovering what I believe to be a natural social pattern encoded within the genes, as basic as an animal's instinct. I believe that in us this pattern is overlaid by conditioning generated from fear of intimacy, and separation from our Earth Mother. I am fascinated that as I discover about other land-based intentional communities around the planet that have been operating for some time, I find that they have developed similar customs to ourselves, even down to some fine details. There are essential patterns in leaves and water-flow, so it is feasible there are God-given blueprints for human settlement, regardless of how sophisticated we think we have become. It is simply a matter of uncovering the clutter.

CONFLICT RESOLUTION IN AN ECO-VILLAGE

by Declan and Margrit Kennedy

Professor Dr Margrit Kennedy (Dipl. Ing., MURP) is an architect and urban planner with a PhD in Public and International Affairs. She has published numerous books, articles and reports on community, school planning and building, women and architecture, urban ecology, money, land and tax systems and permaculture and has also practised urban planning in Brazil, Nigeria, Scotland, the USA and Germany. At present she lives in the eco-village of Lebensgarten Steyerberg and in Hanover, where she works as a professor at the Department of Architecture of the University of Hanover.

In 1995 she undertook research on Large-Scale Ecological Settlements in Europe for the European Academy of Urban Environment. More recently her emphasis has been on ecological design for the workplace, especially industrial production units. Her work on ecological architecture and interest-free money systems has resulted in numerous lectures throughout the world which have been translated into a variety of languages.

Professor Declan Kennedy (Dipl. Ing.) is an Irish architect, urban planner, permaculture designer and ecologist. He is a founder member of the Permaculture Institute of Europe. He has been teaching and practising urban design, landscape and agricultural planning coupled with holistic implementation strategies since 1972, currently in special intensive seminars held in many countries – and formerly as Professor of Urban Design and Infrastructure at the Architectural Department of the Technical University of Berlin. He was Country Co-ordinator for Germany for the Global Action Plan for the Earth (GAP) Household Ecoteam Programme. Since its foundation in Denmark in 1994, he has been Chairman of the board of the Global Eco-village Network (GEN) and now runs their European secretariat and its association GEN-Europe, from the ecological community Lebensgarten Steyerberg, Lower Saxony, Germany where he lives.

Margrit and Declan run a planning office in Hanover and Steyerberg. Their research work on ecological settlements in Europe was published in English in *Designing Ecological Settlements*, Dietrich Reimer Verlag, Berlin, 1997, and later published in German. They have been part of a group of ecological architects and planners known as Gaia International since its inception.

Address:
Ginsterweg 4–5, D–31595 Steyerberg. Germany
Tel: +49 57 64– 21 58 Fax: +49 57 64– 23 68
Email: declan@gaia.org

Why Have We Moved into a Community?

Because we wanted to implement a permaculture model and we realised that this was almost impossible to do alone on a meaningful scale. For instance, we could imagine producing vegetables, but not selling them on the market. By living in a community, this necessity could be taken care of by other community members who needed the produce. But we also wanted a very special combination of community characteristics. Our search for a place went on for exactly three years (1982-85), and we found two distinct types of communities:

The first type was the eco-technological community, like Stanley, Tasmania; Langenbruck, Switzerland; Svanholm, Denmark; or Springe-Eldagsen, Germany. They did a very good job in terms of developing new ecological techniques, such as highly productive, low-work, food production systems, ecological stoves, solar cars and solar collectors, organic food for the local market, zero-energy houses, controlled ventilation, root-zone sewage treatment systems – all in the middle of the 1980s. However, in our view, these groups underestimated the whole question of social relationships, assuming that when all members had the same ideal, i.e. ecology, this aspect would take care of itself. But usually it did not – and, in some of these communities, unresolved conflicts can build in such a way that the more sensitive type of member simply had to leave.

The second type was the spiritual community, like Findhorn, Scotland; Wetzhausen, Germany; some Sanyassin communities in Australia or anthroposophic communities in Germany and Sweden. They usually developed good human interrelationships and practised 'love your neighbour as yourself' as well as producing fantastic vegetables. But, either we found them too limited in their following of one guru and in their implementation of one particular path, or we found them lacking in innovative ecology.

Lebensgarten Steyerberg

We realised, therefore, that we had to be part of creating a new community which would combine social/spiritual aspirations as well as the ecological aspects. The community of Lebensgarten Steyerberg was started when a businessman from Berlin bought a dilapidated housing estate which had been originally planned and built in 1939 as housing quarters for a munitions factory. After the war, it had been used as a barracks by the British army – and then it stood empty for almost eight years. In the Northern German climate, this means everything freezes up in winter. For instance, pipes and heating radiators burst and tiled floors blistered. During this time it had also been vandalised – inner doors and ceilings had been broken and the basements were often full of stagnant water.

On December 17th 1984, together with six other people, we decided to initiate a spiritual and ecological community. It was named 'Lebensgarten' (the garden of life) Steyerberg. But it was not until the following spring that people began to move in – very slowly at first, as the new occupants had to wait for connections to services: water, electricity and natural gas (from nearby gas fields).

The housing area had 65 units that could be converted to terraced houses and various administrative buildings – all dilapidated, but with redbrick outside walls and tiled roofs in reasonable shape. We moved there in October 1985 and were the seventh group to move in. As only seven houses had lights, the settlement was quite spooky at night in the winter of 1985/86 – not to mention the negative vibrations left by the former Nazi and later British army presence which had reigned for more than 40 years on the site. Within three years of our purchase, all the houses had been either bought or rented by people interested in participating in this experiment. There are now over 100 adults and approximately 50 children as members of this community – of different ages, social and professional backgrounds and with different religions and objectives.

The first action that was taken was to move into the settlement, despite its ruined state, and start the renewal of the buildings one by one, with minimal resources except enthusiasm and commitment. Both physical and spiritual renewal was necessary because more than 30 years of war meant that these walls radiated violence and inhuman realities. The steps chosen by consensus were rebuilding, insulating and renovating as well as meditation, conflict resolution and healing.

Many ecosystems around us have been destroyed, even in the decade and a half of our existence in Lower Saxony, and many others are on the brink of collapse, particularly the 16 square kilometres of the original munitions factory, some few kilometres north of our community. Here the original underground production vaults are being used as temporary storage for radioactive waste from hospitals until a permanent depot can be found. But the location of the final depot is one of the political issues high on the agenda both in Lower Saxony and in Germany as a whole, and no decision is expected in the near future.

Pollution in the water table is another problem. 10 years ago the water that we bored for on the permaculture plot was so good that the City of Hanover contemplated having a contract for piping it 70 kilometres to the city. Now it is contaminated with nitrates and nitrites. We assume that these contaminants are derived from the slow seepage into the ground of the widely used chemical fertilisers that are needed to get two to three crops per year from this mainly sandy soil.

During the past 13 years, Lebensgarten Steyerberg has made it a priority to challenge this escalating trend of environmental damage. We are working hard to demonstrate and display concrete examples of cultural, permacultural, economic and spiritual ways of life that do not tax the earth, i.e. passive and active solar energy savings, benign spiritual practices, sustainable gardening and alternative education. We have not got there yet, but the focus of our undertaking is a return to basics. This is not a step backwards, but a step forwards – towards our roots, encompassing the various aspects of simple, mindful and sustainable living to a way of life most people around us consider 'natural'. Sustainable living incorporating natural laws is not in fact inferior, but superior. As work progressed, we planned:

- To work out a concept of new forms of socially and ecologically oriented life as well as the feasibility of transposing these to society at large – this through information, education and example encompassing e.g. the media of exhibitions, specially tailored seminars and experiential tours, etc.
- To prepare the space for these presentations by renovating the parts of the existing buildings that have not yet been refurbished.

Over the last 13 years considerable efforts have been made to use the almost derelict community centre for the association and for educational purposes. The renovation of the whole building complex (including the landscaping with reed bed sewage treatment and tertiary ponds) ought to be finished by the year 2000 in order to accommodate the additional stream of visitors, expected from the nearby EXPO 2000 in Hanover. Lebensgarten is now recognised as one of the major fringe projects of this World Fair.

A number of work activities have been set up by members of the Community, and about one quarter have found jobs in the local area. The educational facilities are used to pass on accumulated knowledge in fields such as ecology, healing, healthy building, mediation and personal development (involving approximately 100 seminars and 3,000 guests a year).

The charitable association was founded in 1986, and currently has 100 members and an annual turnover of approximately DM 900,000. There is a great feeling of neighbourliness, regular meetings are held to solve community problems, circle dancing takes place every morning and there is a variety of different working groups.

Our Links with GEN – the Global Eco-village Network

Over the past ten years, many members of Lebensgarten Steyerberg have had the opportunity to travel to countries all over the world. We have witnessed the degradation of our natural systems, and the rapidly accelerating impact of modern human living on the environment. The planet is already well overstretched and in our present system of over-using natural resources will have difficulty in supporting the next five billion people expected over the coming centuries. Reflecting on economic and ecological realities, we believe that unless we change our direction, our behaviour and our ethics, there is little hope that we and these extra people can survive. It is, therefore, not only a wish but a necessity to re-evolve the relationship between Humans, Nature and Technology – which happens to be the theme of EXPO 2000, the World Fair in Hanover.

In the context of this relationship, the Statutes of our Association, Lebensgarten Steyerberg e.V., also fit in with the ideals of the Global Eco-Village Network (GEN). The aims of the association are defined as follows:

a) Use and preparation of natural ways of nutrition and holistic healing methods.

b) Development and dissemination of ecological models in which plants, animals and people live together in a mutually supporting way even in limited space.
c) Development, experimentation and dissemination of biological building materials and their use by local craftsmen and through artistic design, as well as the development of techniques and production methods which support an environmental approach to raw materials and energy.
d) Use and performance of music, theatre and other forms of the fine arts that support integrative healing methods, training in self-realisation through mediation and training in methods of conflict resolution.

Through its educational programme, the association intends to contribute a human design for everyday life, and to assist in reducing the illnesses of the body, mind and the soul brought about by civilisation. The educational approach aims not only at the human mind but also tries to develop a personal relationship on a heart to heart level.

A rich social and cultural life has developed during these 13 years, leading to the following activities, most of which create business and employment, but also have a significant community component in them:

a) *Community facilities*: Children's group, youth rooms, adventure play area, studios, music rooms, meditation rooms, a café, bio-retail outlet, wholefood kitchen.
b) *Ecological facilities*: Lean-to greenhouses, solar electric and solar hot water collectors, solar car with solar filling station, passive solar roof for energy gain, co-generation heating plant, car-sharing group, and a permanent exhibition on the subject of energy and environment.
c) *Job-creating facilities*: Shop for biological building materials, book-store, school for medical para-professionals, environmental consultancy to industry, ecological architectural and planning office, eco-village institute, school for mediation, eco-publishing, computer consultancy, workshops for precious stones, jewellery and goldsmithing, natural medicine practices.
d) *Public relations*: Co-founders of the Waldorf School in Minden (40 km. away) and the Permaculture Institutes of Europe and of Germany, consultancy and co-founders of new ecological settlements and of international peace work groups, participation in the EU passive-solar programme Building 2000, several reports in the press, radio and television, networking with other ecological communities worldwide as well as active membership of the Global Eco-Village Network, whose secretariat for Europe Declan Kennedy has been running from Lebensgarten for the past 3 years.

The following amenities have been mostly self-financed or partly supported by private foundations and friendly business firms: a solar roof, a co-generation heating plant, community education, a community living room, a solar-heated lean-to greenhouse, the renovation of our seminar building: Heilhaus, our solar filling station, the wholefood kitchen, a Zen meditation hall, connection to the Internet and email, a permanent exhibition: Energy and Environment, a light-meditation room, participation in Peace Trees, Croatia and permaculture design courses in new countries of the former eastern block.

How Did Things Work Out Between Members at Lebensgarten?

Well, there's no denying it was exciting, beautiful and difficult, particularly during the first five years when we experienced severe conflicts among ourselves. None of us were educated to deal with the multi-faceted relationships in a community. We all had come from nuclear family backgrounds. We all had different dreams and visions and we all wanted to implement our vision, and wanted the others to help us.

The first step was to realise that we all had to let go of our dreams... so that we could accomplish them usually in a somewhat modified form, later on. We (Margrit and Declan) dreamt about establishing an ecological technology centre, something like the Centre for Alternative Technology in Wales. That never materialised because most of the members were more interested in their own self-development than being partners in a business and sharing the 'capitalist's risks'.

The second experience was that we all had quite similar problems in accepting others – and, as it invariably turned out, the problems were mainly with those who reflected some unknown shadow side of ourselves.

Once we understood this and looked upon that shadow side in ourselves, lifting it up into the light of our consciousness, the problem within us – and with the other person who reflected the problem – began to disappear, sometimes instantly.

In a larger community – by 1999 Lebensgarten comprised roughly 100 adults and 50 children – many opportunities for this learning process have occurred, and members will have to develop the ability to transform their shadow sides very quickly. Otherwise, individual conflicts will destroy the functioning of the group as a whole.

Fortunately, and this is an important point, it feels really good to learn to progressively accept oneself and others, and to look at conflict in a different way: "Hey! There is something to learn again – be creative and enjoy it!"

Therefore, in the 'pressure cooker for personal development', as the two of us sometimes called the Lebensgarten, we began to be able to communicate with people at a continuously deeper level of understanding. We noticed that learning was beginning to get easier, faster and was happening with more and more fun, instead of pain. That, we feel, is real progress. Our growing sense of love and accomplishment is also reflected in the outside world. Things are not only beginning to look better on the inside, but also our immediate environment is improving from an ecological point of view.

Ecology was certainly not a second consideration in our case, but for a time the human aspects were paramount. Today, however, we can look back and see that they are a lot easier to resolve. Thus, Lebensgarten has also accomplished quite a bit in terms of recycling of its old pre-World War II buildings. We have put them to good use as dwellings and for our seminar programme which includes lessons in conflict resolution in the community and passes on our experience to others from outside.

How Did the Experience Affect our Professional Lives?

In order to answer this question, we would have to explain one other common experience: that we all learned to do what we can do best, and to do it as well as we can. By acting in a way which may seem selfish to some outsiders, we found our contribution to the community grew, as did our giving to ourselves and also to society as a whole.

Margrit, after wanting initially to implement our permaculture model, found out that she really wanted to write a book about money – or a sustainable money system as a basis of a sustainable world economy. After having rejected this idea for five years because she is not an economist, she wrote the first draft of the book in four days. Many other small miracles happened while fulfilling this task, but the most amazing one is how this message is self-perpetuating. The book has now been translated into eighteen languages. The Spanish edition was published in Buenos Aires, Christmas, 1998.

Declan continued his permaculture work and found others to help him. Lots of conflicts during the process often made it feel like sowing and weeding on a human relationship level, and within himself too. His 'real' task was, however, networking and going out into other countries in Europe – spreading the message and the use of permaculture principles in rural and urban settings. He went to countries which had experienced peace for many years like Sweden, the Netherlands, Switzerland, Ireland, the USA, Brazil and Italy, but also countries which were in a state of conflict: Poland before the political changes, Croatia during the war, Slovenia just after the separation from Yugoslavia, places where things had to be built up from nothing. Later, he did Eco-village Design Training in the USA, Australia, Italy, Slovenia, South Africa and Zimbabwe. Almost everywhere the courses and the training were often as much about mediation as permaculture or eco-village design – as he found that conflict is also a learning process in the development of eco-villages elsewhere.

Then came projects in East Germany. After the re-unification, this region was the target for those out to make a quick DMark. Some 'West-Germans' however, tried to implement a complex ecological settlement adjacent to an old town where their ancestors had lived. Declan became the official ecological advisor, but again his main task was to animate and mediate between different planning consultants and also between them and the residents of the old town.

This trust in doing what we enjoy most and where our hearts are, has developed within the community. Not only did we experience this within ourselves individually, but also with others around us in the community which made our lessons much more penetrating and real. Although we see ourselves as professional planners in almost all our projects, often this ability to mediate between people who have not learnt to communicate with each other, or to listen to each other, has become almost as important as our professional knowledge. Both over 55 years of age, we went back to the classroom and did a year's training in mediation so that we would have the right tools with which to work.

What is mostly forgotten is that it is just as important to find a solution at the feeling level as it is to be able to create a rational, satisfying concept. From there, the next step follows – to have fun and to enjoy the path to synthesis, that is, creating situations which integrate rationality, feeling and intuition.

References

Kennedy, M., and Kennedy, D., 1974. *The Inner City.* London.

Kennedy, M., 1984. *Oeko-Stadt – Volume 1 and 2.* Frankfurt/Main.

Kennedy, M., 1988. *Interest and Inflation Free Money – How to Create an Exchange Medium that Works for Everybody and Protects The Earth.* Revised edition with Kennedy, D., 1995. Seva International: Michigan. Now in 17 other languages.

Kennedy, M., and Kennedy, D., 1997. *Designing Ecological Settlements.* Berlin: Dietrich Reimer Verlag, in English. 1998, in German. 1998, in Russian (in parts) on the Internet.

ETHICS AS HEALING

Another Approach to Conflict Resolution

by Cliff Penwell

Cliff Penwell is a long time resident of the Sunrise Ranch Emissary community near Loveland, Colorado. Since 1979 Cliff and his wife have lived in community in five countries, helping to develop Emissary facilities and programs. Cliff is also an editor and consensus facilitator, specializing in cross-cultural understanding. The Emissaries, founded in 1932, are an international network whose primary purpose is to encourage the experience and expression of divine identity. They support community development – both land-based and virtual – through hosting a number of residential communities around the world and by operating EmNet, an international electronic bulletin board network.

Address:
5569 North County Road 29
Loveland
Colorado 80538
USA
Tel: +1 970 679 4229
Fax: +1 970 679 4233
Email: cpenwell@emnet.org
or: cpenwell@well.com

The middle-aged couple, prospective members of our community in northern Colorado, looked admiringly around our dining pavilion. "God, it's great to be here," the man said. "I always feel so much better here at Sunrise Ranch than I do out there." He pointed south, toward Boulder, where he and his wife were successful team-building consultants. "So much conflict, so much hassle, so much craziness!" He outlined his city-life difficulties, and concluded with a statement I have heard before: "Man, I hope you people know how lucky you are here!"

It was a rhetorical comment, but it tempted an answer. In years past I would have hastened to tell him how we have our share of problems, how his rosy view would vanish in time, how we too are part of the 'real world'. But instead I said what I've discovered is more useful: "Thanks. Community living is a lot of work, but I feel it's worth it."

For my friend and his wife, the idea of community represented something precious and inviolate, a reminder of the harmony possible in human interaction. Having seen hundreds of people come and go from our half-century-old intentional community, I have learned to let people have their own experience and, with them, to cherish what they see as possible. I'm less inclined to press upon them the 'hard realities' of communal living; the imperfections, where they truly exist, reveal themselves soon enough.

My own experience in community began 18 years ago, when my wife and I began living at a spiritually based community in England. The facility is operated by The Emissaries, an international non-profit organization founded in 1932 to support integrative work in a variety of disciplines. Over the years, the organization has hosted a number of intentional communities as ways of 'grounding' its creative philosophy in day-to-day living. Our communities vary in population from ten to over a hundred, with an age range of prenatal to late eighties.

Here at Sunrise Ranch we are blessed to live about 15 miles from the nearest city, though urban sprawl is fast shortening the distance. We occupy a long, narrow valley with geographic boundaries that discourage development around us. However, we are by no means isolated. Besides being a village with a year-round population of about 110, we run a conference business that attracts groups from around the country. Also, we welcome several hundred guests each year to experience community first-hand. It can be a highly pressured environment as too few of us scramble to take care of too many of us. And because our demographics are slanted toward the mid adult-to-elder range, many of us bring a considerable amount of experience from 'out there' to 'in here'.

As you can imagine, in one way or another we have experienced pretty much the full spectrum of conflict over these decades of rubbing shoulders. We've tried ignoring it, tolerating it, admitting that it was creative, and confronting it. The only thing we hadn't done, until only a few years ago, was acknowledge it as a door to healing in our community.

Ethics as a Doorway

The discipline of conflict resolution came to us via the trend of 'ethics awareness', which has fully found its place center-stage in the organizational theatre of the Nineties. As our community grew, changed, and made mistakes, we accumulated a backlog of unattended interpersonal business. Like many organizations founded in the earlier half of this century, The Emissaries were governed in a hierarchical format, with a single spiritual leader and various regional directors. As the need for change became apparent, the transition to consensus-based government was abrupt and messy. At Sunrise Ranch the 'old' leaders were replaced by a new circle of governance within a matter of a few weeks. Grievances that had gone unspoken before were offered openly now, and we realized that we had little idea about how to handle the resultant conflict in our community.

So we did what any organization faced with the unknown might do: we called in a consultant! As it happens, we met Cedar Barstow, a remarkable therapist who had just navigated a similar crisis in a similar organisation. She had much good and timely counsel for us. Her central message was to neither be afraid nor ashamed of grievances in community; the fact that they were being spoken rather than swallowed was healthy, and they gave us a doorway into conflict resolution. What we needed, she said, was a mechanism for handling conflict, and a deepening understanding of ethics was the way to get there.

Ethics Beyond Moral Issues

I should make clear here that I am using the word ethics somewhat outside of its mainstream connotation of moral proscription. (Most ethics committees, for example, spend much of their time watch-dogging their organizations for moral and legal violations.) In our work at Sunrise Ranch we have adopted Cedar's definition of ethics simply as "the right use of power". This lifts the topic out of debates about morality versus evil. It has nothing to do with curtailing power or even trying to equalize it – a great temptation in roundtable-style government. Rather, this use of the term acknowledges that:

a) We all have it in varying degrees.
b) Certain roles carry it inherently (in the therapist-client relationship, for example, the therapist carries a great deal of power).
c) It is often when we don't acknowledge our power that we tend to abuse it. Our greatest challenge in becoming ethically sensitized was to face the fact that many of us had trouble admitting how much power we individually wielded.

Sunrise Ranch Pavillion, Colorado

So we set about forming an ethics committee and an ethics educational program for the community, based on the 'right use of power' paradigm. We determined from the outset that ethics would be a medium for healing rather than a tool for punitive retribution. Yet even with that foundation in place, we still found ourselves in the midst of an unsettling time. We discovered, as we started exploring what the right use of power meant in our community, that the very consideration brought a swirl of questions and feelings about trust, abuse, leadership, sexuality and just about everything else. (In retrospect, I have come to the conclusion that the process of forming an ethics committee is supposed to lift all this stuff to the surface so it can be clarified.)

Early on in this process, those of us who were designing the committee decided that we would not primarily be about squelching rumours, providing damage control, passing judgement on past behaviour or being the defenders of morality – though there are always tough issues to face and hard decisions to make. One of the first fears we faced at Sunrise Ranch was the perception that our community would become obsessed with each other's behaviour, initiating witch hunts and creating a moral police force in the process. While this was perhaps a danger, in practice we discovered that we, like any group, already had a highly defined moral code, staked down at the edges by myriad unspoken guidelines. Until the ethics process, a mainstay of the social code was the agreement so many of us seemed to have made not to say anything publicly about what everyone knew and disliked privately. Some of the work yet ahead of us was in dealing with the backlog of things happening in this climate.

Other questions came up around how much power the ethics committee should have, who they are accountable to, and what decisions they could make. These inquiries in turn opened a whole banquet of consideration – again, issues of trust and power brought to the surface because it was time for the community to deal with them.

After electing a committee of six (including myself), we set about creating guidelines for ourselves. We decided to concentrate on developing skill in such areas as sensitivity to the difference between intention and impact, building healthy working relationships, and tracking the effects of our power with each other. We invited guest lecturers to speak to the community, hosted workshops and made ourselves available for consultation. The only thing we were missing was actual experience in handling grievances between community members!

Ethics in Practice

Opportunity to practise came soon enough, and we learned a great deal in a hurry. Because of the transition in government and people's caution about perceived 'power imbalances', our initial work in conflict resolution tended to be between supervisors and team members. As we matured in our process, we began to act as a resource for a much wider range of interpersonal situations. We set up a process whereby the 'claimant' (the one who claims a misuse of power by the other) and 'respondent' (the one responding to the complaint) each have a chance to bring their situations forward in the presence of four neutrals selected from the ethics committee. (Usually this has followed attempts on behalf of both parties to resolve the dispute on their own, without success.) Each person is heard, and opportunity to ask clarifying questions is offered to each of the parties. Questions such as "What have you learned through this process?" "What, if anything, would you do differently next time?" and "What would you like of the other person?" are asked of both parties, and much healing often takes place in the honest answering of these and similar questions.

When this facilitated session is complete, the ethics committee decides what additional action, if any, needs to be taken. Our thrust is educational and preventative, aiming to prevent recurrence of unacceptable behaviour, rather than punitive. It is my experience that both respondent and claimant need a certain level of care; no shaming, victimizing or scapegoating of anyone is allowed in the process.

Because residents at Sunrise Ranch are committed to developing deeper levels of understanding between them, we have a base to draw from when things seem to go interpersonally awry. The ethics process is voluntary and respected because it stems from a base of integrity within the community. Though a mechanism to appeal decisions is built into the grievance system, it is rarely called upon.

When we first introduced the grievance process here, the community (including the ethics committee) was eager to use it, as it was virtually the only tool we could offer. Most of our conflict resolution processes looked like formal grievance sessions, with respondents and claimants meeting with four out of the six committee members. As our training and skill levels increased, however, so did our usefulness in the community. Gradually we have been able to offer one-on-one conflict coaching, 'third-party neutral' listening services, facilitation and mediation. We have developed a good network of associate professionals, including therapists and mediators, to whom we can refer issues we don't feel qualified to handle. Our presence and availability in the community acts as a kind of catalyst for people to address their conflicts, knowing that we are there as a resource when needed.

Ethics as Resolution

These days, we try to spend most of our time on the 'nutritional' end of the ethics spectrum rather than the 'emergency surgery' (grievance) end. However, we still welcome anyone to file a grievance as is deemed necessary. We have learned well that embracing and dealing with conflict, in whatever way possible, helps to build a foundation of respect, regardless of the issues. And by doing so, our ethics committee helps to steward and develop the right use of power in community, rather than just acting as a moral police force.

The deepest root of the word ethics is 'innate essence', the core quality that guides us. I believe that this inner characteristic, given the right care and surround, will always naturally seek resolution in whatever setting it finds itself. Communities of many forms provide a marvellous laboratory for exploring this homing instinct – and plenty of opportunity for proving it out!

SUSTAINABLE ECONOMICS IN ECO-COMMUNITIES

by Jill Jordan

Jill Jordan is a community development consultant, lecturer and cultural development facilitator. She has been instrumental in setting up a number of community initiatives in Maleny, Australia.
Address:
PO Box 87
Maleny
Queensland 4552
Australia
Tel: +61 754 943 312
Fax: +61 754 296 139
Email: manduka@pronet.net.au

Photo: Maddy Harland

When forming intentional eco-communities, it is important to understand the role of community economics, and how personal economics interacts with community economics.

If communities fail, it is usually through a failure in their economic foundation, or a failure in interpersonal processes. This chapter will seek to address the first factor, and the second as it relates to the community's interaction with the 'wider community' within which it finds itself.

To illustrate this chapter, I will draw from my experiences of 25 years learned in my own community, the small rural town of Maleny, Queensland, on the east coast of Australia, and other communities where I have had the pleasure of assisting in their development towards sustainability.

THE BASIS OF SUSTAINABLE COMMUNITY ECONOMICS

The model of sustainable community economics which most appeals to me is that of the Rocky Mountains Institute in Colorado. It is simple, elegant and practical. Combined with the principle of diversity of an economic base as creating stability, this model provides the blueprint which, if followed, can lead to truly sustainable community economics. Combined with a variety of legal structures to ensure the people empowerment which is attained through the development of community-owned businesses, this model can lead to a thriving community where the majority of members are self-employed in work which is both satisfying and useful.

There are four strands to the Rocky Mountains' model for community economic development:

1. **Plug the Leaks**
   This is the first step in creating sustainability within our economic system. It entails undertaking a community audit in order to assess what aspects of the community's needs are currently supplied from within the community, and what needs are supplied from outside the community. This audit will include food, energy, transportation, manufactured goods and all kinds of services, from infrastructure provision through communication, health and education to cultural activities.

   Once this audit has been done, it is possible to assess which of the goods and services that are currently obtained from outside the community can be supplied internally, and begin to create opportunities for community members to supply these needs from within the community.

2. **Support Existing Businesses**
   The second step in the creation of sustainable economics within a community is to support existing local businesses. It is very discouraging for businesses within a local area if the residents do not use their services, and indeed, leave the local community to do business. This practice may result from a lack of thought and understanding by the community consumers of the consequences of such actions, or may come from a dissatisfaction with the level of service provided by the local suppliers. It may also arise as a result of businesses not being appropriate to community needs, a situation which would not occur if potential businesses undertook a community needs assessment before starting up! Whatever the reason, it is important to ascertain why this is happening and remedy it. This can either be through promotion of the benefits of local trade by emphasising the concept of money revolving through community, and the multiplier effect this has, or through feedback to local businesses as to the improvements they need to make in order to win back support from the community. In the case of businesses not needed by the community, a decision would need to be made to focus on export potential, or to retrofit the business so that it fulfils a community need.

3. **Facilitate the Start-up of New Businesses Appropriate to the Character and Needs of the Community**
   It is important to note that in this step, we are talking about 'appropriate' new businesses, and part of this appropriateness involves the assessment from step 1. That is to say, new businesses whose start-ups would be facilitated would fill the niches shown by the audit process, and would assist in plugging the leaks in the community.

   There are many ways to facilitate the start-up of businesses. These can range from a simple 'mentor' system where older, often retired people with particular skills teach their skills to younger people within the community to a formalised system such as those produced with Enterprise Centres or shared workspaces. In the latter situation, a physical venue, tailor-made to suit the individual needs of fledgling businesses, and with few start-up costs, is provided to a number of potential businesses. Technical and moral support are also provided to the potential business by the manager of the Centre, and infrastructure (phone and fax facilities) is shared between the tenants to cut down on costs.

Each community will need to decide for itself the range of strategies that it will employ to assist in this process. This will depend on the size of the community, and the skills base within the local region, as well as the level of motivation within those skilled people to assist in the development process.

4. Encouragement of Appropriate Outside Business into the Area

You will note that this step, which has traditionally been the first step in 'conventional' economic development, is the last step in the new paradigm, and would only be employed when it was assessed that the community did not have and would be unlikely to have the wherewithal to implement the strategy without inviting outside implementation. It is also important to note that the business or industry must be one that is appropriate to the community.

The Process Inherent in Establishing a Community

One of the greatest inhibitors to making a move to a new community is the fear of not being able to earn an income, this often being equated with not being able to 'get a job'. However, once people have made the move, earning an income initially takes a back seat. People's first need is for shelter of some kind and especially if they do not have accumulated capital, to grow some of their own food. It is only when they have these basic necessities that they are able to focus on income-producing activities.

In looking at sustainable economics, a different mind-set from the conventionally accepted one needs to be adopted. If we evaluate conventional economics, its objectives and its outcomes, including the implications for individuals within a community, we will find that, generally speaking, the conventional economy these days focuses on money as the prime goal of our working lives. This money then enables us access to goods and services from around the globe. There is little or no emphasis on the internal effect of this mind-set on our communities or the inherent wastage in such a system. This wastage includes energy, as even the most basic of foodstuffs are transported across the country, and skills, as many people remain unemployed if they do not possess the type of skills required by the (often specialised) industries within their region.

Community economics within an eco-village, town or city focuses on the needs of the community, and looks at supplying as many of those needs as possible from within the community, by employing local people, and having local people fill the gaps in production as they are recognised. In this way, money earned in the community is circulated again and again within that community, thus not being drained away from the area.

It is in this context that the importance of the Rocky Mountains Institute model becomes apparent, with its insistence on the basic tool of community economic evaluation as being the audit. Through this audit, it is possible for community members to see what goods and services are currently being provided, and where there are niches which are capable of being filled, at the same time as providing income for individuals and groups.

The process of 'growing your own job' according to the needs of the local community is a novel one, and can be quite daunting for those used to being employed for a regular weekly wage. For a community which is in its infancy, as well as for those people contemplating moving to a community, it may be heartening to know that, although it is a new experience, the process of 'growing your own job' can be stimulating and rewarding. It can also have very little risk, providing the necessary information is obtained beforehand, and the necessary support is available through the initial stages of the initiative.

It is said that being involved in small business as a sole trader is the most lonely occupation in the world, and it is for this reason, amongst others, that I have spent many years assisting others to start up and run group enterprises. Within our schools we have begun to teach our young people about enterprise skills at last, but I still believe that this is not enough; we need to teach them to be able to work together in groups. In this way, each person can use their specialist skills to gain initial confidence, before going on to learn some of the other plethora of skills necessary to run a successful business. And the responsibility for decision-making is shared, making the process less onerous for each individual. Other reasons for creating group enterprise within a community include the synergy that comes from a well-oiled group process which can manifest both in the ideas stage, as well as in the physical 'jobs to be done' stage.

The following provides a brief description of the stages which need to be taken into account when starting up a group enterprise within an eco-community.

THE PRINCIPLES

1. Start Small – Start From Where You Are

This means beginning with the available skills and resources, and not having grand (and often overwhelming to others in a group) schemes, but ones that have a reasonable chance of succeeding. It is more important when starting out to have a small success rather than a huge failure!

2. Make Use of Role Models

Use the expertise of those who have trodden the path before if at all possible. Have someone from your group spend time learning 'on the job' in a similar venture, even if it means travelling to do so. Most people involved in projects of this nature will be happy to share their insights, skills and lessons with you. They remember what it was like starting up!

3. **Develop a Broad-based Organisation**
This will maximise the chance of sustainability, as it means that not only is there a broad skills base to draw from, but that there is less chance of 'burnout' which can happen easily when only a few people are trying to do it by themselves. Involving people is relatively easy at the start of a project, when people are excited by the newness of the concept, but harder throughout the tough stages of the life of the project. It is imperative to inform the wider community at all phases of the project as it progresses, thus minimising chances of misunderstanding. Such a strategy also opens up possibilities of more recruits.

4. **Build a Base of Mutual Support**
This needs to be accomplished both 'within' your organisation, and, as others with similar values also are started, between those and your own. As more organisations with different functions are begun, it is possible and very beneficial to make use of those different organisations to provide services, e.g. education and training or financing, for your group.

5. **The Elements**
Even though any group economic venture (community business) may perform different functions within the community, there is an essential thread running through them all. Each community will have slightly different needs, and different priorities for meeting their needs. But essentially, each venture needs to be based on a number of common elements if it is to succeed. These are:
    a) *Community Need*: Any project must have as its basis a perceived need in the community. It does not matter how good an idea is, if there is not the need for the product or service within the community, the project will not take off. A simple needs assessment can be carried out by means of a survey, interviews and local talk-back radio.
    b) *Energy*: An assessment of the energy requirements (human and other resources) of any project must be undertaken before starting. It was important, for example, when starting our community Credit Union, our financial institution, in Maleny to assess if there were people who:
        - had money they would deposit with an alternative financial institution;
        - had worthwhile projects that needed capital; and
        - were prepared to commit themselves to bringing up and running the Credit Union.
    c) *Physical Focus*: It is most important that any community economic project has a 'home', a physical space which is identifiable and accessible to the community. This not only ensures a clear identity for the emerging venture, but enables the community to 'own' it more easily, in a way not possible if the project is based in a private' space, e.g. someone's home.

d) *Clear Aims and Objectives*: It is important initially to formulate a clear set of aims and objectives for each project. This will provide guidance not only as the project gets 'off the ground', where it will inform the budgetary process, promotional strategies and provide a focus for the founding group's energy, but also as a clear direction in years to come. This is not to say that these initial aims and objectives cannot be modified as the need arises at a later stage of the project, but emphasis is placed on the importance of strategic planning early in the project's existence.

e) *Commitment to the Vision*: When launching a new strategy, capital will become a pressing issue. There are limited ways to capitalise a project, which I will outline briefly:
   - The first involves putting your own capital into the project, or pooling the capital resources of your group. This is often not an option for small, community-based groups, which are mostly skills-rich, and cash poor.
   - The second involves borrowing the money required to start the venture. If you take this option, you must be aware of the commitment to work at least twice as much as if you had not taken the loan, in order to pay the capital and the interest back.
   - The third capital source is that of Government grants, which again have implications for the project. Firstly, the project may have to be altered, either slightly or substantially, to fit the grant guidelines, and then a considerable amount of energy will be needed to make the application, furnish the periodic reports to the funding body should the application be successful, and keep the project within the government guidelines until the conditions of the grant have been fulfilled.
   - The fourth method, which most community-based groups resort to, is that involving 'sweat equity', where items needed for the start-up are donated or borrowed, and group members give their time in a voluntary capacity until the venture begins to be profitable and can afford to pay wages. This is more difficult now than it was ten years ago in Australia, due to current Industrial Regulations legislation. In all cases, the commitment to the vision which inspired the group to undertake the venture will need to be strong, for it is a well-known fact that the pioneers of any strategy subsidise its success in years to come.

f) *Education and Training*: Given that many people who launch into revitalising their communities have boundless enthusiasm, but possibly have not learned many of the skills necessary to run a group enterprise (see later), the role of education and training in community development projects cannot be over emphasised. In bringing up the business ventures in Maleny, very few of the people involved had business or financial skills to begin with. This is not as serious a deficit as it may at first seem, as, by starting the project in a small, manageable way, these skills can be acquired 'on the job' (action-learning as it is called these days) and grow along with the venture's success.

There are numerous stories of individuals who, before coming into one of the Maleny co-operatives and other community businesses, had never touched a calculator, let alone a computer, had never written a business letter, or had to negotiate with the Government or business community. They are now, after years of training, comfortable running their own micro- or mini-businesses, or helping to manage a multi-million dollar (i.e., the Credit Union) or multi-thousand dollar business. Such is our capacity to learn – given a conducive environment. This is not to say that a group of people with no business skills could magically start and run an enterprise; just that it does not require the whole group to have those skills initially. As long as there are a small number of people with some of the requisite skills, and a commitment to training, it is sufficient to begin.

This commitment to education and training must include multi-skilling people within the organisations and educating the wider community as to the objectives and benefits of any particular venture. This last ensures that anyone in the wider community who can benefit from the outputs of the strategy knows what the project is about and how to gain involvement at the level they are comfortable with.

The Skills

The skills that are needed to build successful community economic ventures are twofold:

1. **Technical Skills**
   Skills such as management, financial, organisational and suchlike. There are plenty of easy-to-read books on such subjects, and others who can point you in the right direction for your particular needs in this area. Do not be afraid to ask 'professionals' for advice and help: many of them are happy to become peripherally involved in community organisations, either as an ethic or as a means of making the community aware of their involvement in other than strictly 'commercial' arrangements.

2. **Interpersonal Skills**
   Skills related to working together. These include democratic forms of decision-making and conflict management techniques. These are the type of skills that have not been emphasised in the past and are still given little weight in conventional business organisations. They are, however, essential for the successful operation of a co-operatively – structured business venture.

Although we have generally not been taught in school how to work together, or how to resolve conflicts, these are some of the most important skills that we can learn. There is as broad a range of literature and techniques available for learning such skills as there is in the range of 'technical' skills. I cannot emphasise this aspect of skills training enough: for, without these skills, your organisation will surely fail to thrive. Just as it will if you do not properly learn how to manage the financial side of the business!

CONCLUSION

This chapter has outlined some of the principles and processes that are important when developing sustainable economic communities, and the skills that are vital in this development. The model provided has been operating over the past twenty years within the small community of Maleny, in Australia, and elsewhere, albeit in a less developed form. The process is one of community empowerment, which generates satisfaction and sense of identity for a community. It exemplifies the principles of 'doing well by doing good', and living lightly on the earth, which are, after all, the cornerstones of sustainability.

THE WISDOM OF THE ELDERS
Communal Conflict and Conflict Resolution
by Dr Bill Metcalf

Bill Metcalf has lived in and studied communities for 20 years in Australia and twenty other countries. He works at the Griffith University, Faculty of Environmental studies.
Address:
50 Mabel Street
Highgate Hill
Queensland 4101
Australia
Tel: +61 (0)7 3844 8922
Fax: +61 (0)7 3844 8922

Photo: Helen Best

INTRODUCTION
The New Age communal movement is now about 25–30 years old. Many communal groups, in numerous countries around the globe, have safely passed the famous 'one generation or 25 years' barrier[1]. While most of these New Age, intentional communities and communes were started as an anarchistic and often hedonistic manifestation of a youth movement, both the participants and those communities that have survived have aged. Considerable research[2] indicates that the average (mean) age of participants is now in the mid to late forties, with as many participants over fifty as under thirty years of age. Researchers, however, too often address the questions of the survival of intentional communities as if they are still filled with exuberant, long haired, youthful hippies, rather than by seasoned communards.

Almost all the hardened radicals of the 1960s and early 1970s, including those who were aggressively atheistic in their radical youth, report an interest in spiritual development, ranging from seeking to reconnect with traditional religions and shamanism to eco-spirituality.

Although facing innumerable problems, this global New Age communal movement is growing and quite healthy. Intergenerational transfer of power and property, provision of support services for an ageing membership and, in some cases, coping with unexpected wealth and comfort are important issues.

Over the past five years I have been researching the life stories and 'wisdom' of communal elders from around the world. Their stories, the stories of communal survival, are both heart-wrenching and encouraging.

What can we learn from the stories of these communal elders?

Conflict and the Wisdom of the Communal Elders

The New Age communal movement is now very much a movement of and for middle-aged people. This means that communal conflicts are now more around issues of relevance to middle-aged and older people than around youth issues. And conflict, as any communal elder will admit, is both inevitable and endemic. What is in question is how to deal with that conflict.

In my research I have been collecting the 'wisdom' and life-stories of long-term members of contemporary intentional communities from around the globe. I ask key participants, with at least 20 years of communal experience, to write their story – to share their wisdom – of why they are involved, what makes their group work (or not work) and what they have learned from the long and arduous communal process of which they are 'the elders'. I did not randomly select respondents, since being a communal elder does not necessarily equate with having wisdom! Instead, I selected long-term members who have maintained their utopian zeal and their radical enthusiasm.

The long-term communards with whom I have worked provide a useful research access to those groups and individuals who are in for the long haul; for whom communal living is a lifelong commitment rather than a historical curiosity or a youthful phase of growing up.

While participant observation, ethnography and social surveys are the standard tools for research into communes and communards, I rejected them for this work. What I have called Biographical Discourse, whereby participants are encouraged to write and rewrite their stories, to share their wisdom, under my guidance, has proved to be an effective, revealing and efficient research strategy. It avoids many of the ethical issues of participant observation and surveys by empowering the participants, and facilitating their presentation of their stories in their own words. It also leads to publishable work thereby promoting the ideas and ideals of these communards as well as the general study of communalism.

This research project has so far resulted in two books. *From Utopian Dreaming to Communal Reality: Co-operative Lifestyles in Australia* is based on ten communal elders from a broad spectrum of intentional communities across Australia. The second book to result from this research is *Shared Visions, Shared Lives – Communal Living Around the Globe.* It is based on 15 communal elders from intentional communities in New Zealand, Japan, India, Israel, Germany, France, UK, Canada, USA, Mexico and Brazil. These communal elders have an average of 33 years communal experience, with several having lived communally all of their lives. One woman, for instance, was born in 1936 in a commune where she was raised, had her children and where she now has her grandchildren.

These 'elders' range in age from late thirties to eighties, and come from religious and secular communes and intentional communities around the globe. Leigh Davison, of Dharmananda, in Australia, asks, "Are we just a bunch of ageing, middle class baby boomers with Buddhist tendencies, trying to maintain a toehold on the 1960s, and will the whole thing just fizzle out after one generation? Or will (we) endure and thus have lasting social relevance?".

Longevity and cross-generational sustainability are important to all serious communards, and must be crucial to any meaningful analysis of the contemporary movement. The history of alternative lifestyles is more impressive in terms of the enthusiasm of would-be communards than in their ability to realise those dreams. The utopian spirit has fared much better that any particular communal experiment.

In her seminal research, Dr Rosabeth Kanter[3] considered one generation as the time for which a group must endure in order to be considered successful. While the question of what success means for alternative lifestyles has been widely debated[4], the indisputable fact remains that if communal groups are to contribute to social improvement, they must at least endure and be sustainable. All these communards talk about what they hope or seek to achieve through their social experimentation. Such achievements can only be greater the longer the group endures. And these groups have endured!

These communal elders are so different, yet so similar in that they have succeeded where so many have failed.

Comparison of Communal Elders and Intentional Communities

Differences:

While some communards had a stable, conventional family upbringing, others suffered class oppression and/or domestic violence in 'dysfunctional' families. Some communal elders stayed in the education system to gain PhDs, while others did not finish secondary school. Some are still involved in mainstream society, holding down professional positions, while others are unemployed and more isolated from the dominant economy and culture. While some had to grapple with their communal role, at times experiencing threats to their self-worth, others have been more comfortable with their own position vis-a-vis their intentional community.

These groups differ in size from only 8 people at Commonground in Australia to about 1,600 members at Yamagishi Toyosato in Japan. Religion is central to Chenrezig in Australia, Christavashram in India and New Meadow Run Bruderhof in USA, while it is peripheral but tolerated in others such as Kibbutz Einat in Israel and Lothlorien in Brazil. L' Arche in France, Los Horcones in Mexico and Mandala in Australia are geographically isolated, whilst Community Alternatives in Canada and UFA Fabric in Germany are in the heart of major cities. Commonground in Australia and Padanaram in USA have clearly enunciated political ideologies, while several others have no common political stance, and may even strive to be apolitical. Economic sharing is a crucial issue at Cennednyss in Australia and Christavashram in India, while it has only a limited role at many others. While a reaching-out, educational function is important at Findhorn in UK, Lothlorien in Brazil and Chenrezig in Australia, education has very little role at many others. Centralised, charismatic leadership is found at Christavashram

Members of Mandala Community, Queensland, Australia. Photo: Helen Best

in India and Padanaram in USA, while others such as UFA Fabrik in Germany, Tuntable Falls in Australia and Auroville in India are better described as anarchistic. The Emissaries in Canada, The Farm in USA and Findhorn in UK have all made the transition from centralised, charismatic leadership to diffuse, semi-consensual decision making, while Yamagishi Toyosato in Japan and Kibbutz Einat in Israel remain more hierarchical and bureaucratic.

Similarities:

Most of these communal elders acknowledge the importance of spirituality within their own lives and within their group. For many, the term 'eco-spirituality' best captures this guiding principle. Most communards have come from materialistic, secular backgrounds, but several also had strong religious convictions. All have found that secularism gives insufficient meaning to life – that a deeper, more spiritual connection, both between people and with the earth, is essential. This spirituality differs from religion, and its expression ranges from what was expressed as 'Earth Dreaming', 'a search for Gaia', 'a quest for the life-enhancing feminine principle' and a 'Spirit of Natural Regeneration'.

All groups have found the dynamics of interpersonal relationships to be one of their biggest challenges. Tuntable Falls and Crystal Waters in Australia, Auroville in India, Kibbutz Einat in Israel and Yamagishi Toyosato in Japan partly cope with this challenge through their large size which means that people who do not get along need not see much of each other. In more intimate communes such as Commonground and Cennednyss in Australia, Lothlorien in Brazil and Riverside in New Zealand, formal conflict resolution processes help promote amicability. At Chenrezig in Australia and Findhorn in UK, group meditation provides a basis for sociability, while prayer meets similar needs in New Meadow Run Bruderhof in USA, L' Arche in France and Christavashram in India.

All intentional communities experience conflict. The groups which endure have learned how to work with and through that conflict rather than hide it, and when conflict cannot be resolved, to at least reach an accommodation. The saddest part of the life stories of these communal elders comes when they admit to the times when their own approach to conflict resolution did not work and members left.

Chris Palmer, who has lived at Riverside Community in New Zealand for 45 years, writes:

> *"I remember, years ago, being amused when Riverside received a letter from another community, suggesting that as we had been going for over 20 years, we should have good advice on solving problems of personal relations and tensions. I was not aware that we had any particular expertise! Looking back, I realise that it was very much a case of 'If it's too hot, get out of the kitchen'. I am sad about that, and I believe that the mediation techniques which we now have would have overcome some of the situations*

> *which arose previously. It is easy to be aware of poor relationships between members but very difficult to know what to do about it. I think that most of those who are attracted to communal living tend to be idealistic and strongly individualistic. This runs counter to the necessity to be prepared to lose some of that individuality for the sake of the common good. For communal living is just that; I can't get away from it while I'm here so I have to make it work."*

Many groups experience a tension between the 'doing' and 'being' aspects of communal life. This tension is particularly important at Commonground in Australia, The Farm in USA and UFA Fabric in Germany where their commitment to social and political goals, and their striving for radical change tend to take them away from just enjoying each other and sharing everyday life. After all, when one is promoting social revolution, it may seem a waste of time to discuss who washes the dishes! Tensions between the doing and being aspects of communal life have no final solution. But when a group devotes more attention to doing, through group projects, members come closer, promoting their sense of being. Most groups find that shared work is often one of the most effective yet underrated means of resolving conflict and reaffirming their commitment.

At Findhorn in UK they state, "Work is Love in Action", while at Padanaram in USA they assert more forthrightly, "One who won't work shall not eat". Rachel Summerton, a thirty-year communal veteran, concludes, "These things affected me right where I lived. Philosophies of 'how to' didn't help. It's what I lived, what I experienced, and sometimes it was raw! It was the nitty-gritty of communal life, the daily ups and down. It is called 'working together'."

Most intentional communities acknowledge a dynamic tension between individualism and communalism, between the centrifugal forces of mainstream society where personal choice and whim are celebrated, and the centripetal forces needed to keep a communal group together. For example, at Moora Moora in Australia it is "easier to make decisions that give something to the individual but harder to do likewise for the collective". Communes persist only when people submerge their individuality into the collective reality. That is why most long term intentional communities are not true communes but are more diffuse 'alternative communities'. The latter attempt to get the best of both worlds, to allow considerable personal autonomy while enjoying the fruits of a richer and more complex social collectively. However, without care and attention, intentional communities tend to lose their radical zeal and devolve into rural suburbs. This process is easiest to see with The Emissaries in Canada, Kibbutz Einat in Israel and Crystal Waters in Australia.

Selection of new members is critical to all communal groups and can lead to very serious conflict if mismanaged. While having people with appropriate motivation and commitment is important in all groups, not all have developed adequate mechanisms to deal with it. The naive notion within New Age circles that communal groups should have no boundaries, and just be open to all and sundry, has been one of the most insidious, nonsensical millstones around the members' collective necks.

Two well-known American researchers recently acknowledged this by observing[5]:

> *"Communities are well advised to screen prospective members carefully... Far from being arbitrary or elitist, screening through a period of extensive dialoguing and apprenticing makes good sense if communities indeed benefit – or suffer – from the degree of fit between their basic vision or purpose and the personality characteristics of their members. Strongly doctrinal communities may benefit from a more authoritarian and less open-minded membership, while new-age, spiritually eclectic and secular communities may require less authoritarian and more open-minded members in order to thrive."*

Riverside in New Zealand, The Farm in USA, Los Horcones in Mexico, Lothlorien in Brazil, and Mandala, Tuntable Falls and Moora Moora in Australia all discuss problems they have faced from having inappropriate member selection procedures.

Most communal elders acknowledge the importance of the socialisation of new members in order to promote thinking in terms of 'we' rather than 'you and/or I'. This process is helped in the large communities by newsletters and formal gatherings. At Chenrezig in Australia, Christavashram in India and New Meadow Run Bruderhof in USA the presence of a clear set of religious

Crystal Waters Permaculture Village, Queensland, Australia. Photo: Helen Best

South East Essex College
of Arts & Technology

principles helps. Having their own school is very important in Tuntable Falls in Australia, Christavashram in India, Yamagishi Toyosato in Japan and Los Horcones in Mexico, although many other groups have no formal educational policy.

While it requires serious, hard work to make an intentional community work, many communal elders also acknowledge the importance of having fun. Most groups have 'trivial' rituals that help bind them together. Shared meals, games nights, group meditation, nude swimming or saunas and, most importantly, working-bees are crucial to developing and maintaining their sense of 'groupness' or 'we-consciousness'. As Albert Bates of The Farm states, "We have to make it all come together for the next generation, which means it has to be relevant, even inspirational, and might even be fun. Actually, it had better be fun or no-one will want to do it." Justin Peters of New Meadow Run Bruderhof tells us, "Particularly when there is too much work to do and too few hands to do it, we find excuses for fun. A few days ago there was so much work to do in the factory that we closed it down and played softball for an hour. What a great way to pump new enthusiasm into our work!"

Just as most families have symbols which, at least in their own eyes, help explain what and who they are, or at least what they want others to think they are, long term communal groups have the same. Most proudly display a 'logo' at their entrance, a classic example of boundary demarcation, as well as a practical way of telling the world that they identify as a 'collective-we', a social-collective rather than being a mere collection of people.

All groups recognise that while a high commitment by the individual to the collective is essential, this must never stifle individual creativity. Several communal elders assert that one's creativity is enhanced within the group's safe confines. While all groups adhere to notions of 'equality', the naive idea of all people being equal has fortunately been abandoned. To be effective, groups must acknowledge and utilise members' unique skills. Not everyone is equally competent at book keeping, resolving conflict, repairing a roof, leading group meditation and prayers, or fixing communal vehicles, but all these skills are critical. The recognition and acknowledgement of the difference between 'social equality' and 'all are equal' in terms of skills has been important to the survival of communal groups.

Several communal elders point to the need for careful planning and detailed research in order to start an intentional community. Communal groups do not just happen, but only result from years of planning and hard work. These communards describe the painful and dreary work required, as well as the rewards when it works.

Is The Quest for Intentional Community Worthwhile?

Several quotes are instructive:

> *"In ten years' time, we fervently hope that we will still be here, living in this rich environment... Cennednyss works for us and there is no other way we would rather live. It enriches our lives immeasurably."*

Members of Dharmananda Community, New South Wales, Australia.
Photo: Helen Best

"Intentional community provides a perfect environment for practical anarchist activity – for 'ordinary' people to... chip away at the edges of the system.... intentional community resists the oppressive, criminal and environmentally disastrous values and practices of state power and bourgeois individualism... Here (Mandala) is the signpost for the remainder of my life journey in intentional community. Why did I take so long to reach this starting line?"

"I've never regretted for a moment my commitment to l' Arche. My roots are here, and here I feel so alive. I want to stay here until my last breath will fly away on the wings of a seagull. Returning to the purest Holy Light... returning to God."

"The knowledge that I will be here (Dharmananda) for the rest of my days has had a settling effect... I am grateful that my communal farming experience in this beautiful, natural setting has enabled me to make contact with my own inner artist and mystic. They now work together with the... inner scientist... I have inadvertently stumbled onto the best of both worlds."

"I love my home, Kibbutz Einat, and many of my fellow communards. My husband and I enjoy our work. I feel that my roots are very deep in Kibbutz Einat, and that no ideological or political disagreement is worth severing these lifelong ties.

"I have but tasted our human need and potential for community (Moora Moora); a taste that feeds and drains me, a taste that cushions me from the harshness and threats of the dominant world, while being a mirror to the wonders of human capacities. I have... become more rounded... playing with the children and working with the land."

"Do the gripes loom large enough to blight my life, sour my community experience, or make me feel I'd like to... live... in a retirement village or in another community?... NO – I'm here (The Wolery) for good!... it's here I want to live, and later on, to die."

Summary and Conclusion

Perhaps the utopian quest for community, for developing more humane ways of living together and with our natural world, is crucial to our survival. Biographical discourse facilitates the wisdom of these communal elders to be better analysed and communicated to a mass audience. As well, the method helps these people to clarify their ideas, to gain self-confidence and to feel and be acknowledged for their life work. They rightly take on the mantle of a 'wise elder' within the communal movement. Their diverse stories from intentional communities around the world demonstrate:

1. Communal living attracts and creates fascinating characters.

2. A spiritual, beyond-self orientation is almost always needed.

3. Leadership is critical, with all forms having problems.

4. Conflict is endemic and will be resolved – somehow.

5. The material, political, spiritual and social planes are entwined.

6. Sustainable communal societies are possible but difficult.

REFERENCES

Metcalf, B., 1995. *From Utopian Dreaming to Communal Reality.* Sydney, Australia: University of New South Wales Press.

Metcalf, B., 1996. *Shared Visions, Shared Lives – Ecospirituality and Social Experimentation.* Scotland: Findhorn Press.

[1] This measure of what is often incorrectly labelled 'success' was popularised by Dr Rosabeth Kanter in his famous book, 1972. *Commitment and Communities*, Cambridge: Harvard University Press . In spite of ample criticism, it remains as a valuable, albeit rough indication of a communal group's sustainability.

[2] For example, Metcalf W., and Vonclay, F., 1987. *Social Characteristics of Alternative Lifestyle Participants in Australia*, Griffith University: Brisbane. IAER.
Questenberry D., and Morgan, M., 1991. *A Demographic Analysis of 186 North American Intentional Communities.* Presented at the International Communal Studies Association Conference: Elizabethtown, USA.
Weggemans, T., eds. D., Hardy and L., Davidson, 1989. Modern Utopia and Modern Communes. *Utopian Thought and Communal Experience.* Middlesex Polytechnic, London. p.44–53.
Cummings, M., and H. Bishop, 1994. Stereotypes Challenged. *Communities – Journal of Co-operative Living.* No. 84. p.10–12.

[3] Kanter; op. cit.

[4] Wagner, J., 1985. Success in International Communities. *Communal Societies.* V. 5. p.89–100.

[5] Cummings M., and H. Bishop, 1996. Open-minded, and Closed-minded Communities. *Communities – Journal of Co-operative Living*, No. 90. p.9.

Part III

Conflict Resolution Techniques

INNER DEVELOPMENT IN SERVICE TO COMMUNITY

by Patricia Michael

Patricia Michael and her family live and work in Austin, Texas, USA where she is co-founder of an earth-bonded non-denominational church. She is an advisor, conflict resolution assistant and elder to a large bioregional community. Patricia has published in the subjects of ecological design, gardening, community, caring for your own dead, and bioregional organizing. She has over ten years experience in teaching, lecturing and conducting workshops in organizational dynamics and design. She has lectured and presented in the US, Central America, Sweden, France, the Czech Republic, Australia and New Zealand. She has significant experience organizing civic, cultural and educational events and communities including: The Other Economic Summit, Houston, Texas, Regional and International Bioregional Congresses, was co-founder and director of a 250-person cooperative community and a founding board member of the Fire House Art Center non-profit art school, Norman, Oklahoma.

Address:
1206 Marshall Lane
Austin
Texas 78703
USA
Tel: +1 512 474 8981
Fax: +1 512 494 0890
Email: patricia_michael@compuserve.com

> *"In any gathering, in any chance meeting on the street, there is a shine, an elegance rising up."*
> Rumi

For a community to create unity its members have to be able to 'Meet'. This may be the most difficult aspect of community and the richest. When a community can 'Meet' conflicts are much easier to deal with and don't arise as often. We have a tendency in community to flee into administration, law, rules. Work, and activity. We hide in doing things for people and the community but not 'Meeting'. To love we have to 'Meet'.

Those of us whose service is leading meetings have to know how to enable 'Meeting' to happen. Too often we facilitate business, and doing things or making decisions, but not 'Meeting'.

There is a particular alchemy, a seemingly magical power or process of transmuting meeting as individuals into 'Meeting' as a unity. When everyone is blended we become invested in nourishment, joy, interest, and the good of the whole. A 'Meeting' is alive when energies are blended. The 'Meeting' in community is a manifestation of the experience of being one. We often learn lots of techniques for facilitation but leave the alchemy of 'Meeting' to chance. Singing and dancing together creates this blend, and so does heart-to-heart communication.

A community can train in sentience and every member can use their perceptions to 'keep the heart' in meetings in order to renew blending and 'Meet' on a regular basis. If this is done, conflicts are very different and are much easier to solve.

The Insight Facilitator

A group facilitator needs to be sensible and in touch with the group. What I mean by 'sensible' is being open to insight from all our body's senses. When the facilitator is in touch with the energy of the group, she or he knows what form, process, etc. will serve the highest purpose of the group and each group member. It is just a mess when the energies of the group are not read by the facilitator or are misread.

Having a few energy-insight people to help the facilitator be sensible to the group's needs helps because it is too easy for the facilitator to get lost in content. Every organization could benefit from a team of mystics to keep vigilance at 'Meetings' for the energy of the group. Intuition and observation are extremely important to protect the group's greatest good.

It is one thing to trust intuition. It is another to know where it is coming from. Blind trust in intuition is as dysfunctional as any other form of blind trust. Perception of something this subtle can be tricky. We need training.

Each of us is a mystic with our own modality of reception and transmission. For example, clairvoyants see images and clairaudiants hear messages in their inner dialogue. Insight mystics just have insights. They simply know information about things that have not been communicated directly to them through any of the standard overt means of communication. Most people are insight mystics.

I define insight as the capacity to discern the true nature of a situation and to make it clear or clarify it. Most of us have had the experience of an insight. We call them hunches or inklings. Many of us have had the experience of not acting on our elucidating glimpse and later wishing we had. Often we do not trust our insights. We don't communicate about them and a valuable possibility for 'Meeting' is lost.

Experiences of an Insight Mystic I am not one of the 'gifted' prophets. I am a simple, everyday person who has had, and continues to do, practices and exercises to develop my subtle side. I have been graced to have some very good teachers and want to share some of the most effective teachings and discoveries here.

My grandparents lived in a neighborhood on the outskirts of Wichita, Kansas, USA, when I was a child. I lived with them much of the time. The neighborhood had as its center a large manufacturing yard that built railroad cars for the Santa Fe Railroad. This was during and right after World War II. Around this yard lived very poor people from many countries who had come to Wichita because the railroad offered them free transportation and a job. You didn't have to know much English to do the hard work in the railroad yard.

This was an exciting neighborhood of rich images of colors, clothes, foods, smells, plants, music, art and exotic (for me) religious practices. Grandma and Grandpa had a small city farm on the edge of the neighborhood, and it was from my grandmother, who was the farmer, that most of the new immigrants received seeds, cultivars and regional garden lessons. Grandma was also experienced in folk medicine and helped to deliver many children and helped out with illnesses. Within this community was a little Quaker silent meeting hall where we did what was called silent communion. Others might call it contemplation or meditation.

I spent a lot of time just being quiet and observing. The subtleties of experiences within myself, the landscape, other animals, my family and our community could fascinate me for hours. My insight teachers were from the Orient, Middle East, Mexico and Europe.

My favorite game with my grandmother was generating plant roots. We would cut a plant branch, put it in the ground and encourage it to root by calling earth helpers to it. We would find worms and other small animals in the earth by feeling/hearing where they were and then gently digging to confirm their position. These were, seemingly, just childish games, but they were fun and built my intuition.

Now my favorite daily practice is to stand barefoot on the earth with my arms in front of me, elbows out and finger tips aimed toward each other, thumbs up, palms toward my chest. I just stand relaxed and feel the sensations in my body. Concentrating on the movement, vibrating, tingling, little patterns within me, my eyes are open and soft and my body very relaxed. The very energy of the earth and sky are keeping me up. I am an antenna and a transmitter between and within nature.

The basis of good sense is rest and nutrition. For each of us that means something different because we are of such varied body types and cultures. The way I can tell if I'm doing it right is how calm and reasonable I can be under stress and how well I can think. It helps me, as the facilitator of a long process, to take a fifteen-minute nap with my legs up on the wall to bring blood to my brains at least every two hours. I carry nutritional supplements, teas, herbs and special little personal nurturing things like fresh plants and good water with me, as well as raw foods, whole grains and sea vegetables.

A long drink of water can bring almost anyone back to their senses. A jog around the room, a fast walk to the rest room and back, or some chi gong, swinging the arms, are respectful enough to pass even in a very formal meeting situation.

The training for good sense is any exercise or practice that balances and hones and grounds our body's senses: seeing, hearing, smelling, touching, tasting, feeling and intuiting.

When facilitating, I make an effort to have my heart open. The heart is the transformer of energy. I make it the size of my body's edges and about a foot beyond. I beam it into the whole room. This gives me more surface for transformation. To do this, I begin in silence and use that space to image my heart growing to the desired size. Quickly rubbing my palms together helps to open up my heart. If during a meeting I forget and then notice that I am not in my heart, I breathe a deep breath and rub my hands together again. I learned this from a social work veteran who told me it is a way to avoid heart stress, which is well known in the service fields.

Sometimes if it is a difficult meeting I ask a friend or two to assist the meeting by sitting in silence and staying in their hearts. They meditate, stay in their hearts, and imagine positive, wonderful outcomes for the meeting. The Threshold Foundation uses this technique, and my grandmother used 'silent communion' people when birthing babies, when people were very ill or dying, or when settling a disagreement. This is a long-standing Quaker tradition.

The energy the 'Meeting' facilitator needs to be most aware of is the energy inside their own body. We are all patterned and changed by the experiences of our lifetime. We all sense differently, and what is sensible for one person is not for another. It is important for us to know as much as possible how we experience energy so we can tell, literally, where we are coming from when we sense. As the inscription at the Oracle at Delphi says, "Know thyself."

The Chakras

The seven chakras provide a convenient matrix for checking the quality of energy in our body. Each chakra is a center of energy in the body, and each is associated with a particular focus. Here is a brief summary, starting from bottom and going up.

	Place:	Energy Focus:
1.	Root/base of spine	Survival, basic needs for food, water, air, shelter.
2.	Genitals	Sexuality, creativity, the beginning of duality.
3.	Belly/Hara	Power, aggression and defensiveness; victim, perpetrator, rescuer.
4.	Heart	Love, transformation, nurturing, feeding.

5. Throat	Communication, sending and receiving, talking and listening, where all the other chakras come together; Satsang, the company of truth.
6. Third Eye	Insight.
7. Crown	Connection.

EXERCISES FOR INSIGHT

To trust intuition for clear communication in serving community, it is helpful to do exercises and practices. These help us in several ways.

We become able to communicate and do reality checks on our insights. We become able to understand our own internal insight process. We become able to select processes, meeting protocols and facilitation tools to act on the insights clearly.

There is an interesting set of exercises a group of people can do over a period of time together to study the experience of energy in their own bodies using the chakra system. These exercises help to build the ability to intuit and to begin to learn how our sensing of an experience is colored, as it were, by our past.

These exercises will require that you imagine sending, receiving and blocking energy. It is a game of make believe that has real results. To send energy you can imagine streams of colored light or sounds or water or air flowing from a particular center of your body to the corresponding center in the other person's body. The idea is to increase sensitivity and awareness. Even the greatest cynics will have experiences because these exchanges of energy are life. It helps to bring them to awareness. It is best to do these exercises under the guidance of a facilitator who has done them before. Do the exercise several times, each time sending and receiving from a particular center (chakra) in the body, such as the survival center (first or root chakra), the sexual center, the power center (hara or third chakra), the love center (the heart, the fourth chakra), and the center of communication (the throat chakra).

THE BASIC EXERCISE

Select a room that is quiet and comfortable, with no distractions. Allow at least two hours for each chakra exercise. Don't wear perfumes or essential oils or burn incense out of respect for the chemically sensitive. Besides, you can have a more accurate sense of smell if you don't.

Select a partner. Take a few moments to relax and feel comfortable with each other. Sit facing each other at the same level. Choose who will be the first sender and who will be the first receiver.

The basic exercise pattern is the same for each chakra:

1. Do a guided meditation to remember a strong experience of the energy of a particular chakra. The facilitator leads the guided meditation.

2. The sender keeps that experience in mind and sends the energy of that experience to the receiving partner. The receiver simply receives the energy. Do this for about five minutes. Experience what it feels like to receive and send from that place.

3. Stop and discuss what it felt like to send and to receive the energy. What did you feel in your body? In your emotions? Talk about it with your partner.

4. Switch roles and do the process again. Stop and discuss what it felt like for each role.

5. Now switch roles again (back to the original roles) and do the process again, but this time with a difference. The receiver, instead of simply receiving the energy, tries to block it.

6. Stop and discuss what it felt like to be sending energy that the other person blocked and what it felt like to block the energy.

7. Switch roles and do the new process again, with the receiver blocking. Stop and discuss what it felt like for each role.

You can repeat this process for each of the chakras.

Often these exercises bring up memories of other times in our lives when we have had similar feelings. Take time to talk about them. It will help you understand the energetics of those times and any in the future. We have learned patterns of energy. For some of us these exercises will show us where it is hard to receive or to send. We may also discover personal patterns of blocking or continuing to send even though the other person is blocking.

The order in which you do the centers is a cultural decision. Start with the energies that the people who you are assisting express most easily. For instance, in the United States I might start with power, then survival, sex, love and finally communication. I do not generally start with the sexual center because it is easier to deal with the second chakra after the group has had some experience with the exercise.

The guided visualizations for each chakra should create a strong, distinct energy. Here are some suggestions for each chakra:

For the root chakra, imagine or remember a time when all was well. Remember a time when all your needs were met – you were well fed, happy, full, felt rich, loved, comfortable and grounded. For the genital chakra, imagine or remember a time when you felt very sexy, very attracted to another person. For the belly chakra, or hara, remember or imagine a time when you felt very powerful. You can do this twice. First imagine having just completed a major piece of work or accomplishment; this is power from within. Then imagine being really angry with another person and forcing them to do your will; this is power over. For the heart chakra it is great to remember a time when you felt so much love that you were just overflowing with it. Sending that love to another person and having them block or receive it are two distinctly different experiences. For the throat chakra, imagine or remember a time when you were truly flowing with clear communication.

I do not do these exercises for the sixth and seventh chakras, because those chakras are more impersonal. They do not relate as directly with other people as the first five.

These exercises are not a test, and there are no right answers. People have very different experiences. One friend felt panicky and recalled a time when she sent a huge heart full of love to another who received it and it was wonderful, but later the receiver betrayed her. Now she felt panicky about being betrayed when she sent her love.

Sending love and having it blocked actually caused pains in my chest when I first tried it. Blocking love when someone sent it to me made me feel a little nauseated. Another friend felt anger, and another felt pressure in her head and described it as like having her head full of cotton. One friend, a very beautiful young woman, was surprised at how familiar the feeling was when someone sent sexual energy to her and she blocked it.

It is not important what the experience is. What is important is that we understand that many of our experiences with other people have energetic symptoms in our bodies, and if we have studied what these are for us, then we know what is happening energetically in the moment and can make choices based on more than words or even body language. It gives us an energy language also.

I observe animals and plants and landscapes to hone my senses. It is there that I sense the patterns of nature that I make an effort to emulate for successful group process.

Over time as we focus on and widen the zone in ourselves between what part of our insight is conscious and what part is unconscious, we develop our own language experiences within that zone. Some folks link with the vibration as their personal code, others link with sounds, colors, tastes or other sensations. It doesn't matter; just find out what works for you. Do not buy another person's language and experiences as your own. In metaphysical, mind-body zones it is very important to know for yourself and be honest and clear.

> *"Learn about your inner self from those who know such things, but don't repeat verbatim what they say."*
> Rumi

Observations of Group Energy

Here are some of my personal observations about groups. Since what I am attempting to describe is not describable in regular terms, I will use synesthesia to elaborate the flavor of my experiences for you. I have developed my own metaphors so I can have a logical relationship to an intuitively felt reality.

Imagination does play a role in intuiting. If the language you develop is truthful to your own inner experience, then it is your truth. I learned that as a studio artist. My truth was communicated through patterns of line, color, saturation and form. The mystic and the artist have in common an ability to communicate the culture's truth.

Every group at any moment has a particular flavor or taste. Some are sweet, others spicy, others salty or bitter. I have been in groups where I could smell the group's fear, disgust, anger or boredom. Boredom smells to me a little like clothes that have been hanging in the closet too long, fear like sharp and sour, and anger a little like sulphur or acid. Disgust will snort puffs of a smell a little like the taste of charcoal, and sadness is thick, almost smothering or stifling the sense of smell.

To taste and smell a group it helps to eat foods that are simple, fresh, raw or slightly cooked, prepared with few spices and little or no salt. Refined flour, sugar and complex chemical foods like packaged mixes and artificial sweeteners confuse the receptors for taste and smell. Alcohol and drugs can heighten the senses, but I cannot trust what I feel to be clear when I am under their influence.

When balance and attunement is happening in a group, the pattern in the room is expanded. There is lots of room, and it is filled out by people. Their very bodies look bigger, faces are more rounded and eyes are wide, yet relaxed. The net pattern also shows up; the group looks like a net, with lots of connections. Arms and legs are spread wide. A person may put their hand on the knee of the person next to them, or relax their arm across their neighbor's shoulder. The group will fill in the spaces between each other with connections like looks, reaches, gestures and jokes.

When any form of fear is present, folks contract and the pattern of the room is scattered. Gestures dart rather than flow, and looks go down or out of the group more.

The quality of light changes with each phase of the group. I like to keep meeting rooms well lit with indirect lighting from the side, many lamps or open windows and doors. Overhead light contracts a group and seems to make it restless. It is not as easy to see the group energy with overhead fluorescent lighting. Light-colored spaces and dark spaces have different qualities. A dark, closed space is good for bringing up archetypes, old memories and psychological 'Meeting'. A lighter space is better for the early stages of a group, for singing, and for safe and less invasive 'Meeting'.

I have my own experience of color in groups. Sometimes the group is golden, either bright sparking twinkly young gold or deeply reflecting dark yellow gold. That is a color of group harmony for me.

I have seen groups go brown and pack up like wet clay soil, each person holding their position with few movements or flows. The energy of the room seems to ooze out of the doors like erosion.

I have seen groups gold and green with fresh enthusiasm and playful rawness. They seem just picked for cross-fertilization and thrusting growth.

Some groups are blue to purple with softness of spirits and widespread energies that are lovely but of little verbal content other than energy. Singing is often one of these beautiful clear blue times. Storytelling is another one of these shades of blue harmony.

Sometimes a group is white. Everyone is putting out energy and receiving energy on a full-blast level. I was once in such a group led by Starhawk. It was a night of group catharsis and great beauty. There was such trust and protection that each person in the group of over seventy women was doing her own business wide open. Starhawk was keeping the spell with a simple drum beat and women were crying, wailing, dancing, nurturing, singing and acting out a tableau of intensity. It was a discharge of such trust that the room vibrated with white light. I was transfixed with wonder while singing a capella harmony with three other women somewhere in the room whose faces I don't even know, but our voices leapt like a cathedral roof over the whole business and was a part of the vessel for the light. Literally and figuratively, all colors of light were there. At one point late in the evening an elderly stick of a woman with well-advanced cancer stepped into the middle of the room and danced with colored chiffon veils a dance of limber, lithe, flowing youth. She was truly in and of that light.

Some parts of nature are so slow that they appear to be not moving at all. It is important for a facilitator to see that kind of movement and not interfere with it. That is the deep, significant grounding of a group that is like rock. That rock movement feels very different from stuck or stubborn entrenchment.

I had an opportunity to attend a Father-Son dance with Carol Whitney of the Jacobsen Foundation in Oklahoma when my daughter, Sarah, was of nursing age. That was the first time I saw people dance like rocks. The men and some women did many forms of high-energy fancy dancing. They were like the dances of plants and animals in the wind or water, especially birds. Then a line of women moved out into the dance space. They were holding their arms out crossed over their breasts, elbows up and parallel with the earth. They had large shawls draped over their shoulders and arms that held a powerful shape. They were in rows of three or four across and spread an arm's length behind each other. They moved ahead with an exact measured step and dipped, keeping their bodies straight, chins up, looking ahead with soft eyes. This powerful, thick line of dancers sent a shudder of recognition through my body as I saw rock, the very earth dance.

That kind of energy happens in a group when there is deep agreement, and a time has to be allowed for it. It is when an agreed-upon truth is sensed by all and that truth is soaking in like dew on rocks. Watch for when you see the rocks move.

Group Facilitation as Spiritual Service

Those of us whose service is leading meetings have the opportunity not only to create a healing and nurturing space for the group but to use our skills as a way to deepen and develop our own spiritual growth. Doing so makes us more effective as group facilitators. We get to embody in ourselves what we hope to nurture in the group: the realization that our greatest good lies in service to the whole of which we are a part, and that we serve best when we are fully nourished and have fully developed our own inner abilities.

Six Ingredients for Forming Communities
That Help Reduce Conflict Down the Road
by Diana Leafe Christian

Diana Leafe Christian has studied intentional communities and eco-villages intensively since 1992. She has edited *Communities Magazine* in North America since 1993, and was former publisher/editor of *Growing Community* newsletter. She has contributed articles for the *Fellowship for Intentional Community's* (FIC) 1995 *Communities Directory*. She has presented her workshop, 'Six Ingredients for Forming Communities That Help Reduce Conflict Down the Road' at sustainable communities conferences, permaculture design courses, alternative colleges, regional educational centers, and for forming community groups all over North America, as well as for the FIC's regional Art of Community gatherings and at the Findhorn Foundation's 1998 Sustainable Communities Conference. Her book on how to form new communities, Together We Can Make It, will be out in 1999.

Diana has written articles on health and consciousness for *New Age Journal*, *East West Journal* (now *Health Consciousness*), *Yoga Journal*, *Shaman's Drum*, and other alternative American magazines. She formerly worked for Fritjof Capra's Elmwood Institute and the Institute of Noetic Sciences. She lives in and is co-founder of a small community in Colorado, in the US.

Address:
Communities Magazine
290 McEntire Road,
Tryon,
NC 28782
USA
Tel: +1 828 863 4425
Email: communities@ic.org or diana@ic.org

According to my estimate, approximately one out of ten newly forming intentional communities or eco-villages in North America seem to actually get built. That's very few, compared to the numbers of inspired and visionary people who make the attempt. Sometimes a community or eco-village disbands because it doesn't have enough money or because mistrustful neighbors prevent the group from getting a needed zoning variance. But mostly, newly forming communities dissolve because its people can't get along with each other.

I've met with, read about, or interviewed hundreds of people involved in newly forming communities and eco-villages, as well as founders of existing ones, and noticed the same thing over and over. Most of the groups that disband do so in conflict. Or conflict and heartbreak. Or conflict, heartbreak, and lawsuits.

A major factor in the dissolution of new communities and eco-villages is what I call structural conflict, as distinct from interpersonal conflict (which I see plenty of too). Structural conflict arises when founders didn't explicitly agree upon certain important issues before they got started. Several weeks, months, or even years later, the group runs into a problem that having had that system or agreement in place would have largely prevented. But now it's a crisis. It's as if a time bomb has been ticking away until the community stumbles over it, then, 'Boom!'.

Communities and eco-villages have had great difficulty, and sometimes floundered and sank on the shoals of such issues as: "What do you *mean* I can't get my money out again when I leave?!" "What, my brother can't live here? What do you mean he has to pass through normal new-member application channels. He's my *brother*!" "Oh, I'm *sure* Raffy didn't bite your child. He wouldn't hurt a fly! I'm not getting rid of my dog; no way!" "I have to move my piles of scrap lumber off the land? But I didn't agree to that! Who decided that?! I didn't vote on this!"

In all the disbanded and dissolving would-be communities and eco-villages I saw this same kind of structural conflict – and much of it preventable if the founders had included six ingredients in the early days:

1. They identify their vision and create a Vision Statement.

2. They learn what things they need to know in order to take on this complex task.

3. They use a fair, participatory decision-making process in which they've had some training, and they have a trained facilitator for their meetings. If they use decide to use consensus, they learn *how* to do it first.

4. They draw up clear agreements, in writing.

5. They learn good communication skills, and they make clear, clean communication a priority. This includes ways of reducing and mediating conflict.

6. They select for emotional maturity in co-founders and members.

1. Vision and Vision Statement: "What We Are About?"

A group's vision is a compelling idea or image that inspires and motivates. It is not verbal, but rather a feeling tone, an 'energetic presence'. It gives voice to the founders' deeply held values and intuitions. It is their group's picture or 'feel' of the kind of life they'd like to lead together.

The vision is not the same thing as a Vision Statement. The Vision Statement is the vision articulated – it's the vision written down.

In my opinion it's most potent if it's short, 20 to 40 or so words. (It can certainly include accompanying paragraphs of description.) The Vision Statement is a clear, concise, compelling statement of overall purpose and goals that everyone can identify with, and which serves to unify the group's effort. The Vision Statement helps focus the group's energy like a lens. It gives them a reference point to return to in decisions or during confusion or disagreement. It keeps the members inspired, as it reminds them why they're creating a community. When times get tough, the Vision Statement helps awaken the vision as a energetic presence. It communicates the group's core purpose to others quickly: "*This* is what we're about; *this* is what we hope to accomplish." It allows the group to be specific about what it is – and is not. It's what potential new community members want to see first. Ideally, the Vision Statement is memorized; every member can recite it. It is the 'who', the 'what', and the 'why' of the forming community. (It doesn't contain the 'when', 'where', or 'how'; that's in the strategic plan). Some examples:

> *"We have joined together to create a center for renewal, education, and service, dedicated to the positive transformation of our world."*
> Shenoa Retreat and Learning Center, California

> *"We are a group of individuals, couples, and families desiring to live and participate responsibly in a cooperative housing community."*
> Nyland Cohousing, Colorado

> *"We are creating a cooperative neighborhood of diverse individuals sharing human resources within an ecologically responsible community setting."*
> Harmony Village Cohousing, Colorado

> *"We are a neotribal permaculture village, actively engaged in building sacred community, supporting personal empowerment, and catalyzing cultural transformation... We share a commitment to a vital, diversified spirituality; healthy social relations; sustainable ecological systems; and a low-maintenance/high-satisfaction lifestyle."*
> Earthaven Eco-village, North Carolina

Notice that these Vision Statements are all fairly concrete and specific. I've found that the greater the amount of generalized, idealistic non-specific language, the greater the likelihood the eco-village or community will disband early or never get off the ground. But when the Vision Statement is concise, concrete, specific, and grounded, the eco-village or community tends to actually get built.

It is quite possible that people in a newly forming group have more than one vision among them – which means they're more than one potential community. It's crucial to find this out early – *before* the group buys land. Imagine the conflict that emerges when people become land partners only to find out they have two distinct visions: "We are a demonstration site that teaches permaculture to others, with regularly scheduled workshops – and we live in community to do it." "We are a community of supportive friends valuing privacy and quiet that practice permaculture together." Once they find this out, who gets to live on the land and who has to move away?

Or, imagine founders of a community with no Vision Statement who buy land, move on, put up a few buildings – and then start to run out of money. Now they must decide how they'll spend their remaining money. But they can't agree on priorities. Some want to finish the community building because they believe that creating a sense of community is the primary reason they're together, and know that having a community building will focus their community spirit. Others want to finish the garden and irrigation system because they see their primary purpose as becoming food self-reliant. Different members have different visions, which they each assume all others share. The group is like a hydra-headed monster in Greek mythology, with each head presuming it knows what the creature wants. Now there's lots of conflict, but at the core it's structural; it's *built into* the system. The group is arguing mightily, and it looks like interpersonal conflict. But at it's core, this is a built-in 'time-bomb' kind of conflict, with members unable to see that it's not 'so-and-so being unreasonable' or 'so-and-so being irresponsible', but each person operating on a different bottom line about why they're there.

I know a small, rural income-sharing community that didn't create a Vision Statement, but launched themselves enthusiastically, borrowing money for their land from a large, successful community nearby. Five years later the bottom fell out of the market for the product they manufactured in their primary community business and overnight they lost 45% of their annual income base. Now under severe financial strain, they had long meetings to figure out what to do. Unfortunately different members had vastly different ideas about this. Major conflict time. The community had no touchstone to return to. With different members having vastly different ideas of their purpose, they couldn't agree. Because they use consensus for decisions, some members couldn't impose their vision on others who saw it differently, unlike a newly forming community in which people with different visions were free to go their separate ways and create neighboring communities. This place was their home, and no members were going to force others out because they had different ideas about what the community should be. Several members saw no way out, and left. Now the community had two crises – not enough money and not enough members to carry out the duties of their other labor-intensive community businesses!

If a community doesn't identify its vision and articulate it in a Vision Statement at the beginning, it inevitably asks for conflict down the road. Please make creating your Vision Statement the *first* thing you do.

2. Know What You Need to Know

Founders of successful communities know the range of skills and information that they'll need to master in order to pull off a project of this magnitude. In my opinion, forming an eco-village or community is like simultaneously starting up a new business, entering into a marriage, and undertaking a long, involved overseas trip. It is a complex and time-consuming process and to not know that – or to not know *what* you will need to know – is another common reason many forming communities and eco-villages fall apart in conflict.

I can't tell you the number of times I've seen spiritually oriented community founders present inspiring ideals and compelling visions, but can't create a budget or timeline, or don't know how to buy land or get a bank loan. Or the number of times I've seen founders with technical or business expertise build a composting toilet or create a strategic plan, but can't get anyone to go along with their ideas and don't know the first thing about effective communication. Or, the times I've seen both crash and burn when it comes to conflict.

These folks didn't know what they needed to know! Forming communities or eco-villages need both kinds of skills – although not necessarily in the same individuals. And not necessarily in their own group. If the members of a forming community don't have these skills among their own members, they can always hire them.

Forming a community or eco-village also takes a great deal of committed time and hard work. Even if the group meets weekly, they often need people on various committees – gathering information, drafting proposals, and so on – in-between regular meetings. In my experience this amount of work is equivalent to one or more group members having a part-time job. Eco-village founders need to know 'heart' aspects and 'head' aspects of forming a community:

- Good communication skills.
- Fair, participatory decision-making.
- Methods for reducing conflict and dealing constructively with conflict when it arises.
- Community agreements.
- Budget, timeline, and strategic plan.
- Legal structure(s) for land ownership, and for any planned community businesses or non-profit activities.
- Local zoning or land-use laws.
- Finance and real estate.
- Site planning.
- The land development process (roads, power, water, sewage, etc.).
- And if it's raw land, building design and construction.

Complex and time-consuming? Yes. Overwhelming? Probably. Can your forming community afford to do without it? I don't think so.

3. Fair, Participatory Decision-Making

Many conflicts occur in communities because people whose lives are affected by certain decisions didn't feel that they had enough say in them. Or, that they participated in the decision, but their input wasn't sufficient to affect it. These people end up feeling powerless, and powerlessness, real or perceived, leads to resentment. And resentment is the acid that can eat away at the heart of any community. So the third 'ingredient' for newly forming groups to prevent conflict later on is to choose a decision-making method that's fair, so that each person has a say in, or can influence to some degree, decisions that will affect his or her well-being down the road.

Most people in the West think 'majority-rule voting' when they think about fair ways to decide things. I'd like to suggest that majority-rule voting isn't the best way to ensure that all community members feel empowered in the process of making a decision. With majority rule, up to 49% of the members can be unhappy with a decision, and that same 49% will have to implement and live with a decision they may have been diametrically opposed to.

On the other hand, many forming communities choose consensus as their decision-making process. Unlike voting, in which people argue for and against a proposal and then cast their votes and it's either passed or not, in consensus, the proposal itself is modified as people express their concerns about it, until, ideally, everyone can unify behind it. If everyone can agree to the revised proposal, it passes. If one person blocks the proposal, it doesn't pass. Consensus is therefore a conservative process, which only passes proposals that the whole group feels fine about, and can implement without resentment.

Unfortunately, groups who believe they're using the consensus process are often practising what I call 'pseudo-consensus' – when they are untrained and doing it incorrectly. Pseudo-consensus can drive people right up the wall. Some examples of pseudo-consensus:

- *Everything* we decide on must be decided by consensus. It betrays consensus to use any other method. (*Consensus is our religion.*)
- *Every* group should use consensus; it's the best way to decide things. (*Consensus is the only religion.*)
- We're going to stay in this room until we make a decision – no matter how long it takes! (*We must go from initial proposal to final decision in one fell swoop. Consensus is a tyrant.*)
- *Everyone* in the group must be involved in every decision, no matter how small. (*Once we've chosen consensus, we must use it for everything.*)
- "I block! This proposal just won't *work* for me." (*One blocks for personal reasons, simply because one personally dislikes the proposal.*)

Consensus is like a chain saw – it can chop a lot of wood; it can also chop your leg. So while majority-rule voting can create conflict in communities because almost half the members can be unhappy with a decision, improperly learned consensus can *also* create conflict.

Keep in mind that other decision-making methods exist: 75% voting, 85% voting, 95% voting, consensus-minus-two, consensus-minus-one, and so on.

My favorite method is pure consensus, however, in a group well-trained by a professional consensus teacher and facilitated by a skilled facilitator. Ideally everyone in the group has equal access to power: one person isn't the landlord, and the rest tenants, or the boss, and the rest employees. If the group can't agree, the proposal is dropped or sent to committee for further refinements. Blocking is used rarely, and only when someone feels that the proposal would be morally, ethically, financially, legally or in some other way harmful to the group in the long run. Whatever the decision-making process a forming community chooses, it will help reduce 'structural' conflict later on if the method is fair and participatory. And if it's consensus, *please* get good training in doing it properly.

4. Clear Agreements, in Writing

As you can imagine, many eco-villages and other communities have floundered and broken down when people don't have a written agreement as a reference, and simply try to remember what they agreed upon months or years before. Unfortunately even those with the greatest goodwill can recall a conversation or an agreement in such divergent ways that each group in a dispute may wonder if the other is trying to cheat or abuse or manipulate them. This is one of the greatest stumbling blocks in newly forming communities and eco-villages – yet so easily prevented. Please, write out your agreements, read them, and *then sign what you've agreed to.* Keep these agreements in a safe place and refer to them as needed.

Many agreements must be in writing, because they're embedded in legal documents such as corporation bylaws or lease agreements. Others are in private contracts, which are legally binding in a court of law. Others are simple agreements with no legal 'teeth', but which still help the participants stay on track with each other nevertheless.

Forming communities need to agree who their members are. What are the qualifications to become a member and what is the process to do so? Do people need to attend a minimum number of meetings to be approved by the others? How are new members brought up to speed? How are decisions made, and who gets to make them? How will your meetings be run? How are records kept? Who takes notes, how are they distributed, and to whom? Does your group have a record of decisions to show new members? How are tasks assigned to members, and how are people held accountable for them? What are expected expenses and how will they be paid? Is there a dues structure? Many groups have found that a non-refundable investment of some minimal amount such as US $100 differentiates the 'just looking' folks from those willing to commit time and energy to the project. Who will keep records of what has been paid? Are such monies refundable? A forming community with these and other issues in writing (as well as all legal issues in writing) can save all kinds of misunderstandings in the months and years ahead.

5. Good Communication Skills

Some people are naturally skilful and effective communicators. Others, probably most of us, need to unlearn many of our habitual ways of communicating. Unfortunately, Western culture tends to systematically train people away from any innate tendencies toward cooperation, open-heartedness, and compassion. We're taught to be competitive, to seek to win at all costs, and that we're either winners or losers. It's no wonder that nine out of ten attempts to create cooperative communities often end in conflict and heartbreak.

Fortunately, however, there are plenty of books, courses, teachers, and workshops on methods of communicating that are heartful, inclusive, and not conflict-provoking. In my experience, the higher the degree of communication skill a forming community or eco-village group has, the higher its chances of success. I recommend that a forming community agree upon and practise some form of conflict resolution – ideally learned in a workshop with a trainer – early on when there's little or no conflict, for the same reason school children practise fire drills when there is no fire.

This is also a way of preventing structural conflict because, if mastered at the beginning of the group's life, it can help reduce the severity of conflict later on. Members of every community and eco-village experience conflict, even (especially!) those who mistakenly believe, "In true community, there would be no conflict". I believe a healthy community or eco-village is one that views conflict as normal, and, if handled right, as a bridge to further harmony and closeness.

Conflicts usually arise as the result of a misunderstanding, or when someone wants something he or she is not getting (or wants something to stop), and refuses to speak up about it, or, asks for it in a way that alienates others. The actual conflict is the misunderstanding, or a request for a change in a situation, or in someone's behavior or attitude. Unfortunately, most people's unskilled way of communicating about these issues generates far more conflict than was there in the first place.

My favorite conflict resolution method is Nonviolent Communication[1], developed by Marshall Rosenberg. He suggests that the way most of us respond to conflict is with an attitude and language that, directly or subtly, threatens, judges, or criticizes the person we're communicating with, even if that's not our intention. Nonviolent Communication is a four-step process using certain kinds of words and phrases that disarms the other person by offering openness, understanding, and non-reactivity, and thus defuses the level of conflict in the situation. We can still discuss the core conflict – the misunderstanding, the thing we want changed or that someone else wants us to change. But we're doing so neutrally and compassionately, eliminating the 'secondary' conflict that arises out of the way most of us handle conflict.

6. Select for Emotional Maturity

This is controversial, because some feel it's not really 'community' unless we're inclusive and open, and anyone can join. I heartily disagree. I have seen, over and over, forming communities (with great Vision Statements, fine communication and business skills, and good training in consensus) break apart in conflict and lawsuits because someone didn't have the minimum level of self-esteem to get along with others.

When a person is wounded and having a difficult time in life, he or she can certainly benefit from living in community, and, ideally, can heal and grow because of the support and feedback offered by others. But a certain level of wounding appears to be too deep for most groups to handle. One deeply wounded person appears to be far more powerful than ten healthy people, in terms of that person's destructiveness to the group, and ability to derail its agenda and drain its energy.

This is especially true of someone who has been seriously abused as a child and hasn't had much healing before walking into your community meeting. The person may be desperately seeking community, perhaps assuming it will be a safe haven that finally makes things right. Such a person frequently feels needy, and tends to interpret other people's refusal or inability to meet those needs as further abuse. The person expects to be victimized, and tends to trigger anger and annoyance in others and then concludes, "See, I knew you'd abuse me".

How can you determine the level of emotional maturity in prospective members? One way is through interviews. Irwin Wolfe Zucker, a psychiatric social worker and former Findhorn member (writing in *Communities*, Fall 1997), suggests asking: "How have you supported yourself financially until now? Can you describe some of your long-term relationships? What was your experience in high school or college? How much schooling did you complete? If you chose to leave, why was that? Have you pursued alternative educational or career paths such as internships, apprenticeships, or on-the-job trainings? Where, and for how long? Did you complete them?" I also suggest asking for references, from former partners, employers, landlords, housemates, and former traveling companions. I also recommend 'long engagements' – provisional memberships of six months to a year, where the group and the prospective member can continue to get to know one another. "If your community front door is difficult to enter," writes Zucker, "healthy people will strive to get in. If it's wide open, you'll tend to attract unhealthy people, well-versed in resentful silences, subterfuge, manipulation, and guilt trips." Once these people become community members, the energy of the group may be tied up in getting them out again. In my view, creating healthy, viable communities is one of the finest projects we can undertake. And, we can learn to set systems in place – right from the beginning – that give us the best chance of succeeding at this.

1 *Center for Nonviolent Communication*; Barbara Kunz, Orchidea Lodge, Postfach232, CH–4418, Reigoldswil, Switzerland.
Email: cnvc@compuserve.com

Consensus

A Tool for Building Harmony

by Betty Didcoct

Betty Didcoct is founder and president of TIES Consulting, a group which offers its services to facilitate meetings, gives training in consensus facilitation and team-based decision making, resolve conflicts, and work with organizational change and revisioning. Betty has worked in the USA, Canada, South America, and Europe as an organizational consultant, meeting and conference facilitator, certified Dynamic Consensus trainer, and educator. For the past 10 years, she has served on the board of the Fellowship for Intentional Community, an international networking organization which promotes community living and co-operative lifestyles.

Address:
TIES Consulting
PO Box 1007
Langley
WA 98260
USA
Tel: +1 360 221 3064
Fax: +1 360 221 7828
Email: Betty@ic.org

Everyone goes to meetings... but most people don't like them because "they are too long and boring", "we get mired down in too many details", "nobody cares what I have to say anyway", "all we do is argue", "my ideas are never used", "a few people dominate all the discussion", or "the decisions won't get carried out anyway, so why bother".

We probably have all participated in organizations and groups which were doing wonderful work to find creative solutions to some of the challenges in our society – only to see the group dissolve or become ineffective because of ego battles, people feeling left out or becoming frustrated by unproductive meetings. Meetings often become competitive battlefields to 'win' a decision and gain just enough votes to put an idea through.

In the early '70s I was fortunate to be part of the staff for Argenta Friends School (AFS), a small residential Quaker high school in the mountains of British Columbia, Canada. I had always been interested in meeting structure and process, and I often conducted meetings or served as parliamentarian in groups where decisions were made by a majority vote. But my time at AFS opened a whole other way of conducting business – consensus.

Consensus is about people making decisions *together*. It is based on cooperation rather than competition and seeks solutions where everyone benefits. Consensus decisions build unity from diverse viewpoints by honoring and integrating the contributions of each person.

For the most part, our ways of making decisions together have changed little in the last 400 to 500 years. We still operate with competitive 'win-lose' styles and 'power-over' structures. We have been well conditioned by our competitive cultures and hierarchical power structures. We have learned to focus on getting results. We do not value how we do things (the process), but judge ourselves and others by the results we get. Even though we might leave a meeting with hurt feelings and angry thoughts, if the results were acceptable, the meeting was considered a success. Getting results is primary – more important than the people and their feelings.

We have convinced ourselves that voting is the most efficient way to make decisions, when actually it can be wasteful of time and result in inferior solutions. Voting generally leaves a dissatisfied minority, which can make implementation difficult and time consuming. Because everyone's point of view is not integrated, we may not have reached the best and most creative solutions possible. Certainly our decisions will not be as long lasting if some members of the group do not feel heard and become alienated.

But things are changing. Today, all over the world, we are being asked to give up old ways of hierarchical decision-making structures and seek new methods of sharing responsibility and power. Many corporations have shifted to team-based management. In this climate, I have found a rising enthusiasm for working with consensus and other participatory decision-making structures because they offer systems which are inclusive and encourage the participation of all.

Consensus is not an easy meeting form nor a panacea for all meeting ills, and its pathway is paved with many misconceptions which can result in unsatisfying experiences. We are so deeply steeped in other styles of decision-making, most predominantly autocratic or majority voting, we tend to mix up these styles with the consensus philosophy and process. This can lead to trouble.

Many groups desire to be inclusive and use consensus, but work with it as if it were a unanimous voting process. Or pressed by time and impatience, they adopt decision-making styles such as 'consensus minus one' (or two or some number they feel they can live with) which ultimately defeats the core value of respecting everyone. It can still leave a disenfranchised minority. Commonly groups fall into demanding agreement around tiny details as we learned in working with *Roberts Rules of Order* and other parliamentary procedures.

Until I experienced how much better decisions could be when using consensus, I must admit, I was skeptical. At first I was frustrated with the extra time it took to resolve concerns and differences, but I soon learned that once we *had* reached a decision, implementation went much more smoothly and decisions were much longer lasting.

I learned how a decision does not move forward until everyone finds it acceptable. Our AFS meetings were attended by students, who were in grade 11 and 12 (aged 15-18), by faculty, and occasionally by members of the larger Meeting community. Even though the group was diverse in age, viewpoints, experience, and wisdom; the input of everyone was encouraged and honored. I saw the process stimulate-creativity to find much better solutions than anyone dreamed possible before the meetings began.

What is Consensus Decision-Making?

Consensus is a decision-making technique in which all members of a group actively participate in reaching unity (agreement). It is based on the belief that each person holds some part of the truth of the group; no one person holds it all. It is not a unanimous voting process; in fact there is no voting at all. It eliminates majorities and minorities and avoids the potential polarization of 'yes' and 'no' factions created by voting.

The consensus process seeks the synergy of the group to reach the highest and best solution, rather than compromising to a middle ground or settling for the lowest common denominator. While it works best in an atmosphere of cooperation, the process itself can build trust and create a spirit of community within the group.

What Are The Advantages of Using Consensus?

- There is no disenfranchised, unsatisfied minority.
- Consensus gives the opportunity to reach carefully considered and more creative decisions because all viewpoints are explored.
- It motivates more participation and a higher level of investment in the decisions because everyone participates.
- It saves time in the implementation of the decision.
- It uses disagreement to help develop a clearer understanding of the issues and to resolve conflicts.
- It reduces polarization. When concerns are explored, it is rare that issues are only two-sided with a yes-no answer.

What Are The Disadvantages of Consensus?

- Meetings can take longer, as there is more input to consider.
- It can be too conservative for some, because consensus is needed to make a change (although there are mechanisms to try out decisions).
- If the facilitation of the meeting is poor, time can be wasted in unfocussed discussion, the group being dominated by outspoken participants, or issues not drawn out of conflict situations.
- If trust is low in the group, it is more difficult to come to a consensus. You will need to count on extra time to build the trust.

WHAT IS THE FOUNDATION OF THE CONSENSUS PROCESS?

Consensus is based on a clear set of values which serve much more than just a decision-making system. Central to consensus, as expressed in its Quaker roots, is the spiritual belief that there is 'that of God' in each person. When the Quaker meeting process was moved to the secular world in the USA during the protest days of the '60s and '70s, this core value was translated to 'everyone has a piece of the truth', which did not necessarily communicate the essence or importance of respecting one another.

Deep respect fosters the participation of everyone, encourages careful listening (on many levels), builds trust, gives everyone equal access to power, and invites a holistic integration of the head, heart, and spirit. The process builds a sense of community and enhances group spirit.

Embodying and *practising* the core belief of deep respect and that 'everyone has a piece of the truth' is no easy task, but in it rests the potential for us to truly experience the spiritual philosophy 'we are all one'. If we believe there is God (or spirit, or a higher self, or good, or whatever expression you are comfortable with) in each person, then we can be open to hear insights and understandings from the most unexpected sources.

I realize these are idealistic words. If I read this description with newcomer's eyes, I can hear myself saying, "It sounds great, but how can it possibly be done?" Our years of training in competitive structures are hard to break. It has become 'natural' to constantly divide our worlds into 'we/they' groupings and to fiercely protect our individuality so we don't get lost in the group. As we grow spiritually to more fully understand our oneness, we do not always bring the fruit of that understanding into our daily lives – much less into our everyday meetings.

WHAT ARE THE REQUIREMENTS FOR CONSENSUS TO WORK WELL?

- The group should be clear about and have agreement about their purposes. These agreements are the foundation from which consensus is built.
- Each person needs to act with respect for others, and a trust that each person is doing their best.
- Each person needs to be willing to work for the good of the group and engage on the issues.
- There needs to be sufficient time to work. Good decisions cannot be rushed.
- The group needs a skilful facilitator who can hold a neutral position and understands they are a servant to the group. The facilitator does not lead the group to a decision, but assists the group to explore its differences and to build *its own* solutions and decisions.

In my experience I have seen that with a little education, an openness to the possibility, and the willingness to make a good faith effort, any group can put consensus decision-making into practice. When people join their commitment and their energy, the results can be truly amazing!

How can you be a productive and supportive meeting participant?

- Respect the input and opinions of others. Don't assume there is conflict just because there is disagreement.
- When someone disagrees with you, don't avoid them or make them into the 'other side'. Explore your differences together. I have been inspired by Stephen Covey's book, *Seven Habits of Highly Effective People* and his habit which says, "Seek first to understand, then seek to be understood."
- Value differences as an opportunity to gain more insight and clarity about the issue. (Rather than "That idea can't work", what about, "Help me understand how you see that working"?)
- Put your ideas into the center of the circle, then break your emotional attachment. When you give an idea to the group, it becomes the property of the group.
- Let go of petty hurts. The greater the maturity level of the group, the more efficient the process will be.
- Be flexible, keep an open attitude. Be willing to 'sit in the other person's shoes' and understand their perspective.
- Be responsible for contributing your piece. Decisions will not be as good as they can be if you withhold your insights, reservations, or ideas.
- Look at solutions and decisions with two viewpoints in mind:
    a) Is this decision something I can live with, even though every detail does not meet my greatest desire?
    b) Will this decision serve the group? (Rather than, does it serve me?)

After you have experienced quality and power of consensus decisions, it will be difficult to go back to voting.

But How Do You Respect Others When You Don't Agree With Them?

The essence of consensus lies in the way disagreement and conflict are handled. Differences, emotions, and conflict are natural in any process of decision making. They cannot and should not be ignored. In fact, they are the 'grist' for finding clarity and opening the door for more creative solutions.

It is important for the facilitator to encourage the group to view differences and conflict as an opportunity to get clearer about issues, to be more creative about embracing a wider point of view, and to improve the quality of decisions.

As disagreement emerges, you can ask yourself some questions: "When someone disagrees with me, do I cave in, smile sweetly and agree only to withdraw my support behind their back? Does disagreement become 'me against them'? Do I try to sway everyone I can to my side, without first understanding their point of view?"

What would happen if you approached those who disagreed with you with a curious, open mind? What if first you tried to understand their position before asking them understand yours? Can you find the good points in their ideas? Can you find ways for your ideas to work together?

Do you know the 'whys' behind their position? Do you understand fully the motivations behind your own position?

What If, After All This Work to Explore and Integrate Differences, We Still Can't Agree?

Each person has the responsibility to express concerns throughout the discussion, so the group can work with the reservations. But if these are not satisfied and you do not feel in accord with the decision, you have two choices: to stand aside or to block the decision.

Standing (Stepping) Aside

When you feel the decision is acceptable for the group, but you are personally not comfortable with it or unable to support it due to other commitments, you can choose to 'stand aside'. A person who steps aside may be excused from carrying out or supporting the agreement. Too many people stepping aside is probably an indication that the decision still needs more work.

Blocking

If you feel that *the group* is making a mistake by the decision, then you have the right and the responsibility to 'stand in the way of' or block the decision. A block will stop the decision from moving ahead. This is a position of great responsibility and conscience and is rarely used in groups which fully understand the consensus process. A block only appears after considerable work has been done on the issue. (I have seen it used only twice in 25 years of working with consensus and both times it was proved that the wisdom of the block was correct.)

The person who holds a block must state their reasons. Generally the group will see a block coming and can alter the proposal to address the concerns, refer it to committee for further work, or agree to let the proposal drop.

Some people are fearful that a person might block repeatedly, preventing the group from getting anywhere. If this happens, it often is appropriate to explore the possibility that the person is not in alignment with the purposes of the organization. This might not be the group for them.

Consensus as a Tool for Transformation

It is a radical notion that everyone can agree. It is radical to satisfy the minority view. If we can create a world (or just a piece of the world) where everyone is truly heard and truly respected, we could revolutionize the way people interrelate and the way people relate to the planet. The way we work together – our process – is a key to transformational ideas becoming a reality. Good process can open up the doors for miracles to happen.

The consensus process is more than just a decision-making technique. It is a way of being, a way of listening, and a way of understanding. Working with consensus has given me hope that we *can* overcome our differences and difficulties and create a more harmonious world.

Practicalities of Creative Collaborative Community Living

by Catherine Widdicombe

Catherine Widdicombe has been a member of the Grail community for over forty years. She was recently President of the English Grail, an extended network of people in Great Britain with a residential community near London. The Grail is basically Christian but open to people of all faiths. She was co-founder of Avec, an ecumenical agency for church and community work and for the past twenty-five years has been engaged in consultancy, training and facilitation work with clergy, religious and lay people. She is co-author of *Churches and Communities – An Approach to Development Through the Local Church*[1], author of *Group Meetings That Work – A Practical Guide to Working with Different Kinds of Groups*, and is currently writing *Setting Up Small Religious Communities – A Practical Handbook*. For her M Phil she researched over thirteen years work with those trying to implement the changes of Vatican Two in the Roman Catholic Church.

Address:
The Grail
125 Waxwell Lane
Pinner
Middlesex
HA5 3ER
England
Tel: +44 (0)181 866 2195 and +44 (0)181 866 0505
Fax: +44 (0)181 866 1408

In the Grail one of our growing interests is in living more ecologically and using our ten acres in suburban Pinner[2] to explore with others how we can live more harmoniously with the earth. This desire led me to participate in the 1995 Eco-villages and Sustainable Communities week at Findhorn. As I listened to the speakers, led a workshop, and conversed with people it was increasingly born in on me that the ideas which have become central to my life and work in building community, have a practical application to those in eco-villages and communities.

Living in community involves a plethora of activities: hammering out aims, working at tasks, making decisions, eating and celebrating together, tackling problems, sharing hopes, dreaming dreams, discussing and thinking, dealing with tensions, organising events, having meetings, settling conflicts. All are done through a variety of formal and informal exchanges. Working collaboratively through all this is at the heart of building satisfying and effective communities.

Many people subscribe to working collaboratively but to most of us it seems to come neither naturally nor easily. Usually the theory and the desire to do so out-paces good practice. For most of us to truly work in this way requires a conversion of heart and the acquisition of skills, and we must be convinced that people are capable of thinking things out and making good decisions in relation to their own lives and work, and that they will grow as individuals, groups or communities through doing so.

I am therefore focusing on the work which people in communities need to do in order to participate in and contribute to the wellbeing and development of community life. By 'work' I mean that which needs to be done to promote the sort of relationships that enable people to live satisfying and purposeful lives together; which gives individuals confidence and the freedom to be themselves in community; and which has a positive outcome in terms of decisions made and activities undertaken. Developing ways of working which stimulate people to share their unique ideas and insights on an equal basis calls for ingenuity and sensitivity. What I attempt to do is to suggest some practical ways in which this can be done. Communities are living systems, made and broken through the interaction of complex inter-related and overlapping factors. There are, however, some basic methods which have helped me and other people to work with these complexities and bring out the uniqueness of each community. Here I focus on:

- Working to purpose.
- Analysing and designing work situations.
- Making good decisions.
- Tackling problems.
- Reviewing and evaluating
- Approach and method.

Working To Purpose[3]

Frequently people sense that they have common aims, and proceed to work together. This can cause confusion. People are more likely to work together effectively if they articulate their purpose and differences. An easily said but demanding task. A clearly formulated purpose which is agreed, reviewed and reformulated periodically in the light of experience as people and situations change can be invaluable as a touchstone during planning and decision-making.

By purpose I mean that which people aim to achieve: those changes for the better which they want to bring about in their situations, but more especially in the lives of people: themselves and others. Purpose comes from deeply held beliefs: those things which determine the direction of life, which motivate them, by which they make sense of life. Listening to members of any group who are endeavouring to build community in their neighbourhood, it becomes clear that their purpose is something they work towards but never fully achieve, although there may be indications that people are moving in that direction as they become more caring and responsible. Stepping stones towards purposes I call objectives.

Working to purpose can transform people's lives and work. The steps below may be used or amended to help a group or community in the difficult task of formulating and agreeing a statement of purpose.

1. Personal Reflection

Get people reflecting on the changes for the better they want to bring about or would like to see in their own lives, in the lives of others, and their environment. Encourage them to be specific. Time for individual reflection is important. It can vary between a few minutes, half an hour or be done over a week in preparation for a meeting. One or more of the following ideas or questions may begin to get people thinking:

- What do you want to avoid happening? These are sometimes called noxiants.[4] To state them clearly can heighten your awareness of what you do want to achieve.
- Put down your hunches and gut feelings about what is needed.
- Ask yourself 'why?' or 'what for?' in relation to things you would like to see in your community. For instance, why do you want to set up a drop-in centre or an agricultural co-operative? What is it for? What do you hope will happen as a result?
- Do a personal 'brainstorm' on paper allowing yourself to jot down anything that occurs to you without censoring yourself. This can loosen up your thinking. Once you have done this you can sort out what you see to be of central importance.
- Think about and possibly jot down your deep motivation, the beliefs you hold, that which is burning within you. Then think about your situation, community, organisation or neighbourhood. Now compare them: what are your beliefs and values saying to your situation? What is your situation saying to your beliefs?

2. Gathering Ideas

When working with a large number of people, the next step could be to ask people in subgroups to share their ideas by listening to each person without discussion before amalgamating them on a large sheet of paper.

3. Formulating Your Ideas

What you now have is an initial formulation and may well be something of a mixture between purpose, objectives, methods and beliefs. In order to move towards a clear formulation of purpose you might ask yourselves:

- Have we differentiated between purposes, objectives and methods? An objective could be, for instance, building a community centre. A purpose would be related to what happens in people's lives as they use the centre. One way of sorting these out is to add to the statement of purpose a list of objectives or methods, each one prefaced with 'by' or 'through'.
- Have we separated our beliefs and purposes? To include in your formulation of purpose the beliefs which motivate you can be confusing and make the statement so wordy that it loses its cutting-edge. Stating your beliefs and purposes separately means they can be more easily handled when you come to make plans.
- Is our purpose so general that it loses touch with the reality of our situation? For instance, 'to bring peace and love into the world' would be more useful if it is stated in terms of what doing that means in this particular neighbourhood, where it might have to do with racial or class harmony, healing divisions, or engendering an atmosphere of freedom rather than fear. It is easier to think of objectives for these latter formulations.
- Have we been succinct and used plain language rather than technical terms and jargon? Writing in simple everyday terms helps to earth your purpose and makes it easier to keep it in mind as you work.
- Have we stated our purpose in terms of people and their relationships rather than in terms of things, material and impersonal?

4. Using Your Purpose

Once you have a succinct, clear and agreed statement of purpose, it can be used in a variety of ways. It provides a reference point in planning work, in tackling problems and in reviewing. Ask questions such as "Will this activity help towards our purpose?", "Is this likely to avoid noxiants we have identified?" Recall your purpose when making a decision to ensure that what you plan is in line with it. This also helps to avoid specious arguments when deciding what to do to overcome problems (*see p. 208*) and when evaluating work (*see p. 210*)

Analysing and Designing Working Situations[4]

Community working situations are complex, composed of many parts which are related to each other. A small community is part of larger entities, such as a neighbourhood, town or city and of a global network of eco-villages.

Analysing a community systemically in relation to its internal make-up and environment helps people to understand what is working, where there are gaps, where things overlap, and how the various parts relate to or impinge on each other. Ideally there is a creative interdependence between the parts which promotes both mutual support and challenge. Of proven value to many community groups is a particular way George Lovell and I have developed of analysing complex working situations.[5] This method may be used to consider the overall situation of a community or organisation, giving proper respect to the parts, or to work on one part of the situation in relation to the whole. It can be used with individuals, groups and communities. It promotes both overall wellbeing and development and enables members of a community to understand and empathise with areas of work in which they are not directly engaged. Doing this as a group exercise ensures that people are working to a common understanding of the situation and makes use of everyone's insights. The steps are:

1. **Build Up a Picture of the Working Situation**[6]
   Describe the situation as accurately as possible. Include not only factual details about the place, programme, people and so on but also the feelings, hopes, ideas of those involved and difficulties they are up against. It can help:
   - To circulate a brief written description as a basis from which to start exploring in more detail.
   - To sit around a large sheet of paper or flip chart and use diagrams, charts or graphics to model or clarify the interaction between the various parts. Conceptualising a situation on paper not only provides a focal point for discussion and an aide memoire but will often disclose hitherto unseen elements or relationships.
   - To concentrate on the one situation rather than engage in a comparative analysis with other similar or dissimilar ones.
   - To enter into the situation in order to understand it as fully as possible before highlighting what is working well and what is dysfunctional or problematic. No situation is perfect: it is in working to make it better that community is formed.
   - To realise, particularly if a common picture is being built up by those involved in the situation, that everyone has different perspectives and feelings about it. These differences are part of the picture and need to be recognised and taken into account.

2. **Decide On Your Development Agenda**[7]
   This involves deciding what needs to be done about key issues, difficulties, opportunities and identifying points of potential development. It is important to identify that which, if worked at, will have positive effects on all the parts. That helps to determine priorities. This is a reflective exercise and not one to be hurried over.

3. **Design and Plan What You Will Do**[8]
   These are two distinct and very different activities. If you are landscaping a garden you think out your design before you work out the steps by which you will execute the finished product. Designing a work programme can be described as 'workscaping'. This step requires creative thinking, it can be both demanding and exciting. It involves calling on everyone's experience, expertise, insights and hunches, tentatively suggesting and then exploring possible ways forward so that the various elements relate

smoothly and creatively together, giving a flow and balance to the whole.

Times of seeming chaos and confusion, wintery periods of seeming stagnation, are painful characteristics of creative activity. Head and heart both need to be engaged. Gradually or suddenly a pattern will emerge and a way forward will seem right.

PRINCIPLES OF GOOD DECISION MAKING[9]

There are however certain principles which communities would do well to take seriously, and some practices which are destructive of community.

In this section I outline some key principles which could well be used by a community to review their decision-making procedures. No community gets decision-making 100% right for all time and no individual, however skilled and well-intentioned is exempt from making mistakes. Such a review, though it could be painful, if entered into openly can make for community health. The following factors are interdependant.

1. Allow Adequate Time for Reflection and Discussion

The following may be useful:

- Provide information about the issue well before the decision-making meeting.
- Discuss on one occasion and decide at another.
- Assure people a decision will not be made until all are ready. Check carefully that people are ready to make it.
- When discussing a series of inter-related decisions, make provisional ones as you go along. When the proposals can be seen as a whole, go back and check each decision.
- Contract with those involved to take the time and energy to search for the way forward – make a tentative date by when you will make the decision.
- But be prepared to change it as necessary.

2. Motivate Participation

For people to own the decision they need to participate in making it and not be passive observers of the process. In order to motivate people to engage in making decisions:

- Clarify why a decision is being considered or is needed and allow time for people to reflect and respond before proceeding.
- Encourage people to think creatively and contribute their ideas and feelings. Working in small groups often helps quieter members to speak.
- Take all ideas seriously. If a contribution is ignored or rubbished, it can cause not only that person but others to realise it is safer to keep silence if one does not want to be hurt or put down.
- Emphasise that everyone has a unique contribution to make and a responsibility to make it. We each have our own background, experience, perceptions and needs.

- Contract with people to 'stick with it' during periods of confusion, depression or a seeming impasse.

3. **Use Your Purpose and Beliefs**
   Keep in mind your overall purpose and the purpose behind the particular matter to be decided upon. You may want to check your decision in other ways: how does it fit in with your basic beliefs? Is it likely to contribute to the wellbeing of the community, even if made in the interests of a few?

4. **Consider All Aspects**
   If people are confident that all aspects will be considered they will be more likely to relax with the process and allow themselves to really listen to all points of view. Where this is not so, tension and argument, pressurising and persuasion can enter in and be dysfunctional and destructive. Considering all aspects involves:
   - Ensuring all necessary information is available or giving time for it to be found.
   - Examining all options and working out the pros and cons of each as objectively as possible. Doing this may enable other options to surface, or ways of ameliorating some of the disadvantages can be seen. Are there any positive or negative side effects?
   - Calling in one or more experts to provide information and guidance. Beware of being swayed by their eloquence. You are the experts on your situation and what is realistic for you. Be both open to and critical of others' expertise.
   - Exploring who else will be affected by this decision. Do you need to talk to them, get their views, formally or informally, or let them know what is in your mind?
   - Reflecting on who will bear the cost, not just in monetary but also in human terms.
   - Asking: have we forgotten anything? Pause long enough to allow any other factors to surface.

5. **Implementation**
   Thinking about how the decision will be implemented is a necessary part of the process. The following questions form a decision-making and implementation check list:
   - What will be involved in implementing the decision?
   - Who will do so? This may be one or more persons or groups. Are they clear as to their brief? Have we the resources and personnel needed? Is training or outside help necessary?
   - When do we expect it to be carried out? When and how will people be kept in touch with progress?
   - Have we a clear and agreed record of the decision made?
   - Do we need to discuss how it will be implemented?

- What happens if problems arise?
- What happens if someone else gets an idea and has information which has a bearing on the implementation?
- When will we review and evaluate things? Not every decision will be implemented. Some may be forgotten or be found to be unworkable. A lot can be learned by exploring why a decision was not implemented, and asking yourselves: Do we want to do anything about it now? What is this teaching us?

6. Work For Consensus Wherever Possible

Clearly this is the ideal but it is not realistic to expect this on all occasions. When some people cannot go along with certain decisions, there are choices to be made:

- Put the decision 'on hold' for a period, as the time may not be ripe for it now.
- Have a vote, but ascertain beforehand that those who are unhappy about the decision feel able to commit themselves to go along with the outcome.

7. Communicate Decisions

Ensure that all who will be affected by the decision know what has been decided and why. The detail in which this is done will depend on the nature of the decision.

Decision-making is not a purely rational process, the feelings are also involved. For a good decision head and heart need to play their part. In some people the head takes the lead and the heart lags behind, in others the reverse is true. It is important to allow time for the one to catch up with the other.

Where decisions are proving really difficult, it can help to 'live with' one alternative for a day or longer, and then live with the other, on each occasion imagining that you have made a definite commitment to that option. It is always possible to have a 'trial period' or time of experimentation, followed by a review.

Above all, keep hopeful. It is possible to work through the quagmire of decision-making and to come out of it not only with a good decision but with renewed vitality and unity.

Tackling Problems[10]

Any human situation is inherently problematic. The higher the purposes of a particular group or community the greater the difficulties to be faced in achieving them. Climbing Ben Nevis, the highest mountain in Britain, is as nothing compared to climbing Everest. It is to be expected that any eco-village, community or group will meet problems and experience failures. Tackling these aspects of community life can be enormously enriching both individually and corporately. To ignore or bury them can be soul-destroying as they fester within.

The Problem Tackling Sequence (*opposite*) is one way of working through

Problem Tackling Sequence[11]

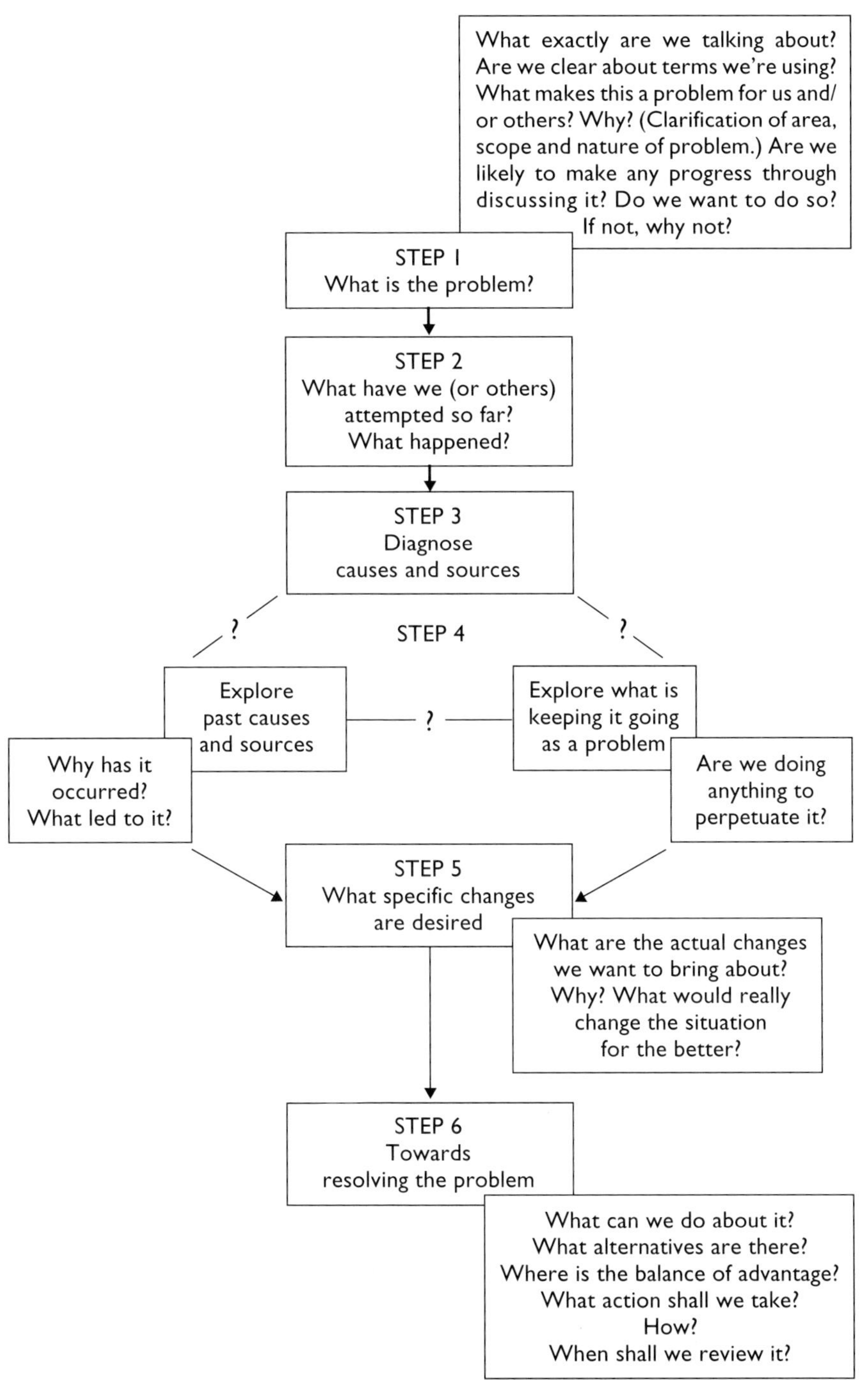

a difficulty. This may be done alone or with a group. If using it with a group it may be appropriate to make the steps overt or simply keep the overall structure in mind and use it to facilitate and to summarise the discussion.

Some difficulties are best considered in story form as a case study[12]. This is particularly so when, either alone or with others you set out to do something, and it has been a failure. I constantly find it a great learning experience when I face and work through such incidents. Doing this as a group exercise with others who may or may not have been involved, brings additional insights. These are the steps:

1. **Tell The Story**
   Write down exactly what happened: what you wanted to achieve, how you set about it and all the actions you took and what happened as a result.

2. **Analyse What Went Wrong**
   Note or underline all those things which you did or did not do which led to the unsatisfactory outcome.

3. **Look To The Good**
   List all that is going for you in the situation, your allies and things you can build on.

4. **Decide How to Redeem The Situation**
   In the light of the above diagnosis work out what you now need to do in order to ameliorate any damage you may have done. The questions below may seem simple but they open out onto the complexity of the decision-making which will affect the outcome. Instead of fixing on the first idea which comes to mind it is useful to list several options and spend some time looking at the pros and cons of each, before deciding what action to take and how to take it. Who do you need to approach first? What are you hoping to achieve by doing so? How can you make contact and what can you say or do?

5. **Learning For The Future**
   Spending a few minutes asking yourself 'what have I learnt from this incident?' can lead to a whole heap of practical points tumbling out for later use.

Reviewing and Evaluating[13]

Building community goes on for ever. No community can ever rest on its laurels having attained the goal. In fact I believe that it is in the daily struggle to live in communion with people who have the same goals and purposes but whom I would not otherwise have chosen to live with, that I find my salvation, growing as a human and spiritual being. This means on a personal level that reviewing and evaluating is part of the on-going life of a community, and being able to handle day to day feedback a necessary ability. It is also important for a community to make time and review and evaluate its life and work. Several steps are involved.

1. **Receiving Feedback**
   Feedback may come as unsolicited comments and is more likely to do so if you show that you value it in order to learn from it.

2. **Evaluation**
   Evaluation is a critical assessment of the feedback received. The following models may be used or adapted with community groups.

   Evaluate feedback in relation to purpose rather than objectives. If your purpose is to do with change for the better in the lives and attitudes of people, evaluation is difficult because inner change is not discernible. It will however result in behavioural change, so the question to ask is "What indicators show that inner changes of the kind we seek have actually taken place?"

   A Historical Model
   Using this model will give you a picture of the flow of change over a period of time.

   The Community and/or its work 5 years ago (describe its key features)
   The Community and/or its work now (describe it as it is now)
   List the key changes (and areas of no change)

   Discuss which have been changes for the better and which changes for the worse. Ask yourselves:
   - What do we think about these changes?
   - What shall we do as a result?
   - Where do we want to be in 5 or 10 years time?

   A Decision-making Model
   In this you need to plot and explore the key decisions your community group has made, why and with what result.

   Options before us (list them)
   Why we chose to do X (give reasons)
   What happened (describe)
   What we think about it now (describe and discuss)

   Ask yourselves: What are the implications for us? What do we wish to do for the future?

Approach and Method[14]

To work collaboratively in the various ways described above requires the use of the non-directive approach. This is far more than a tool to be used at meetings: once internalised it becomes a way of life. Put simply it involves working *with* people rather than *for* them. Clearly there are occasions when it is necessary to do things for people, to provide and make arrangements for them when they are unable or not prepared to do things for themselves, or when it is an economic use of time and effort. However, it is the use of the non-directive approach which promotes development. The non-directive approach was conceived by T R Batten during his years in Nigeria and subsequently used worldwide. It is crucial to working collaboratively and building community. Working non-directively as a facilitator or member of a group entails:

- Creating the sort of atmosphere where everyone feels free to speak so that full use is made of the potential of the group. This means listening to what people are saying, exploring it by asking questions and building on it rather than by ignoring them or immediately allowing people to deny or criticise what has been said.
- Ensuring that everyone is clear and agreed on the topic to be discussed and helping people to keep to the point or decide what to do if the discussion wanders from it.
- Clarifying the discussion as it progresses, noticing when people are confused, at times rewording and testing out what a person is trying to say. Clarity can avoid unnecessary argument between people who misunderstand what the other is saying.
- Getting points stated and discussed objectively. This is facilitated by asking open rather than loaded questions. It involves helping people to explore differences of opinion rather than allowing people to push their own views to the detriment of other peoples.
- Summarising the discussion briefly at appropriate intervals so people can see what progress has been made and what areas still need to be explored, and it gives a chance for anyone left behind in the discussion to catch up.
- Ensuring that any relevant information is obtained and considered.
- Structuring the discussion by putting the points in logical order so people are helped to discuss things systematically, and by clarifying any emerging relationship between ideas.

In adopting the non-directive approach you aim to avoid:

- Unduly persuading or pressurising others to accept your point of view.
- Exercising control in a group in such a way that it stifles thought or overrides other opinions.
- Seeing only one side of an argument
- Asking loaded questions and belittling others.
- Being rigid and inflexible in your thinking or judgmental about those in other positions.

Working collaboratively and non-directively depends to a large extent on your attitude and intention. You need to want the wellbeing of the community and those with whom you work and you need to believe that everyone has a contribution to make and that they are capable of making good decisions about matters which affect their lives and work. Working at community issues, projects, and problems in these ways not only achieves results in terms of decisions made and work planned but it stimulates reflective communities, commitment to the common cause, and human and spiritual development.

REFERENCES

1 Catherine initiated an action research project in 1970, Project 70–75, which has been written up in *Churches & Communities – An Approach to Development and the Local Church*. 1976. London: Search Press. With the Revd Dr George Lovell she then co-founded and was Associate Director of Avec, a service agency for church and community work, based in London from 1976–1992.

2 The address of the Grail Centre is Waxwell Farm House, 125 Waxwell Lane, Pinner, Middlesex HA5 3ER. Tel: +44 (0)181–886 2195. Fax:+44 (0)181–886 1408.

3 *Analysis & Design – A Handbook for Practitioners and Consultants in Church and Community Work*. 1994. cf. Lovell, G., Burns & Oates. p.122–125. Lovell describes how he helped a local church to define its purpose in a church, youth and community centre, in the *Parchmore Partnership*. 1995. Grundy, M., ed.. Chester House Publications. p.22–23.

4 ibid. Lovell, G., 1994. This book gives detailed descriptions of the theoretical approaches I outline and describes graphically their use in a variety of community situations.

5 ibid. p.71.

6 ibid. p.117.

7 ibid. p.119.

8 ibid. p.159f.

9 For a further description see my book, *Group Meetings That Work – A Practical Guide to Working With Different Kinds of Groups*. 1994. St. Pauls. p.161–167.

10 ibid. p.74–76 op cit Lovell; 1994; p.51f.

11 op cit Widdicombe p.128.

12 op cit Widdicombe p.75.

13 In this section, including the diagnosis, I draw heavily on the work of George Lovell. I have found it useful with community groups.

14 *The Non-Directive Approach*. 1988. cf Batten, T. R., Avec; op cit Widdicombe, 1994. p.37–38.

The above books are available from: Avec Resources, 125 Waxwell Lane, Pinner, Middlesex HA5 3ER, England. Tel: +44 (0)181–866 2195 and +44 (0)181–866 0505. Fax: +44 (0)181–866 1408.

SOUND
A Tool to Bridge Individuals Into Society
by Bolette Schiøtz

Photo: Jeroen Bouman

Bolette Schiøtz was born in 1942 and has a formal training as a physical therapist. For seven years she held the position as director of one of the seven schools of physical therapy in Denmark. Her interest in holistic medicine and alternative therapy started in 1981 and three years later she established her own practice as a massage therapist working with energy balancing, visualization and dreams. Bolette's voice unfolded spontaneously into overtone singing in 1988 as a fruit of intense personal growth work and disciplined meditation. Now she helps others get in contact with the healing potential of the voice. She works with group structures through a combination of toning, dance and meditation. She offers workshops, lectures, meditative concerts and individual sessions in Denmark and Norway. She has also visited USA and Canada with her soundwork.

In 1996 she released her first CD, *Lyd fra Bjergene* (Sound from the Mountains) with overtonesinging and soundhealing. In 1997 she published a book in Danish, *Blå Lyd* (Blue Sound) about her experiences with soundhealing, toning and spiritual growth.

Address:
Egebjergvej 20
DK 8751 Gedved
Denmark
Tel: +45 75 66 58 60
Fax: +45 75 66 40 70

QUALITIES OF THE VOICE

Of all musical instruments the voice is the most ordinary and the easiest to use. It is a powerful wind instrument and it can make an extraordinary variety of sounds. It can be programmed, consciously or unconsciously, with a wide spectrum of qualities such as destruction, hate, violence, sympathy, love and healing. The voice reveals character structures, psychological problems and traumas and its tonality and timbre changes with age, training and emotional condition. When you explore and work with the voice as a source of energy and vibration, it will not only affect your physical body (listening ability, digestion, respiratory capacity etc.), but it will increase your general sense of vitality, it will open up for hidden treasures of creativity and it will influence your relationship to other people.

Toning – Migrating Birds Moving in Unison

Toning is a natural and spontaneous way of using the voice to bring balance and free the body and the breath from tension. We yawn, we sigh, we moan.

Toning as a conscious group activity consists of vowels sung in a monotonous fashion and in a meditative state of mind. The monotonous vowel sounds operate on a level free of entertainment, emotions and meaning, and this can help the consciousness to extend from an active ego-related state to a deeper collective state. There are no requirements of musicality or experience with singing. Everyone can take part.

The instructions are very simple: The toning should be monotonous, oriented towards a collective blend of voices and done with great attentiveness and concentration. All sound is energy and each individual makes the sound he or she finds appropriate at the time. You sing the vowels in an elongated manner and while you sing, you can change slowly from one vowel to another. The change of vowels makes the overtones or harmonics more audible. You try to keep the same note through a full breath, but you can change note while inhaling, whenever you feel like it. You don't strive for beauty or harmony and there is no concern for being on or off key. The toners work with energy and vibration, and dissonant sound can have an amazing transformational effect. The group is in a process of creation while they tone. Having the eyes closed facilitates attentiveness and concentration. There is no room for soloists or boosting egos in a good toning group.

Usually a toning group sits in a circle, but other positions should be tried: Standing or lying on the floor, toning in combination with slow-motion or slow-walk is also a very energizing experience.

The intension behind the toning activity is an important factor. From where does the sound vibration come? What quality does it carry? If all members of a group center their energy in the heart chakra and let the toning come from that level of their energy systems, it will be easy for the group to become like one organism with one voice, like a flock of migrating birds moving in unison.

When there are conflicts or crises in the group, or when there are individuals that cannot let go of their personal ambitions, it is much more difficult to get the toning improvisation to work in a true communitarian manner. The group can determine the intention of the toning activity before they begin, and through their sound they can transform and raise the energy.

The monotonous toning brings out a massive flow of vibrations that have a tremendous transformational potential for the singers as well as the listeners. The toning can change an atmosphere of intense emotionality to one of peace and compassion in a surprisingly short time. Used with awareness, the toning activity can heal, build bridges, create community and raise the level of awareness.

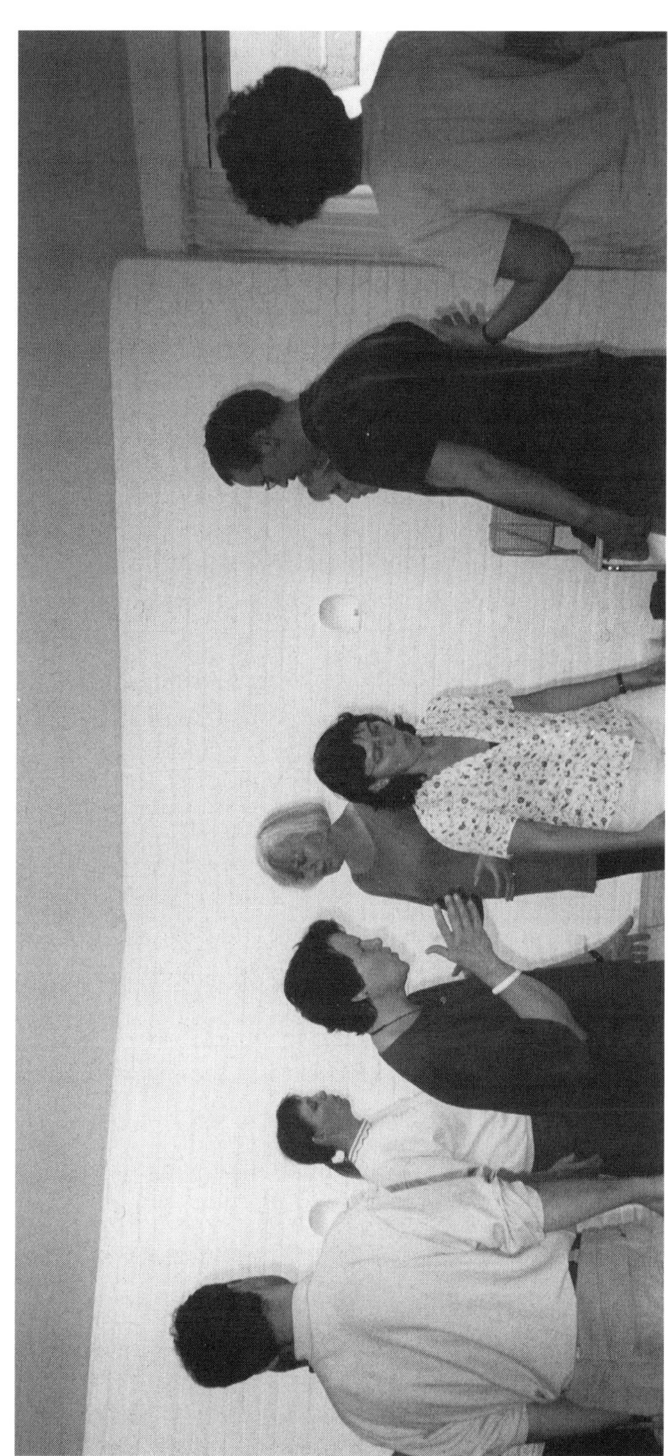

Toning in slow walking. When a group of people walks very slowly among themselves while toning, the sound transcends the personal level and the group becomes one organism.

Horizontal and Vertical Use of the Voice

In the normal activities of daily life a lot of our energy is projected out in a horizontal dimension. Here the voice is mostly serving the ego in a satisfying and confirming way. Through speech, song, whisper, screams, scolding and howling the voice creates contact, communicates emotions, feelings, thoughts and information, and it releases tension and repressed psychological energy. The voice is a wonderful instrument for these purposes. But the voice is also a place where a lot of energy can be leaked and spilled through useless jibber and chitchat.

When we extend our awareness upwards to the spiritual levels of energy or downwards to the primordial and deep instinctive levels of energy, we come in contact with the vertical dimension of human consciousness. This dimension is related to transpersonal levels of energy of which we have little awareness. Again the voice is an excellent instrument for expressing impulses and energy from this dimension. The voice gives you awareness of your powers and qualities by grounding them in an audible expression.

There are many ways of getting in contact with these deep layers in the vertical dimension of our consciousness. Most of them involve meditation, intensive breath work and intensive body work. My approach is an integration of toning, dance, visualization and meditation. The following exercises, suitable for groups, give a taste of this combination. But be aware that the deeper you work into transpersonal structures the bigger the demand for awareness, responsibility and grounding. It cannot be recommended for people with deep anxiety or other psychological imbalances without qualified supervision.

Exercise A

The vertical dimension of your system.

1. Vigorous dance to loud, rhythmic music (15 minutes).

2. Sit down and turn your attentiveness downwards to the energy in or around the pelvic area, the legs, the feet and the energy below the feet (5 minutes).

3. Express through elongated vowel sounds what you experience – feel free to change the position of your body (5–10 minutes).

4. Turn your attentiveness to the energies around and above your head (5 minutes).

5. Express through elongated vowel sounds what you experience – feel free to change the position of your body (5–10 minutes).

6. Take paper and crayons and make drawings of your experiences.

EXERCISE B

Your personal Tree of Life projected into a communal Tree of Life.

1. Vigorous dance to loud, rhythmic music (15 minutes).

2. Stand with feet apart – visualize yourself as a Tree of Life. You have a great root system down in the earth – your body is a big, stable tree trunk – above and around your head you have a huge crown with flowers and leaves (5 minutes).

3. Listen to and feel the flow of energy in all parts of your tree (3–5 minutes).

4. Express through elongated vowel sounds what you experience (5–10 minutes).

5. All group members project their personal tree into the center of the group and visualize a communal 'Tree for Life' (3–5 minutes).

6. Through elongated vowel sounds you give nourishment and energy to the center structure of your community. (10–15 minutes).

7. Take paper and crayons and make a drawing of your experiences.

After such exercises toning improvisations tend to be much more creative and collective.

The two dimensions of the human consciousness can be illustrated in the following cross structure, where the horizontal axis is the dimension of the ego and the vertical axis is the dimension of the self:

Spirituality
Angel
Heaven
Father
Crown
Head

The personal level with ego-related expressions, communication, projection of energy, emotions, catharsis, etc.

Body
Root
Mother
Earth
Reptile
Primordiality

The herb garden at Munach, Denmark, with 50 beds designed as an organic structure. The garden is a symbol of many individuals as part of a whole. Photo: Karl Ravn, © *Familie Journalen*

Both dimensions are a natural part of the human consciousness, and it is very important, that there is a good balance between the two dimensions. In our western culture, the horizontal dimension has grown completely out of proportion at the expense of vertical dimension. The more attention and nourishment we give to the personal level, the more craving and energy consuming it becomes. When we begin to give greater priority to collective structures, communitarian values and spiritual growth, we must give less to the personal level. It is not an easy process, because it involves changes on a deep unconscious and transpersonal level.

By combining toning, dance and meditation we can get in better contact with transpersonal levels of our consciousness, more respect for nature and other living beings, better grounding and higher awareness of our spiritual potential. In other words, we can become more vertical humans in a horizontal society.

Munach – Spiritual Community

I live in a spiritual community – Munach – in a village in Denmark. Munach is a center for meditation and spiritual growth started in 1988 by the couple Anne Sophie Jørgensen and Jørgen Høher Ovesen. Their professional background is respectively theology and psychology. The name Munach was given to Jørgen in a dream as the name of his life's mission. They are responsible for the meditations and 95% of all the work shops offered at the center. During its 10 years of existence the Munach community has grown to 80 adults and 38 children living with their parents. Of these 80 adults 36 live in couples and families.

Meditation is the core and inspiration of all activities in the community. Besides the meditation center, there is an art school and a big organic herb garden ($4000m^2$). Most of the community members support themselves through ordinary mainstream jobs such as nursing, social work, teaching, playing music professionally or therapy. Most of the members are employed and a few have their own businesses. The economic structure of the community is based on individual enterprise and personal responsibility. The housing is also, as of today, based on personal property and publicly supported rental apartments.

The objective of the community is to bring awareness and spirituality into all aspects of daily life; to train people to be able to sense, understand and convey energy on a high level and to work with collective consciousness.

Being Part of a Community

As in all other situations where many people are together, there are a lot of emotions, projections, crises, periods of introversion and extroversion, periods of excitement, creativity and activity and periods of stress, weariness and hopelessness. In our community everybody works intensely with their personal process through dynamic breath and body work and 1 to 2 hours of daily meditation. Over the years a very high level of energy has built up – we call it a strong light – and this always brings out a lot of shadows and emotions. Our goal is to handle this in a balanced and dignified manner with both feet on the ground. We consider emotional activity and projections a personal

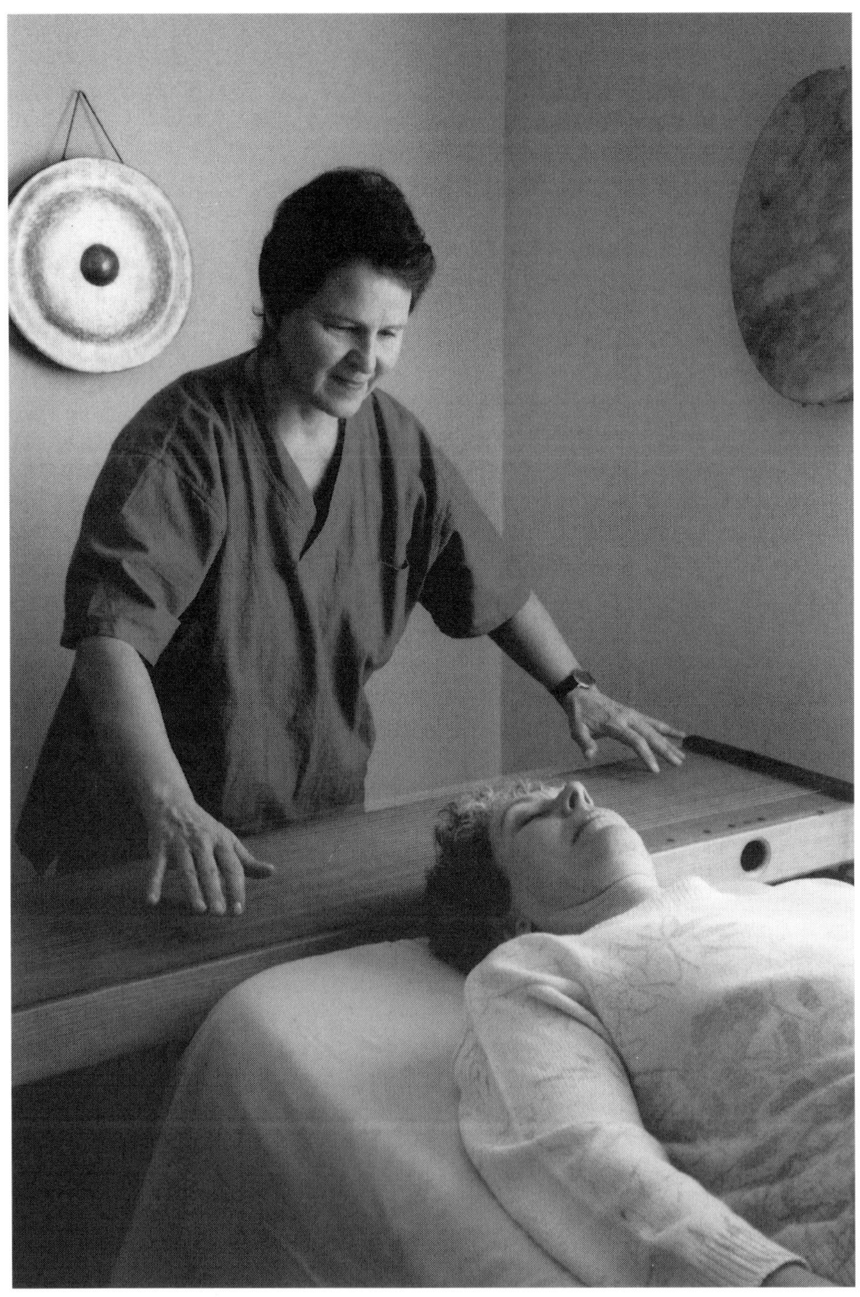

Bolette Schiøtz soundhealing using a monochord.

responsibility and, within our community, there is a frequent exchange of dreams, massage, energy balancing, toning and sound healing.

Sound in the Community

Since the beginning in 1988, we have used monotonous humming or toning as an element in meditation and healing. It has been used with many different intentions in a variety of situations: healing, comforting, celebration, childbirth, death, 'energy cleaning' of a house, blessing of food, sound for growth in the herb garden, peace meditation, moon and solstice rituals etc. Some people are very keen on sound work and do it a lot; others prefer silence. The latest development is a small choir, where we experiment with the voice and improvise with toning and overtoning.

Birthday Celebration with Soundhealing

Let me describe in detail how we celebrate birthdays in our community with toning. Let it give inspiration to many other situations, where it could be appropriate to raise the energy level and communicate without words.

1. The person we are celebrating lies on a mattress in the middle of the meditation room. The rest of the group sits in a circle around. There can be 8, 20 or 50 people.

2. Everybody centres their awareness in their heart chakra and contact the qualities of love, acceptance and light, and let them flow towards the person in the middle.

Birthday celebration: Communal soundhealing.

3. One person walks slowly behind the circle sounding a bell or a singing bowl to gather and build up the energy.

4. The toning starts as a soft hum. Then it opens up into different vowels and different tones. The volume and the intensity raises and the toning keeps going if possible for about 10 minutes.

5. The toning fades out and everybody is quiet for 3 to 5 minutes.

6. One person sounds the bell or the singing bowl a couple of times to mark the end of the sound healing.

Sound and World Peace – An Empowering Vision

When my voice evolved in 1988 it was like a volcanic outburst. It took a while to find out how I could use the power of my voice in the therapeutic work. I felt that this new healing energy was a loan from a deep source in the collective unconscious. Somehow this energy had to be recirculated for a communal purpose. This feeling was reinforced by a vision I had in 1990 during a two day retreat in silence:

> *A cut crystal with nine sections, the size of a large tower – stands on the end in the middle of an amphitheatre with an audience of hundreds of thousands of people all around. In slow motion, one section at a time, is illuminated. This allows the audience to hear and to see the contents. The first section contains a Catholic nun singing the Ave Maria; the second a Tibetan monk in meditation posture singing the typical Tibetan overtone chant; the third a whirling dervish accompanied by a flute; the fourth a shaman drumming to a huge, green snake, and the fifth a faint structure of a dancing Chinese. There are a few more sections of the crystal, that are not illuminated.*
>
> *The crystal slowly fades away and a huge cut diamond appears. A male deity descends from above, stands on top of the diamond and declares: "This is important for world peace."*

This vision shows the old religions and their specific sacred music and symbols. They are pictured with equal importance in a common structure with nine sections. The eclectic evenness in combination with the sacred sonic vibrations builds up the energy level in such a way, that it can transcend to a much higher level of insight – the diamond level.

My interpretation of this vision is that only from a level higher than the individual religions – a level of enlightened community – is it possible to create peace on earth.

This vision gives me inspiration in my work, and I share it in the hope that others can feel the energy and gain insight from it.

HUMOUR AS A TOOL FOR CONFLICT RESOLUTION

A Glue for Community Life

by Patch Adams MD

Patch Adams MD is the founder and director of the Gesundheit! Institute, a 25+ year old project to address all the problems of health care delivery in the USA. From 1972 to 1983, 21 adults used his home as a hospital 24 hours a day. Fifteen thousand people passed through. He never charged any money and he never accepted health insurance, or carried malpractice insurance. He integrated all the healing arts and to present a wellness context, he integrated medicine with performing arts, fine arts, crafts, agriculture, nature, education, recreation and social service.

From 1989 to the present, Gesundheit! has been raising funds to build its fantasy communal home, a 40 bed hospital based on those principles. This project and its philosophy are introduced in Dr Adams' book, *Gesundheit!*. The institute's newsletter, *Achoo!* is also available from the Institute.

Patch has been a public clown for over thirty years, using humour and joy as potent tools for conflict resolution. A film based on the life of Patch Adams, starring Robin Williams as Patch, has recently been released to critical acclaim and the proceeds from this have enabled Patch to realise his dream and begin building his ecologically designed community hospital.

Address:
Gesundheit! Institute
6855 Washington Boulevard
Arlington
Virginia 22213
USA
Tel: +1 703 525 8169
Fax: +1 703 532 6132
Email: hread@micron.net

Humour is one of the most important tools in social intercourse. There are no areas of human endeavour that are not improved upon with a healthy use of humour. It is commonly said that 'laughter is the best medicine'. I would like to suggest further that humour is also potent medicine for a healthy community.

Whether one's conflicts are with oneself or others, humour can soften conflict and help move the dialogue along. A humourless person can put a great damper on conflict resolution. If we are unable to laugh at ourselves, many unnecessary conflicts will rise and fester. A common theatre trick, and great social tool, comic relief, is there to speed resolution in the most profound of situations. (One never says 'love relief' or 'wonder relief'. The word relief is reserved for humour, the great worker for peace.)

That it is often called disarming, implies humour's potential to wage peace. I recall Monty Python's great comic skit about the funny joke, so funny that whoever heard it laughed to death. The military got hold of it and war stopped.

Laughter has been called infectious, implying it spreads rampantly in its environment, another useful characteristic for a conflict resolution tool. There are laughers that can turn whole rooms of people into a laugh-along. When people are laughing they are physically and emotionally vulnerable – maybe even to new ideas, and thus the resolution of conflict.

Humour has been seen as so important in human relations that for centuries in the west, ruling courts had fools and jesters to break tensions and create certain moods. The fool was the person privileged to be honest and confront royalty.

I have been an intentional clown for over thirty years. I live in clown clothes on a day to day basis. Selfishly, I want to create a context of humour, fun and play around me, for the raw fun that grows out of such behaviour. However, the commitment to daily clowning publicly grew out of my life as a social change artist. Once I saw the social potential of joy and laughter and how it helps people relax, become more talkative, and softens the tension of strangers, I decided to *be* joy and fun as a political act to help prevent conflict and speed the germination of community.

I have this theory that public playfulness prevents violence. In over thirty years, every time I have seen an adult and a child fighting in public, slipping into my clown self usually stops the fight instantly. I know my playfulness has stopped fighting in rough bars and protest marches. I think we also see this pacifying effect of fun and laughter at places like Disneyland where people tolerate endless lines with glee; and at Mardi Gras where even though many are drinking heavily and are tightly packed, violence rarely breaks out.

The first thing I would like to emphasise about the value of humour in conflict resolution is its role in the prevention of conflict. Human relationships are very complicated and we get little to no education in growing up on how to do human relations well. Good communication is often a behaviour learned after many horrendous mistakes. It rarely occurs without precious intent. Conflict arises out of misunderstanding, fear, or mistrust. It is best handled in a context of close human intimacy – friendship where one has a vested interest in the wellbeing of the other. When long term marriages and friendships have been studied to see what factors help keep them together and vital, a sense of humour has been found at the top of the list, before love and security.

Patch in a consultation in fun in a Russian hospital.

Patch pacifies guards outside the Kremlin walls.

I lived communally for twenty-five years. I started the community and in the mission statement, one of our seven principles was that all activity would be infused with fun. Ours was a very intense, crowded community that was also a hospital for its first twelve years. I knew, especially since we charged no fees, that to prevent burnout and keep my staff, I had to make the life in the community more fun than the alternatives.

Out of this grew the first silly hospital in history. Huge ridiculous events, often centred around staff birthdays, were staged as rituals to bind the community together. Everything was fodder for fun. There were meals served out of pig troughs, silly dances in the gardens. We enjoyed rooms filled to the ceiling with balloons, a wedding where gender roles were reversed and the groom wore a bridal gown, The human relations grew very intimate and I am sure this intimacy is at the core of why these relationships still thrive twenty-five years later. I know the fun has been what has kept me thrillingly involved.

> *"In every job that must be done, there is an element of fun, you find that fun and snap, the job's a game..."*
> Mary Poppins

Of course, humour is very individual. There is no universal humour. Each group must find their own sense of humour and play, and then do it. Ideally the group would see the value and allocate time and funds for the raw pleasure of play for its members. Ideally, each group would value this equally with the work of the community. Work done in a context of fun moves more smoothly and can be sustained longer. A certain amount of caution and rigidity must be abandoned in order to play and laugh; this relaxation can make for softer conflicts. One can hope that each group has several funny people to see to it that humour comes to every meeting and conflict. Other options are to take very sensitive subjects and make playful games, skits etc. around them. Jokes play this role in our society where the most frequent jokes are about our most sensitive areas.

Our communal home was a hospital and many who stayed with us had some mental illness. Profoundly unusual behaviours peppered our group life. It was our wish to deal with these problems without medication. We let very anxious, even disturbed (dangerous) people stay in our home in large numbers. Some of our most creative medical work was done in these situations. By relentless compassion, humour and vulnerability, we often saw horrible conflicts resolved. We made it fun to work with people that most of the society shuns.

We found humour was appropriate to life's greatest turning points, toughest conflicts. It was not unlike me to go into a dying patient's room dressed as an angel with a harp and wings and say "Coming attractions!"

I've done field research on conflict resolution and humour. For thirteen years I've taken an annual tour of 30 people (ages 12-80) to Russia to clown. In two weeks of 10–16 hour days, we visit hospitals, orphanages, prisons and public places. No clowning experience is required. I take thirty strangers and put them in a new and potentially stressful situation: very long hours with profoundly sick and dying youngsters, and heart-rending exchanges with children saying "please take me home." Yet humour turns painful into positive. The clowns get a relentless graphic experience that humour is a powerful social context – whether planned or spontaneous. I believe the humour given and received and the results seen have made these trips magical for most.

I would like to offer a few suggestions for individuals and groups who wish to put more humour into their lives and conflicts:

1. Each person might embark on a journey of self-discovery. Find what is fun for you, and put these findings into practice. If indeed humour is important, it's essential for each person to develop and act on their own sense of humour, and expand its borders at all times.

2. Make laughter, fun, and play a basic ethic of your community. This is not a frivolous decision. Time and money must be allotted for this humour in action. A party is not an indulgence, rather the liturgical celebration of community.

3. Design into your environment places that are for play. There are all the obvious, indoor and outdoor playgrounds, but also costume trunks, toy closets (child and adult), stage prop collections. Places like lakes, tree houses, fields and gazebos are fertile ground.

Clowning around with J T Ross Jackson (right) of Gaia Trust. Photo: Hildur Jackson

4. Nurture and attract those members of the community who bring a natural sense of play. Make an effort to find and keep guests whose presence leaves the same impression. This new fun blood is very important over the long haul.

5. Creativity attracts humour and play. Value all aspects of art and creativity as essential to community life, not as luxuries.

6. Put great effort towards the deepest of friendships. Watch the role that humour has in making that possible. You may notice that, among friends, especially long-lasting ones, humour is a cement. So much humour is tied up in the memories of a community.

7. Have a fantasy jar and encourage group mates to put into the jar descriptions of fun events they would like. Dip often into the jar and act accordingly.

8. Take a huge number of risks toward being foolish.

9. Once conflicts arise, do not belittle them by 'laughing them off'. Communicate them in several ways. Make sure everyone has their chance to speak. The point of humour is not to gloss over the intensity, rather to provide a ground where all can be communicated and resolved. Be receptive to lightening up on the subject no matter how involved. I've encouraged couples fighting to go ahead and say things, but try it all while naked, and jumping up and down.

10. Be patient with people who are not funny. Everyone can be.

PASSION AND PERSISTENCE

by Patch Adams MD

Patch's biography and contact address can be found at the start of the previous chapter on page 225.

Passion and persistence can change the world! I'm talking about hanging in there joyfully. That last part is extremely important. I'm travelling around quite a lot now, both to build our hospital and to stimulate service. Whether I'm speaking to Chief Executives of hospitals or to university students, I encounter amazement. When I probe, because I would like us to be commonplace, not amazing, I hear not amazement for our ideals and the breadth of our work, but for the passion and persistence I display in its pursuit. This is disturbing to me, because I have a great desire for tremendous social change. I don't want people amazed at our passion or persistence. I want them inspired to work their butts off.

Our society is suffocating under powerlessness, bereft of self-esteem. I want to make these precious gems commonplace, so that it is no longer interesting that people are full of passion and persistence, because it is the rule. These are not attributes of special people, blessed to possess them, rather extremely important tools for change.

To show you the company that they keep, some of their cousins are: desire, intensity, inspired, obsessed, commitment, compelled, insane, crazed, relentless, dauntless, consumed, raging, energised, concerned.

I'm not sure passion and persistence can be taught. In our community I used to try. I'd collect jigsaw puzzles, the harder the better. I would say, "You want to learn passion and persistence? Do this puzzle and don't get up until it is done. Don't want to get up until it is done." Passion and persistence can be inspired, studied, desired, pursued, but taught? I think that's why I am me. I consider myself a designed person – I don't have very many unintentional acts. I'm trying to be a person that might inspire passion. I get good feedback, which is why I do it. Get involved!

Can passion and persistence be found, through revelation, vision, or rational thought? I think so. The shy and quiet exhibit passion and persistence in equal depth as the loud and obnoxious, though I'm more familiar with the latter.

I believe passion and persistence are incompatible, in fact dramatically damaged by cynicism (probably my greatest pet peeve with modern society), apathy, discouragement, whining. If you are going to be a social crusader you must eliminate these from your vocabulary and behaviour. They are pernicious.

Passion, of course, implies glorious scenes: the future grand opening of our hospital building, or getting a bill passed that you worked on for 10 years. But that kind of passion needs no encouragement. The passion that tips the scale is the passion to hang endless posters one more time, to yet again call a meeting where almost no one shows up, though they promised. And to be feverishly enthusiastic for those two people. The passion that actually loves scutwork.

As a communitarian you want to say, "What are the jobs that people like the worst?", and you find the seduction so that people can love them. That is passion.

I represent extreme bias: mostly my own experience as a crazed person. I think I can say that I have spent my entire 50 years exploring passion and persistence in other people as well. I'll list some pointers:

- Ground yourself in missions of higher good. Service. In my office at home I have photos of murdered children, and children on the day they died of starvation. I have a personal ritual. I stand in front of those pictures until I am sobbing to remind myself that in my luxury, right this second, men are taking pleasure in pure torture. Ground yourself deeply in this mission.
- Couple it not with pain and tragedy. Unite your mission with your personal, perpetual experience of the miracle of life. Celebrate and be thankful to be together enough to step out of your selfish self, giving yourself to others and the world.
- Make it fun! As Emma Goldman said, "If I can't dance, I don't want to be part of your revolution!" Feel your path as a rich, varied and uplifting experience. It needn't be my kind of fun—make it your own brand.
- Persistence is a by-product of passion. If you see persistence, passion is at work. To me passion feels like surrender, a freedom from doubt, a zest for pursuit.
- Try to live as close to your authentic self as you possibly can. As a friend of mine says, "It's redundant to say 'authentic self' because self is authentic." Say what's on your mind – that day. No more lag time for perspective. Do what you want to do. No more sacrifice.
- Find creativity in every act, and do not sacrifice your need to be creative. Creativity is one of the greatest medicines ever. Exercise it in the way you wash dishes, in the way you walk down the street, and in the way you make art. Creativity is essential nourishment. It is not a cute thing to add to your community. It is not a luxury, as our government implies. It is the very soul of our sense of self worth.
- Responsibility, sacrifice, struggle and whining hurt passion, each in their own way. They are horrible reasons to move yourself forward. There's a very good chance if you are motivated by a sense of responsibility, sacrifice and struggle that you will grow to blame the thing you're passionate about as some kind of excuse for it's not happening, or for your pain around it.
- Passion is not a final product, like world peace. Passion is the name of the process. This confusion is one reason so many people quit passion, or never even join on to a Big Dream. They quit because achieving the final product is too slow. Certainly the single tragedy in Gesundheit's work is the loss of great people because it's taken so long to get our final product. "How is Gesundheit! doing?" always implies the final product, rather than the process. You must feel that passion today, in the process

– don't tie it to a finish line.

- Invite co-travellers, unless you are clearly hermetic. Co-travellers are the juice. Is there anything in your life more important than your friends? Live your lives that way! Commit yourself to your friends and colleagues! They are your pillars of persistence. Acknowledge them, support them, go for the intimacy of your wildest dreams with every human being you meet. It'll get easy.
- Live the life of an enthusiator. A seducer. Yes, that is my job. Pumping and seduction. I want all of you working around the clock, every day for the rest of your life, for your dreams. Not because you're paid to, but because you can't help it. It's that good.
- Feel the thrill of the quest all the time. Dream the impossible dream, fight the unrightable wrong... Corny stuff, and the best.
- See life itself as a break. I'm not a break person. As Weird Al Yankovich says, "I'll be mellow when I'm dead." I want you to find so much delight with your co-travellers, so much thrill in the quest, that a break is an irritation. Now if you need a break (and this is Dr Adams speaking), I want you to take one THAT DAY. I don't want you working under stress. The reason there are so few social activists is that in the history of social activism, it looks like it's not any fun! It looks like sacrifice, struggle. It looks like everyone you know in it needs a break. Burnout? You know, we should be burned out from selfishness, from vacations, from breaks. Life, your life, needs to be designed so that the idea of

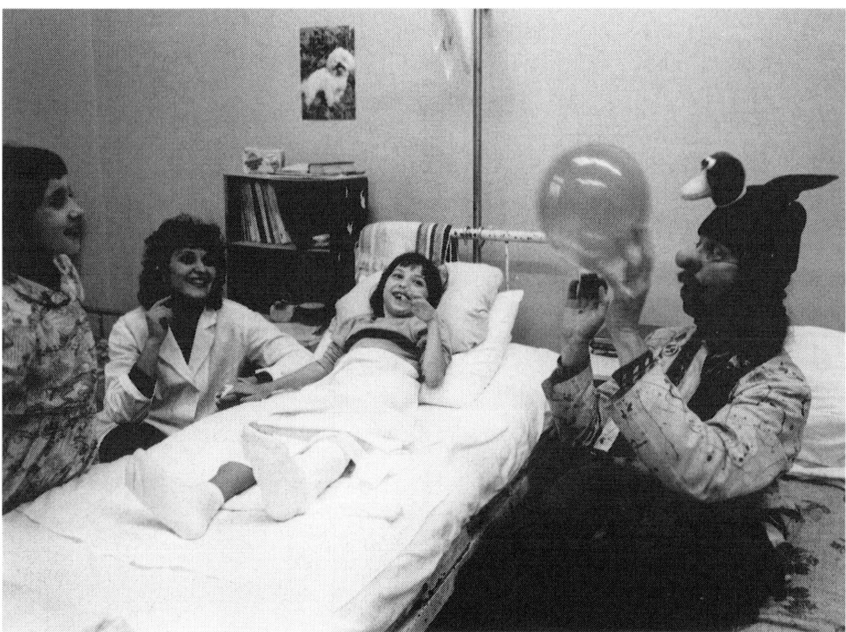

Taking away pain with laughter in a Russian hospital.

Mealtimes with Patch are liable to be fun. Trough meals bond community in play.

Mud pits are a potent tool for collective fun.

a break is an unwelcome interruption. Until you reach that point, take a break the day you need it.

- Exercise your wonder, curiosity and imagination at all times.
- Exercise as exercise. Be physically fit. If you're not, your community will have to take care of you. In order to be a passionate worker, if you have a big project, you'd better stay physically fit. It's going to take a long time! (Unless your project is... dinner.) Make fitness part of the ethic of your effort. Rest when you need it. Otherwise spend your time wisely.
- Define success as something achievable. For myself, I define success as: Did I try? Did I give my time? Did I never give up? All very easy to do. Do not put success in things or outcomes.
- Don't borrow much money. Over the course of our work trying to build a free hospital countless people have urged us to borrow money. The weight of borrowed money can cause you to lose your dream.
- Delight in compromise wherever you can. Have the shortest possible list of non-compromising points. Say, "Sure. I like your way."
- Be cautious about the power your passion brings. Passionate people are given a lot of power in our society, whether they ask for it or not. Because we have so little self-esteem, such boredom and loneliness and fear, passion is extremely attractive. Be cautious.

Quotes Taken from Question and Answer Sessions

"Love children; yours and others'. It's our insurance for the future."

"Passion exhibits itself in performance. Talk is cheap."

"I'm of the servant leadership school, myself. Just do, and look like you like what you do, and you'll be given power in the week. Respect, passion."

"Every time someone says something nice about you, believe it! Show your love and appreciation for others."

"All single parents are doing the single most passionate act in the world, bar none. Passionate people are all around you."

"Want self-esteem? Spend half an hour a day in front of a mirror, until half an hour isn't enough! Clothes on, clothes off, making faces. Until you're going, "If I just had 5 more minutes with myself..." Look yourself in the eye until you really understand why those friends of yours keep coming back."

"Follow your interests. Put passion in everything you do. My first paper was on the delight of washing dishes: there's a stacking thing that you can do that is breathtaking!"

"See yourself as a pioneer to reseed enthusiasm as a positive cultural context."

Betrayal, Revenge and Forgiveness
A Life Initiation
by Ben Fuchs MA

Ben Fuchs is a psychotherapist, trainer and organisational consultant. He is on the faculty of the Findhorn Foundation, where he has developed courses on intimacy, community building and conflict facilitation. He teaches conflict resolution and consults to organisations internationally.

Photo: Brian Young

The author wishes to acknowledge Robin Shohet whose contributions made this article possible.

Address:
11 Fyrish Road
Findhorn
Forres
1V36 OVT
Scotland
Tel: +44 (0)1309 691105
Fax: +44 (0)1309 691301

An earlier version of this contribution first appeared in *Changes – International Journal of Psychology and Psychotherapy*; Volume 15, No. 1; John Wiley and Sons.

Since I first started talking and writing about the psychology of betrayal and revenge, I have had reactions from people ranging from appreciation to hostility. The topics seem to touch a nerve for many people. What I have found interesting is that the strong reactions have come more often from people with high ideals for themselves, their organisations and for the world. While I am not against high ideals, I often see a gap between these ideals and reality (between an idealised self and actual self). Observing this incongruence in myself can easily fuel self criticism, while pointing it out to others is seldom appreciated by them. Yet, I believe that within this gap lie the very issues and feelings which we need to work with in order to develop.

In this article, I will look at two such issues – betrayal and revenge – which frequently operate below conscious awareness, fuelling dissatisfactions and conflicts in relationships and organisations. I will also look at forgiveness and its implications for individual and collective healing.

Betrayal

Betrayal happens in a context of trust. Where there has been a betrayal, there has been trust, otherwise there wouldn't be anything to betray. The two concepts give each other meaning. It is in our closest relationships that we can feel the most betrayed; when we have trusted and our trust has been broken. Most often this happens within the context of marriages and families, but we may also feel betrayed by our colleagues, organisations, religions, or life in general.

We are born with a basic, pure trust because we have not yet had experiences which teach us not to trust. This is what the Jungian analyst James Hillman would call primal trust. When my daughter was two, she used to climb up the steps, saying, "Daddy, catch me", and then jump. She didn't say, "Are you sure you are going to catch me?". Sometimes I had to be quick because she would just jump without considering the possibility that I wouldn't catch her. Now she is eight and no longer jumps quite so freely. The possibility of falling is in her awareness. What happens to this primal trust is that we all get let down. Metaphorically, we jump one day and find that we are not caught, and we end up falling, getting hurt and we experience this as a betrayal. We are let down by parents, teachers, friends, spouses, who for whatever reason, hurt us or are unable to meet our needs.

Often we enter a new relationship or job situation with our highest hopes and dreams (perhaps not articulated, even to ourselves) of how it could be. These high dreams can represent our values and ideals, as well as our goals, aspirations and longings. Our high dreams can be very powerful, inspiring us with a vision of how life could be, giving us a purpose worth struggling for. They can also keep us in painful situations where we refuse to give up on a relationship or an organisation, believing it will change in spite of all evidence to the contrary. We often feel betrayed and disappointed when our hopes and dreams are not met, even if we are not always consciously aware of it. The disappointments of our fallen dreams often lurk in the background, fuelling the more obvious conflicts in our relationships and organisations.

We can feel betrayed by teachers, religious leaders, therapists, governments, doctors, teachers, even God, to the degree that we place our trust in them. The more intimate or important a relationship, the more intensely a betrayal will likely be felt. An organisation or community can also feel betrayed by its leadership. There has been some press recently about a guru who preached celibacy and then had affairs with several of his students. The whole community felt betrayed. Afterwards, we realise how naively we trusted. We seem to set ourselves up for the experience of betrayal and yet respond with surprise and indignation when it happens. Why do we misplace our trust?

From an archetypal perspective, the myth of the Garden of Eden, may say something about betrayal in our lives today. Eden represents that place where everything is safe and perfect. The promised land. It is that place of primal trust, where a child jumps, oblivious that Mum or Dad (God) might not catch her. In the Garden, the concept of trust has no meaning, because without the possibility of betrayal, there is no need for trust. The fall from Eden can be seen as analogous to the knowledge of betrayal. Once we experience betrayal, primal trust is broken and we have left the Garden. Betrayal awakens us painfully from our naivete, teaching us about the world as it is; not completely trustworthy. It is not something that just arbitrarily and unfairly happens to us. It is an unavoidable and potentially valuable step in our psychological development.

What happens to us emotionally when we feel betrayed? After eating from that tree of knowledge we feel vulnerable and exposed, becoming aware of our 'nakedness' and of our human frailty. Betrayal leaves us feeling powerless, which can damage self-esteem and cause feelings of humiliation and shame. These feelings can become unbearable and we may look for a way to restore our power and sense of dignity. It can feel as though a part of our selves, a part of our wholeness, has been taken from us. We begin making choices (often unconsciously) about how to deal with the betrayals of life. We develop strategies – patterns of thinking and of behaving to help us cope with painful experiences. Our responses to betrayal are, in some way, attempts to feel more powerful again, to feel more whole.

I have often wondered why some people seem to be damaged by past hurts and abuses while others seem not only to put their painful experiences behind them, but also develop an inner strength and wisdom because of these experiences. This question brings us to the heart of the healing process for both individuals and organisations. I believe that how we respond to our betrayals determines our life patterns, more than the actual betrayals themselves. We cannot change our past experiences. But we can change what we do with those experiences. The choices we make can lead us towards integration, healing and creative change, or they can keep us stuck, repeating painful experiences. I see the choices involved as an integral part of our life experience – a soul's journey faced by each of us in our own way.

Let's look at two fundamentally different responses to betrayal; one which I call 'revenge' and the other 'forgiveness'. Each has a completely different definition of power. Within its own paradigm each system of power makes perfect sense. The revenge paradigm is much more common, but ultimately keeps us in pain. The forgiveness paradigm allows us to heal.

Revenge

In the revenge paradigm there are many different strategies for responding to betrayal. In his classic essay on Betrayal, James Hillman names five such strategies; revenge, denial, cynicism, self-betrayal, and paranoia. In my own work I have noticed many additional patterns, such as: moral superiority, blaming, withholding, and success.

Overt revenge is the most commonly understood definition of revenge. The talionic law, 'An eye for an eye' is one of the primary ways in which we attempt to restore our wounded pride and find 'justice'. While it is historically popular, this kind of direct revenge is usually not considered acceptable in our Western culture. So this response may become denied, while the desire to get even comes out in more subtle ways.

One form of denial is to minimise the hurt – "It wasn't so bad". The price of this is loss of sensitivity to our own suffering. Alternatively, we can deny the emotional investment in the relationship to the other person. If I deny that you are really important to me, then your betrayal doesn't count.

Cynicism or bitterness is another reaction. We can become scornful of our previous innocence by acting tough and cynical about our own dreams. It appears as a hardened, street-wise philosophy of life. Trust is naive, only for fools. Behind the toughness lies the broken ideals and the broken trust.

While cynicism expects no better of the world, paranoia tries to insure against any possible future betrayals by controlling others. Forever on guard, paranoia demands absolute commitments and loyalty from others and is constantly suspicious. This behaviour often drives others away, proving that the suspicions were well founded.

Self-betrayal is another choice which results in undermining ourselves and betraying what we hold precious. It is a way of turning the anger and revenge against ourselves, perhaps believing we deserved the betrayal. It can also be used to punish others, making them feel guilty. We may use failure, incompetence, illness, or even suicide as a way of dealing with our hurt and anger.

Another way to deal with pain is the consolation of moral superiority "I'm not like you, I wouldn't do what you did". With this comes a certain self-righteousness, which claims the moral high ground. In the famous Old Testament "Love thy neighbour as thyself" passage, it says "Do not revenge" twice, using two different Hebrew words for revenge. One of the words for revenge *kanaout* also means jealousy and zealotry. The Talmud explains: If you ask to borrow your neighbour's axe, and he says no, and the next day he comes and asks to borrow your hammer, you then say, "You wouldn't lend me your axe yesterday, I'm not lending you my hammer today!" That's the first kind of revenge. But, if you ask to borrow your neighbour's axe and he says no, and then he comes the next day and asks to borrow your hammer, you say, "I'll lend you my hammer, because I'm not the kind of neighbour you are!", that's the second kind of revenge – moral superiority.

Another powerful choice is withholding. It can be used punitively by shunning or ignoring someone – disowning them. More subtly, and more commonly, we hold ourselves back, not risking too much contact and intimacy. We keep distance from others so we won't get hurt as badly again. In an attempt to protect ourselves, we withdraw and partially cut ourselves off people and life in general.

If there is pain, there must be someone or something to blame. We can blame circumstances, parents, spouses, the 'system', even God. Blame gives meaning to pain that would otherwise seem arbitrary. Somebody must be made responsible for life's disappointments. This strategy can keep us putting responsibility onto past events and people, while living with resentment or regret. In organisations, an atmosphere of blame can stifle creativity and lead to scapegoating.

Success often translates into achievement; "I'll show them, I'll be more successful, gain more power, and then I won't be vulnerable". There is an old saying that the best revenge is living well.

The strategies we use to deal with feeling betrayed is by no means limited to this list. Most of us use some combinations of strategies, although we may have one which is most familiar. We learned them to protect us, or to help us cope with our hurts. Yet holding on to them as our primary stance towards life inhibits creativity and our ability to function well in personal and professional relationships. Our strategies can be a way of living in reaction to past injuries, subtly becoming a form of revenge.

When I started thinking of revenge in these terms, it changed how I understood the meaning of the word. I had previously thought of revenge as being primarily overt revenge. But as I looked at how revenge presented itself in conflicts between people I was working with and in my own life, I began to see it as a motive in ordinary interactions which are neither violent or extreme. I began to notice how often I wanted to say or do something that was subtly hurtful, when I felt slighted or put down. Sometimes I didn't do something that I might have done, withholding something nice, or not giving somebody a break, out of pride. These are not gross forms of revenge like shooting somebody, but the mini revenges that we experience every day with families, friends and colleagues. This kind of revenge comes in many subtle, often unconscious, forms.

Psychologically, revenge is significant. When we feel betrayed, we feel a loss of power, of dignity. Revenge is an attempt to reclaim that power through aggression or manipulation. Through retaliation, we restore our dignity and belief in justice, however arbitrary. Within its own system of logic, revenge may work. It avenges injustices and acts as a deterrent, while making us feel more powerful. Revenge may accomplish this, but only in the short run. The price of revenge is high.

The problem with overt revenge, 'an eye for an eye', is that it does not get us even. It generates more feelings of powerlessness and wounded pride, and with it, the need for additional retaliation, which escalates tit for tat. Revenge can also be collective. If you harm my family, friends, or taken to a larger extent, someone in my group, nation, or race, I may also feel vengeful. It becomes 'us' versus 'them'. Through group identification, each time one is hurt, many seek retaliation, as in wars, riots or feuds. As Gandhi rightly observed, 'an eye for an eye' only leaves the whole world blind. While the price we pay for this kind of revenge is huge, it is also obvious.

The price we pay for the more subtle forms of revenge, such as denial and withholding, may be less demonstrable, but is also highly destructive to ourselves and others. Instead of trying to reclaim power through direct revenge, we try to gain it more covertly. Yet, the very strategies we adopt to feel more powerful again, or at least more in control, can prevent us from healing. These strategies may defend us against feeling our powerlessness, vulnerability, shame, grief and loss. But in doing so they also prevent us from living our potential and from being in contact with ourselves and others. We end up acting against our own self interests, negating life. Some of these costs include: an inability to take responsibility for our lives, feeling owed something, chronic relationship problems, addictions and physical and mental health problems.

Revenge is often unconscious. It remains in the shadows and is usually denied as a motive because it is taboo in our culture. It is much more socially acceptable to appear to be defending oneself or seeking justice than to be taking revenge. So vengeful feelings are often disguised, even from ourselves, while being acted out in covert ways. Unacknowledged revenge is more difficult to let go of. If we are not conscious of our vengefulness then we lose the ability to choose anything else.

Clearly, the revenge paradigm does not work very well. What alternative is there in dealing with our wounds and restoring our power and sense of dignity? How can we let go of the pain associated with feeling betrayed?

FORGIVENESS

One difficulty in exploring forgiveness is that we don't have secular models for it and many people have been put off by the religious models. The teachings of Christianity, Judaism, Buddhism, 12 steps of Alcoholics Anonymous and A Course in Miracles all provide spiritual models of forgiveness. What these different models have in common is empowerment through acceptance, compassion and inner authority. This is a completely different paradigm of power than that of revenge.

Forgiveness is about letting go our emotional attachment to past injuries and the patterns and pay-offs which accompany them. It is not about either condoning or forgetting, but about understanding. It may be the only non-destructive choice. It is one thing to recognise the need for forgiveness, another to really let go. It can seem like a jump across the ocean to let go, even when we want to.

Forgiveness is a constant act of releasing oneself, which brings about healing. Offering forgiveness can seem sanctimonious, putting oneself in a morally superior, one-up position by having the power to forgive or not. But healing is not a power play and only happens when we give that up. Unless we work consciously on our revenge patterns, there is a danger of a premature forgiveness that doesn't really let go. I once had someone tell me that they had completely forgiven their parents – several times. Genuine forgiveness cannot be faked.

Forgiveness comes when we reconcile with the events which have hurt us, and let go of the patterns of living in reaction to those events. It is not always possible to reconcile with the other person or people involved, although this can heal relationships. The issue is one of making peace within oneself with what has happened. Letting go is a very individual process. While revenge can occur both at the individual as well as collective levels, forgiveness is solitary. We can feel vengeful on behalf of others, but we can not forgive on their behalf. When a group or community of people take this journey together, I believe it can bring about collective healing.

Although there are no formulas by rote for letting go, I have found that there are several understandings which help that process: a willingness to give up the secondary gains of holding on; a willingness to understand our betrayers by exploring those parts of ourselves which are also capable of betrayal; and a willingness to understand the archetype of betrayal in a wider context than only from our own individual suffering, but also as a necessary part of psychological maturation, bringing us from naive trust, to sober trust.

Before letting go, we need to accept our feelings of anger and revenge. After all, our patterns have helped us get through life, when we felt wronged and hurt. If our revenge patterns are working well for us, it may be hard to give them up. Letting go of revenge can seem very unattractive because it may be our most familiar way of having power or getting our needs met. It may even feel like a betrayal of oneself. Our patterns may seem to provide us with the benefits of being able to control others, get support, intimacy, a sense of community and feel more powerful. It may seem very frightening to let go of past hurts if we believe that we will have to give these things up as well.

For example, I attended a conference where issues like racism, sexism, anti-semitism, homophobia and classism were addressed in a large group. I noticed how uncomfortable people in the group, myself included, were with being identified with the one-up position. If one was identified with the one-down, oppressed minority, one could take the moral high ground with a certain righteousness. When the issue of sexism came up, the women in the group expressed to the men how they, as women, have been oppressed by a patriarchal system. The next day, when the people of colour were challenging the white people about the oppression of racism, those same white women did not easily identify themselves as being part of the group of oppressors. In that context, they were no longer the oppressed group. During the conference, the groups which have historically been abused, had the majority of air time, attention and compassion. As a white man, I was uncomfortable being in the group that was mostly identified as the oppressors. My feeling was temporarily relieved when the issue of anti-semitism came up. Then I could stand with the other Jews while we confronted the Gentiles on their historic mistreatment of us. The moral high ground generally goes to the oppressed, not the oppressors, the betrayed, not the betrayer. I began to understand the power of being the one who was wronged, and how that can be used to hold onto power.

Letting go means giving up the moral high ground which comes from identifying ourselves only as the person betrayed and the other only as the betrayer. It means giving up the pay-offs that go with being in the one-down, victim position and the certainty of being the only one who is morally right. The Course in Miracles poses the question, "Would you rather be right, or happy?". For many of us, this seems a difficult choice.

So far, I have addressed betrayal from the viewpoint of being betrayed. Most of us are so identified with feeling betrayed that we rarely consider the role of the betrayer. In workshops and lectures on betrayal I ask groups, 'How many people have been betrayed?". All hands go up. Then I ask,

"How many of you have also betrayed others?". Very few hands go up. If betrayal is an archetypal experience which touches us all, who is doing all the betraying? We all are. Not because of malicious intent, but because we cannot avoid hurting or disappointing others – which they may experience as betrayal.

If we think about how we may have betrayed others, their ideals and dreams for us, then from that vantage point, the betrayal looks very different. Can we guarantee that we would never betray another? I can't. Even with the best of intentions not to do harm, we still end up in the role of betrayer. We are unable to prevent this from happening – not from malicious intent – but because of our differences and our limitations are sometimes stronger than our wish not to hurt others. Understanding this may help us to put our feelings of being betrayed in perspective and not to take it so personally. The 'betrayer' is not just in another, but is also in ourselves. This may be difficult to accept, but I believe we are more like those who have betrayed us than we are different from them. We are all betrayers, even if we don't consciously intend to be. When we hurt others, it's often fuelled by some kind of confusion, distress or pain we are in. Acknowledging our own ability to betray makes it easier to see the people who have betrayed us as being human too. Part of the journey of forgiveness is recognising that the people who have betrayed us were expressing an aspect of their distress and pain. Our compassion, for both ourselves and others helps us to let go.

Betrayal is an archetype that is so prevalent in our mythology, it is important to see its significance, beyond simply being a cause of personal suffering. If we can view betrayal as a teacher, then we can begin to understand the usefulness of its difficult lessons. In fact, if we do not view it as a teacher, we are more likely to either repeat its painful lessons or remain stuck in one of our revenge strategies. So what can be learned from it? The experience of betrayal is part of our psychological development, something not consciously chosen, yet essential in our understanding of life. If we can avoid the pitfalls of revenge, then we can see it as an awakening to consciousness, an initiation into our own inner strength, wisdom and maturity.

This initiation means coming to terms with the world the way it is. For many people, there is a desire for the world to be completely safe, to be able to trust absolutely and to have satisfactory outcomes guaranteed. But this is naive, a longing to return to Eden. A return which is not possible and actually sets us up for further experiences of betrayal and disappointment. Primal trust is a naive trust.

In contrast to this, sober trust is the ability to see and realistically assess an individual or situation. To what extent is it safe? How realistic are my expectations in this relationship? Sobriety means recognising the world as it is, rather than as our dream of the way it 'should' be. People are capable of both love and of betrayal. Life is not completely trustworthy. It doesn't come with guarantees. The forces of life are stronger than our wish for it to be safe, stronger than our ability to prevent betrayal.

There is a moving story by Flora Kalman, about the liberation of Bergen-Belsen concentration camp. She survived the death factory and was in a state of shock and numbness after the British Army arrived to liberate the camp. She describes a day when she was watching her former captors, the SS guards, who had become prisoners themselves, forced to do the grim work of clearing up the corpses. On this day, she watched, feeling nothing. She was unable to feel: the sadness of the tragedy; the relief of it being over; even the sunlight on her face. Then as she watched one guard, she understood that his world had just turned upside down and suddenly she felt compassion for him. She was shocked at herself. How could she feel for the murderers of her family? Then she was flooded with the realisation that her feelings were not disloyal. This awakening was her personal victory. Her spirit was not broken. Even in this Hell, she could feel compassion, even for a German. Suddenly, she could feel the sunlight on her face, hear the birds singing. She felt alive again, part of the human race. Compassion allows healing.

I had a conflict with a friend recently, where I felt very hurt and angry. As I worked through the many layers of blame and then shame, suddenly it occurred to me that actually, there was nothing to forgive. Perhaps that's what forgiveness is. Accepting something just the way it is, accepting the person as they are, without having to fight, be a victim, or need it to be different. That's where the healing is. This is a very different model of empowerment than the one offered by revenge because it has nothing to do with getting even or being superior. It has to do with making peace within ourselves.

If our mythology teaches us anything about betrayal, it is that betrayal is an initiation, a necessary step in our growth, which brings us out of a naive, unconscious state of primal trust, painfully awakening us to greater consciousness. If we can avoid the pitfalls of revenge which negate life and keep us bound to our wounds, we can forgive, which brings maturity, wisdom and compassion. Without betrayal, we could experience neither trust or forgiveness. The awareness that comes with forgiveness brings us into an acceptance of the world as it is – an important step in developing the ability to be truly effective in our personal lives and in the world.

Elemental Help

A Guide for Community Living

by Kay Kay

Kay lived at Findhorn for seven years where she founded the Stewards of the Findhorn Foundation and the global organisation SEEDS (Self-empowerment, Education, Development, Systems). Having divested herself of home and possessions (except those she can carry), she now travels the world to wherever her intuition leads her. She enjoys writing, broadcasting, and coaching individuals or organisations through times of transition.

Address:
123 Findhorn
Forres
Moray
IV36 0YJ
Scotland
Tel/Fax: +44 (0)1309 671736
Email: kaykay2@compuserve.com

Of all the many components which could be considered necessary to the sustainability of communities, in my opinion, three components are of greatest importance:

- Clarifying the purpose of the community.
- Using resources appropriately.
- Integrating new members.

Purpose

It is essential to clarify and keep checking the primary purpose of the community. There are many possible purposes: spiritual, ecological, educational, religious, and many more. The primary purpose may change with the years. If the purpose is not clear, it will be difficult to identify priorities and allocate resources. This is likely to create conflict, disharmony, frustration, and lack of progress on both personal and project levels. It could lead to disaster.

There are a variety of methods for clarifying purpose. Much depends upon the kind of people participating in the process – their approach to, their willingness for, and their experience of the process. One method is to create a simple and concise vision statement that encompasses the visions and intentions of all those involved. A mission statement could be used as a means of alignment for both existing and potential members.

RESOURCES

The most valuable resource for a community is its members. Identifying their strengths, their skills, and the elements of their personalities helps us to allocate their roles for the greatest benefit of the project and the empowerment of the individuals.

As the basis for living an harmonious life, many of us long to be among like-minded people. It is an important criterion when choosing partners, friends, and workplaces. It is especially significant in the development of communities and eco-villages.

Sometimes, however, we confuse like-mindedness with personality similarity. We are often surprised and disappointed when people who seem to be aiming for the same objectives that we are, and who we believe think as we do, don't behave as we do. This can lead to disharmony and conflict, with sometimes serious and painful results.

In our personal development as individuals, we learn that it is helpful to identify our personality type. When creating a community, a company, or a group, it can be extremely beneficial to be aware of the different personality types of potential members.

There are many systems for identifying personality types, from Myers Briggs to the Enneagram. Most of them are comprehensive, and some of them can be time consuming. However, there is a very simple and effective system based upon the elements that Hildur mentioned in her introduction.

The elements of earth, fire, air, and water are to be found in all of us. However, one element is always predominant in each person. Each element has specific characteristics that determine how we behave in the world, which roles we are most likely to play, and which functions we may wish to perform. Here are the characteristics that I attribute to each element in the tables that follow:

Input: (How we most effectively acquire our information)
Action: (Our preferred kinds of activity)
Output: (What we will want to create)
Physical: (Which part of our body we most frequently utilise)
Communication: (Our style; words often used)
Result: (What we can achieve)
Detrimental traits: (The down side)
Traditional professions:
Most effective in areas of:
Most needed in times of:

The identification of a person's predominant element can be quick and easy in an environment of openness and honesty (especially with oneself). It can also be a lot of fun! Here are some suggestions:

AIR

Input: Auditory, study.
Action: Planning, talking, decision making, writing.
Output: Structure, systems.
Physical: Head, perhaps not always grounded.
Communication: Gives a lot of information, comes to, and delivers, conclusions.
Result: Efficiency.
Detrimental traits: Too much talking, overwhelms with information, blinds with science.
Traditional professions: Professor, teacher, engineer, civil servant, accountant.
Most effective in areas of: Research, education, logistics, accounts.
Most needed in times of: Chaos.

WATER

Input: Kinaesthetic, feelings.
Action: Integration, communication, emotional support.
Output: Systems of co-operation and support.
Physical: Heart, open-heartedness.
Communication: Listening, mediation.
Result: Creating co-operative teams, sense of family, support.
Detrimental traits: Collusion, closed systems, tangle, confusion.
Traditional profession: Consultant, social worker, therapist.
Most effective in areas of: Personnel management, mediation, facilitation.
Most needed in times of: Conflict.

FIRE

Input: Visual, intuition.
Action: Creating.
Output: New ideas.
Physical: Throat and power-centre.
Communication: Positive, "I will / let's do it".
Result: Innovation.
Detrimental: Too many ideas, not following through, chaos.
Professions: Entrepreneur, designer, entertainer.
Effective in areas of: Sales, marketing, public relations, vision creation.
Most needed in times of: Decline, new beginnings.

EARTH

Input: Experience.
Action: Doing.
Output: Products, creating stability.
Physical: Standing on two feet, grounded.
Communication: Direct, "I see and I do".
Result: Effectiveness, maintaining tradition.

Detrimental: Dictatorship, stubbornness, unwilling to change; this is how it must be or always has been done.
Professions: Farmer, builder, maintenance engineer.
Effective in areas of: Food or material production, maintenance, sustainability.
Most needed in times of: Stability.

To achieve personal effectiveness and peace of mind, it is useful to identify one's own primary element. Recognizing other people's primary elements helps when assigning their roles in the community. It also helps distinguish opposing elements, which could become antagonistic.

This can be a wonderfully learning and growing process for everyone involved. Openness is the key: open minds and hearts, honest feedback, open communication, and loving support. In an established group, this process helps explain former conflicts, a lack of progress, or previous disempowerment. It helps clarify the roles people need to play, and may lead to a redistribution of those roles among the group.

For instance, if the primary purpose of the community is personal and spiritual development, it is likely to attract a high proportion of air and water elements. Therefore, high ideals and visions may be created, but very little may be achieved in terms of physical infrastructure – the construction of buildings, for instance.

On the other hand, if it is a physical or pioneering project, such as land reclamation, reforestation, or eco-village building, then more fire and earth – the elements of the pioneering spirit – may turn up. Things may get done, but high ideals, tolerance, communication, and loving support may not be in abundance.

Putting square pegs into round holes can be a growth process, and can also be fun for a time, but it rarely leads to efficiency, harmony, or personal and group empowerment. A sustainable community is more likely to be one that rejoices in the individuality of its members, and encourages people to flow freely with their natural elemental energy. This could make a very effective contribution to Gaia.

Integration

In spite of the desire among most humans to have connection with others, we have an astonishing capacity to create separation. How long it takes for 'them' to become 'us' in a community depends upon several things: how long the community has existed, how many people are needed to do the work, the personal development of the existing members, and the criteria set for 'acceptability'. For example, during the early days of the Findhorn Foundation, when a newcomer arrived, Peter Caddy would hand over a spade and say "Dig there". When I arrived twenty-eight years later, a commitment to two years of spiritual, community, and personal growth education was required before a person would be considered a member of the Foundation.

We are becoming increasingly aware that we are moving into an age of self-responsibility. Eco-villages are most likely to be–and indeed probably need to be–created and inhabited by self-empowered individuals with a strong sense of personal responsibility. This can cause problems in the development and maintenance of the 'community glue'.

In the early years of community development, eco-villages will need to attract and integrate a wide range of skills and experience. For some people, joining an already established community-even a relatively new one-can be a stressful experience, particularly if this presents a totally new way of living. Once a culture has been established, it becomes commonplace to those who created it, while to a stranger it can be bewildering and intimidating – sometimes to the point of disillusionment and departure.

There is an argument which says that newcomers should be left alone to work it out for themselves; if it is too difficult for them, then they are not the appropriate people for that particular community. This seems to me to be unnecessarily harsh as well as self-defeating. At worst, this sink-or-swim attitude can deprive the community of valuable resources; at best, it can lead to time wasting, frustration, and disempowerment as people go through their own learning curve and the probable re-invention of the wheel.

Of course it is important for people to learn whatever they need to know in their own way and at their own pace. Equally, it makes no sense to leave folk struggling in unnecessary ignorance. Although ideally many activities will take place within a group setting, there will be many occasions when people will be required to work alone or make personal judgments. A newcomer to a community, or even someone stepping into a new function, will learn more quickly, feel more confident, and become efficient and productive with the help of someone to act as guide, coach, and source of support. In fact, a mentor!

The mass educational approach to skills training has led to the disappearance of most of the apprentice systems. This resulted in a diminished role for the mentor, which until recently had gone out of fashion in much of the developed world. Now, however, in many of the new people-oriented businesses around the planet, mentoring new recruits is once again a high priority. In newly forming communities, it could prove to be the most caring and efficient method of introducing newcomers to the principles and practices of the established group.

Mentors could be assigned the role of imparting information about the community: the history and traditions, the goals and plans, and how things are done. But most importantly, mentors would provide personal support as the new person goes through their process of integration. Whilst that process will be of a very personal nature on many levels, it does not need to be the baptism of fire that it has been for people in some communities in the past. Personal responsibility will be much safer for us all to achieve if our environment is one of care, compassion, and mutual respect.

In choosing a mentor for a newcomer, it could be beneficial to match elemental types. Two people of the same elemental type are likely to be interested in the same kinds of activity, and they are likely to communicate more easily because they absorb information in similar ways.

Mentoring can enrich the lives of both participants and lead to fulfilling relationships. Those who have been mentored in the past are usually very willing volunteers to be mentors themselves. This kind of continuity is a great contribution to the sustainability of community.

Resource List

Global Eco-village Network (GEN)

In spite of all the difficulties some people have actually managed to succeed in building eco-villages. Not least because it is fun. It is invigorating to start to 'walk your talk', it makes sense in a crazy world and there are many wonderful eco-villages to visit. The Global Eco-village Network (GEN), links all these projects in a global network. GEN was inaugurated in Istanbul in 1996 and is now on the Internet. Look up their 1,500 pages under http://www.gaia.org and gain all the information you want about their three regional offices, the national networks, individual projects, how to become a member, and plans for the future. Details are available of many exciting places to see worldwide, of education related to eco-villages, and there are numerous links to other relevant initiatives.

Eco-villages in the South

75% of the world population still live in villages which have been ecologically sound for millennia, although there is plenty of room for improvement. The social fabric may be intact for now, but they are threatened by urbanisation and globalisation, and a new social is needed to dissuade people from migrating to the megalopolises either for simple survival or because they are tempted by 'the American Dream'. This rural exodus must be prevented, and life in the rural areas made more attractive and 'modern'. The mega-polises also need to be part of this by moving out to new settlements and finding other solutions that are more sustainable. Forging links with the eco-village movement is a process which is just beginning for these people. Rashmi Mayur from the International Institute for Sustainable Futures in Mumbai, India has been working with the Gaia Trust and GEN for some years now, and GEN has just established a link with the Sarvodaya Movement of Sri Lanka (linking 13,000 villages in a sustainable development). In Africa the NAAM Movement in Burkina Faso works along the same lines. We hope to strengthen this work in the years to come.

GEN – International Secretariat
Contact: Philip Snyder
GAIA Villages, Skodsborgvej 189
Nærum 2850, Denmark
Tel: +45 97 93 66 55. Fax +45 97 93 66 77
Email: gen@gaia.org
WWW: http//www.gaia.org

GEN – Europe
Contact: Lucilla Borio
Torri Superiore, Via Torri Superiores 18039, Veutimiglia, Italy
Tel: + 39 0184 21 52 90
Email: torrisup@rosenet.it

GEN – Oceania and Asia
Contact: Max O Lindegger
MS 16, 59 Crystal Waters Permaculture Village, Queensland 4552, Australia
Tel: +61 754 944 741. Fax +61 754 944 578
Email: ecosol@peg.apc.org

ENA – Americas
Contact: Albert Bates
556 Farm Road, PO Box 90, Summertown, TN 38483-0090, USA
Tel: +1 931 964 4324. Fax +1 931 964 2200
Email: ecovillage@thefarm.org

Eco-villages in the South

Contact: Vinya Ariyaratne
The Sarvodaya Movement
Dam Sak Mandira, 98 Rawatawatta Road, Moratuwa, Sri Lanka
Email: ssmplan@sri.lanka.net

Contact: Rashmi Mayer
International Institute for Sustainable Futures
73A Mittal Tower, Narriman Point, 400 021 Mumbai, India
Email: iisfb@giasbm
Tel: + 91 22 204 57 58

Contacts: Silvia Ballado, Gustavo Ramirez
Almafuerte 1732, Villa Maipu, 1650 San Martin, Argentina
Fax: 541 752 2197
Email: gaia@wamani.apc.org

Other Useful Organisations and Networks

Canadian Healthy Communities Network
541 Sussex Drive, 2nd Floor, Ottawa, ON K1N 6Z6, Canada
Tel: +1 613 562 4646
Fax: +1 613 562 4648

Centre for Alternative Technology (CAT)
Machynlleth, Powys SY20 9AZ, Wales

CoHousing Center Inc.
103 Morse Street, Watertown, MA 02172, USA
Tel: +1 617 923 1300
Comprehensive development management and architectural services for cohousing groups throughout New England.

CoHousing Company
1250 Addison Street, #113, Berkeley, CA 94702, USA
Tel: +1 510 549 9980
Email: coho@cohousingco.com
Architectural design and consulting services for new and established cohousing communities. A clearinghouse for cohousing activity in the US. Offers predesign workshops for site, common house and private houses.

CoHousing Network
PO Box 2584, Berkeley, CA 94702, USA
Tel: +1 510 486 2656
Email: cohomag@aol.com WWW: www.cohousing.org
An informal association involving cohousing and their regional umbrella groups around the country. Sponsors local and national cohousing events. Publishes *CoHousing* (*see p. 258*) journal of The CoHousing Network.

CoHousing Resources
Contact: Chris Hanson, 174 Bushby Street, Victoria, BC V8S 1B6, Canada
Tel: +1 604 480 4815
CoHousing development consultant with skills in land acquisition, feasibility analysis, group formation, consulting with new cohousing groups. Offers custom workshops.

Cooperative Resources and Services Project (CRSP)
Contact: Lois Arkin, 3551 White House Place, Los Angeles, CA 90004, USA
Tel: +1 213 738 1254
Email: crsp@igc.apc.org
Resource center for small ecological cooperative communities. Membership organization providing book and video loans. Offers workshops and slideshow presentations on its work with the Los Angeles Eco-Village.

EcoDesign Centre
Contact: Shelley Penner
#208, 2130 West 3rd Avenue, Vancouver, BC V6K 1L1, Canada
Tel: +1 604 738 9334
Email: ecodesign@freenet.vancouver.bc.ca

Eco-Home Network
4344 Russell Avenue, Los Angeles, CA 90027, USA
Send SAE for Publications List.

Ecological Design Association
The British School, Slad Road, Stroud, Gloucestershire GL5 1QW, England
Contacts: David Pearson, Herbert Girardet, Victor Papanek
Tel: +44 (0)1453 765575
Fax: +44 (0)1453 759211

Ekoboforeningen Njord
(Swedish National Association for Ecological Living)
Contact: Chris Druid
Blynøsvøgen, 15 Vaxholm, 18534 Sweden

Fellowship for Intentional Community (FIC)
Contact: FIC, Rt. 1, Box 155, Rutledge, MO 63563, USA
Tel: +1 660 883 5545
Email: fic@ic.org
North American association, publishes *Communities Directory* and *Communities – Journal of Cooperative Living* (*see p. 256*). Also hosts the Intentional Communities Web Site (www.ic.org) and produces the biannual Art of Community Gatherings.

Folkecentre for Renewable Energy
Contact: Preben Maegaard
Kammersgaards 16, 7760 Hurrap, Denmark

Gaia Trust
Contacts: Dr J T Ross and Hildur Jackson
Storkevænget 8, 2840 Holte, Denmark
Fax: +45 42 42 55 91

International Centre for Sustainable Cities
Contact: Alan Artibise
#1150–555 West Hastings Street, Harbour Centre, PO Box 12071, Vancouver, BC V6B 4N5, Canada
Tel: +1 604 666 0061
Fax: +1 604 666 0009

International Eco-village Design Society
Contacts: Sim Van de Ryn and friends
PO Box 11645, Berkeley, CA 94712, USA
Tel: +1 510 869 5015
Fax: +1 415 332 5808
Email: ecodesign@igc.apc.org

International Sustainable Development Network/Daybreak International
Contacts: Nancy Skinner, Rob Gilman, Pliny Fisk, Robert Berkebile
3914 North Marshfield, Chicago, IL 60613, USA
Tel: +1 312 880 1391
Fax: +1 312 880 1367

LOS
(The Danish Association of Sustainable Communities)
Secretary: Thomas Seiersen
Munach, Egebergvej 46, 8751 Gedved, Denmark
Tel: +45 75 66 41 11
Fax: +45 75 66 41 21
Email: los@pip.dknet.dk

Out on Bale
Contacts: Matts Myhrman & Judy Knox
1037 E. Linden Street, Tucson, AZ 85719, USA
Tel: +1 602 624 1673
Information on strawbale construction. Publishes newsletter, *The Last Straw* (*see p. 259*).

Shared Living Resource Center
Contact: Ken Norwood
2375 Shattuck Avenue, Berkeley, CA 94704, USA
Tel: +1 510 548 6608
Helps facilitate the creation of living environments that integrate ecological design, affordability, and cooperative self management. Publishes *Rebuilding Community in America*, by Ken Norwood and Kathleen Smith (*see p. 263*).

Urban Ecology Center
405 14th St, #701, Oakland, CA 94612, USA
Tel: +1 510 549 1724
Email: urbanecology@igc.apc.org

Magazines and Newsletters

Achoo!
6855 Washington Bd., Arlington, Virginia 22213, USA
Newsletter of the Gesundheit! Institute

Clean Slate
Machynlleth, Powys SY20 9AZ, Wales
Quarterly journal of the Centre for Alternative Technology (CAT).

CoHousing
PO Box 2584, Berkeley, CA 94702, USA
Subscription: $60/4 issues, low waged $30.
The journal of the CoHousing Network.

Common Ground
Castelbaldwin, Co. Sligo, Ireland
Tel: +353 71 657 37. Fax: +353 71 657 38
Magazine of alternative living in Ireland.

Communal Societies
Contact: Don Pitzer
Email: dpitzer.ucs@smtp.usi.edu
Journal of the Communal Studies Association. Published annually.

Communities – Journal of Cooperative Living
Contact: Diana Christian
290 McEntire Road, Tryon, NC 28782, USA
Tel: +1 828 863 4425
Email: communities@ic.org or diana@ic.org
A quarterly magazine, published by the Fellowship for Intentional Community, on all forms of intentional communities, for communitarians and people interested in community living. Single issue: $6 (in US), $7 (outside US). Subscriptions: $18 (in US), $22 (outside US).

Community Sustainability Exchange
P.O. Box 11343, Takoma Park, MD 20913, USA
Tel: +1 301 588 7227
Published quarterly by the Community Sustainability Resource Institute. $30.

DX: The Design Exchange
PO Box 90, Summertown, TN 38483-0090, USA
Suggested donations for subscription: $25/year
Newsletter of the Eco-village Network of the Americas from the Eco-village Training Centre in cooperation with Global Village Institute for Appropriate Technology.

Eco-Design
20 High Street, Stroud, Gloucestershire GL5 1AS, England
Journal of the Ecological Design Association.

Eco-village at Ithaca Newsletter
Eco-village/CRESP, Cornell University, Ithaca, NY 14853, USA
Tel: +1 607 255 8276
Subscription: $15/4 issues

Eurotopia – Journal of Ecological and Cooperative Living
(for Germany and Europe)
Hasenhof 8, 71540 Murrhardt, Germany
Tel/Fax: +49 7192 3218
Publishes a good listing of European projects. Published by Eurotopia.
Price: DM48 per annum

Gaia Villages
Gaia Villages, Skodsborgvej 189, Nærum, 2850 Denmark
Annual newsletter from the eco-village wing of Gaia Trust, Denmark.

Global Eco-Village Network (GEN) Europe Newsletter
Ginsterweg 5, D–31595 Steyerberg, Germany
Published three times a year for members and subscribers.

Global Eco-Village Ne*twork (GEN) Oceania Newsletter*
59 MS 16 Crystal Waters, Queensland 4552, Australia
Quarterly newsletter of the Global Eco-Village Network in Oceania.

Global Eco-Village Network (GEN) America
The Design Exchange, 560 Farm Road, PO Box 90, Summertown,
TN 38483-0090, USA

In Context's Sustainability Library
– A Vision of a Humane Sustainable Culture
Creatura Books, PO Box 718, Point Reyes Station, CA 94956, USA
Tel: 800 306 1778 (in the USA)
or +1 415 663 1778 (outside USA)
No.'s #9-39 available.
#14, #29, #33 and #35 are especially community oriented. $6.00 each.

Integrations
PO Box 1411, Queanbeyan, NSW 2620, Australia
A quarterly for cohousing, eco-villages and social change.

Klokken
Astaldo Raahede, Silkeborgvej 932, 6462 Harlev, Denmark
Newsletter of the Co-Housing Association for Denmark

The Last Straw
1037 E. Linden Street, Tucson, AZ 85719, USA
Tel: +1 602 624 1673
A quarterly newsletter published by Out on Bale Ltd.
Single issues: $8.00; subscription: $28.00/year

Living Lightly
c/o Positive News, 5 Bicton Enterprise Centre, Clun
Shropshire SY7 8NF, England
Tel: +44 (0)1588 640022

LOS–net
Contact: Thomas Seiersen
Munach, Egebergvej 46, 8751 Gedved, Denmark
Tel: +45 75 66 41 11
Fax: +45 75 66 41 21
Newsletter of the Danish Organisation of Sustainable Communities

One Earth
OneEarth Ltd, The Park, Findhorn, Forres IV36 0TZ, Scotland
Quarterly magazine of the Findhorn Foundation Community.

Permaculture Activist
PO Box 1209, Black Mountain, NC 28711, USA
Journal of the permaculture network in North America.
Subscription: $15/4 issues

Permaculture Magazine – Solutions for Sustainable Living
Permanent Publications, Hyden House Limited, The Sustainability Centre, East Meon, Hampshire GU32 1HR, England
Tel: +44 (0)1730 823311
Fax: +44 (0)1730 823322
Email: hello@permaculture.co.uk
WWW: www.permaculture.co.uk
Quarterly temperate climate permaculture magazine, networking throughout Britain and Europe with links to permaculture worldwide.
Subscription: £10 ($16) U.K.; £12 ($19) Europe airmail and Rest of world surface; £16 ($26) Rest of World airmail.

Resurgence
Ford House, Hartland, Bideford, Devon EX39 6EE, England
Tel: +44 (0)1237 441293

Yes – A Journal of Positive Futures
PO Box 10818, Bainbridge Island, WA 98110, USA
A new magazine developed by former staff of *In Context* magazine.

BOOKS AND REPORTS

† Denotes books available from Permanent Publications' *Earth Repair Catalogue*, containing over 350 books and videos on many different environmental subjects. The Catalogue is available free of charge or can be viewed in colour on the World Wide Web, address as below.
Contact: Permanent Publications, Hyden House Limited
The Sustainability Centre, East Meon, Hampshire GU32 1HR, England
Tel: +44 (0)1730 823311
Fax: +44 (0)1730 823322
Email: hello@permaculture.co.uk
WWW: www.permaculture.co.uk

Adams, P., 1998. *Gesundheit!*†. Vermont: Healing Arts Press.

Alexander, C., 1981. *The Linz Cafe*. Oxford: Oxford University Press.

Alexander, C., et al., *A New Theory of Urban Design*. Oxford: Oxford University Press.

Alexander, C., 1964. *Notes on the Synthesis of Form*. Cambridge, Massachusetts: Harvard University Press.

Alexander, C., et al., *The Oregon Experiment*. Oxford: Oxford University Press.

Alexander, C., et al., *A Pattern Language*†. Oxford: Oxford University Press.

Alexander C., et al., *The Production of Houses*. Oxford: Oxford University Press.

Alexander, C., 1979. *The Timeless Way of Building*†. Oxford: Oxford University Press.

Bunker, S., et al. eds., 1997. *Diggers and Dreamers - The Guide to Communal Living*†. London: Diggers & Dreamers Publications.

Campbell, S., 1983. *Earth Community – Living Experiments in Cultural Transformation*. Evolutionary Press.

Canfield, J. C., and Register, R., eds. 1996. *Third International Eco-Cities Conference Report*. The Yoff conference in January, 1996. CA, USA: EcoCity Builders.

Christensen, K., *The Green Home – How to Make Your World a Better Place*†. London: Piatkus Books.

Context Institute, 1991, *Eco-Villages & Sustainable Communities.* Contact: 306 Louisa Street, Langley, WA 98260, USA. Tel: +1 360 221 6045.

Conrad, J., ed., 1997. *Eco-Villages & Sustainable Communities – Models for 21st Century Living.* Scotland: The Findhorn Press.

Conway, R., *The Rage for Utopia.* London: Allen & Unwin

Dorit, F., and Van Nostrand, R., 1996. *Collaborative Communities.*

Greco, T. H., 1994. *New Money for Healthy Communities.* Contact: Thomas H Greco, PO Box 42663, Tucson, AZ 85733, USA.

Hall, K., and Warm., P., 1992. *Greener Building – Products and Services Directory*†. Association of Environment-Conscious Building.

Hawken, P., 1993. *The Ecology of Commerce – A Declaration of Sustainability.* NY: Harper Business.

Henderson, H., and Koehler, B., 1996. *Building a Win–Win World.* San Fransisco.

Communities Directory. A guide to co-operative living. Lists over 540 North American Communities; more than 50 communities on other continents; also over 200 alternative resources and services; and 35 articles about community living. Contact: Fellowship for Intentional Community (see above).

Jackson, H., ed., 1996. *The Earth is Our Habitat – A Proposal for Creating Demonstration Eco-villages.* Denmark: Gaia Trust. Contact: Gaia Villages, Skodsborgvej 189, Nærum, 2850 Denmark.

Jackson, H., and Jackson, J.T. Ross, 1998. *A Spiritual Journey.* Copenhagen, Fjordvong. Contact: Gaia Villages, Skodsborgvej 189, Nærum, 2850 Denmark.

Jackson, H., and Jackson, J.T. Ross, *1999. Building An Eco-Village Future. Soon to be published.* Contact: Gaia Villages, Skodsborgvej 189, Nærum 2850, Denmark.

Kennedy, M., 1995. *Interest and Inflation Free Money*† *– How to Create an Exchange Medium that Works for Everybody and Protects The Earth.* Michigan: Seva International.

Lindegger, M., *Conceptual Plan for Crystal Waters.* Contact: 59 Crystal Waters, MS16, Maleny 4552, Australia. Fax: +61 74 944 578. Email: ecosol@peg.apc.org

Lindegger, M., *Crystal Waters Owner's Manual.* Contact: 59 Crystal Waters, MS16, Maleny 4552, Australia. Fax: +61 74 944 578. Email: ecosol@peg.apc.org

McCamant, K., and Durrett, C., 1994. *CoHousing – A Contemporary Approach to Housing Ourselves.* 2nd ed. Berkeley, USA: Ten Speed Press.

McLaughlin, C., and Davidson, G., 1985. *Builders of the Dawn.* USA: Book Publishing Co. PO Box 99, Summertown, TN 38483, USA.

Metcalf, B., 1995. *From Utopian Dreaming to Community Reality – Co-operative Lifestyles in Australia.* Sydney: University of New South Wales Press.

Metcalf, B., 1996. *Shared Visions, Shared Lives – Communal Living Around the Globe*†. Scotland: Findhorn Press.

Near, H., 1992. *The Kibbutz Movement – A History.* Oxford: Oxford University Press. Contact: e-mail: 100067.1576@compuserve.com
Or: orders@ISBS.com

Norwood, K., AICP, and Smith, K., 1995. *Rebuilding Community in America – Housing for Ecological Living, Personal Empowerment and the New Extended Family.* Shared Living Resource Center. Contact: 2375 Shattuck Avenue, Berkeley, CA 94704, USA. Tel: 510 548 6608

Oved, Y., 1988. *Two Hundred Years of American Communes.* Transaction Books.

Pearson, D., 1994. *Earth to Spirit – In Search of Natural Architecture*†. Gaia Books.

Pratt, S., (compiled by), 1996. *Permaculture Plot – The Guide to Permaculture in Britain*†. Hampshire: Permanent Publications.

Scott Peck. M., 1990. *The Different Drum*†. London: Arrow.

Shaffer, C., and Anundsen, K., 1994. *Creating Community Anywhere – Finding Support and Connection in a Fragmented World.* Tarcher/Putnam.

Talbott, J., 1995. *Simply Build Green*†. Scotland: Findhorn Press.

Van der Ryn, S. and Calthorpe, P., 1986. *Sustainable Communities – A New Design Synthesis for Cities, Suburbs and Town.* Sierra Club Books.

Van Der Ryn, S., and Cowan, S., 1996. *Ecological Design.* Island Press.

Verlag, D. R., in conjunction with the European Academy of the Urban Environment (EAVE). Kennedy M. and D. Kennedy, eds. *Designing Ecological Settlements.* Verlag., D. R., Unter den Eichen 57, D–12203 Berlin, Germany.

Whitefield, P., 1996. *How to Make a Forest Garden*†. Hampshire: Permanent Publications.

Whitefield, P., 1996. *Permaculture In A Nutshell*†. Hampshire: Permanent Publications.

Whitmyer, C. et al, eds. 1983. *In the Company of Others – Making Community in the Modern World.* Tarcher/Putnam. Available from the Fellowship for Intentional Community (see above).

Electronic Resources

Web Sites

Bagno di Lucca: http://www.urra.it/cyber.wwwvi
Cohousing Network: http://www.cohousing.org
Context Institute: http://www.context.org
Developing Ideas: http://iisd1.iisd.ca/didigest/
Eco-village Information Service: http//www.gaia.org
Eco-village Training Center at The Farm: http://www.gaia.org/dx
Energy Efficiency and Renewable Resources: http://solstice.crest.org/social/ eerg/index.html
Fellowship for Intentional Community: http://www.ic.org
Foundation for Conscious Evolution: http://www.cocreation.org
Framework Convention on Climate Change: http://www.iisd.ca/linkages/climate/climate.html
Global Ideas Bank: http://www.newciv.org/worldtrans/BOV/BOVTOP.HTML
GreenClips: http://solstice.crest.org/sustainable/greenclips/info.html
International Society for Ecological Economics: http://kabir.umd.edu/ISEE/ISEEhome.html
New Civilization Network: http://www.newciv.org/worldtrans/newcivnet.html
Office of Research Services: http://solar.rtd.utk.edu/default.html
Permaculture FAQ: http://csf.colorado.edu/perma/faq.html
Permanent Publications: http://www.permaculture.co.uk
Pete's Pond Page: http://reality.sgi.com/employees/peteo/index.html
PlanetKeepers: http://galaxy.tradewave.com/editors/wayne–pendleyplankeep.html
Sustainable Communities Network: http://www.cfn.cs.dal.ca//Environment/SCN/SCN_home.html
Sustainable Earth Electronic Library: http://envirolink.org/pubs/index.html
World Scientists' Warning to Humanity: http://newciv.org/worldtrans/whole/warning.html

List Servers
These are electronic conversations in which an on-going dialogue is carried on by many people with a common interest. If you subscribe, be prepared to receive up to 15 to 20 messages per day.

ecovillage-l:
On-going discussion on eco-villages and sustainable community issues: Send email message to: ecovillage–l@gaia.org. In message, write only: subscribe [enter your name here]. To unsubscribe, the command is: unsubscribe. When unsubscribing, do not put anything else in the text of the message.

SUSTAIN–L:
On-going discussion on sustainability issues: Send email message to: MAILSERV@PIMACC.PIMA.EDU In message, write only: SUBSCRIBE [enter your name here]. To unsubscribe, the command is: UNSUBSCRIBE Note that all commands to the server must be in upper case. When unsubscribing, do not put anything else in the text of the message.

Magazines On-line
In Context Magazine on-line. Developed by Robert and Diane Gilman, founders of the Context Institute. To subscribe, enquire at: http://www.context.org.

Special Publishers and Booklists on Sustainable Communities

Centre for Alternative Technology (CAT) Publications
Machynlleth, Powys SY20 9AZ, Wales
A complete catalogue of environmental books and products.

Chelsea Green Publishing Co.
PO Box 428, White River Junction, VT 05001, USA
Tel: +1 800 639 4099
Books for Sustainable Living. A wonderful list and descriptions of directly relevant publications. Free catalogue.

Community Bookshelf
East Wind Community, Tecumseh, MO 65760, USA
Tel: +1 417 679 4682
Books by mail order on community, co-ops, group process, ecology, social change, etc. Free catalogue.

Cooperative Services Books
PO Box 243, Yellow Spring, OH 45387, USA
Tel: +1 513 767 2161
A good selection of books on small communities from the Community Service Inc.

Creatura Books
903 Marylyn Circle, Petaluma, CA 94954, USA
Tel/Fax: +1 707 762 5143
Email: mollyeco@aol.com
Can provide any book in print and specializes in books on sustainability, deep ecology, systems thinking, ecopsychology, social justice, etc.. They donate 5-10% of every order to one of a list of transformative non-profits, according to the customer's choice.

Eco-Home Network
4344 Russell Avenue, Los Angeles, CA 90027, USA
Send SAE for Publications List.

Edge Of Time
BCM Edge, London WC1N 3XX, England
Tel: +44 (0)7000 780536
Email: coherentvisions@compuserve.com
Publishers of *Diggers and Dreamers – The Guide to Communal Living* and other 'alternative' titles.

Findhorn Foundation's Phoenix Community Stores Ltd
Phoenix Community Stores, The Park, Findhorn Bay, Moray, IV36 OTZ, Scotland
Tel: +44 (0)1309 690110
Fax: +44 (0)1309 690933
Booklist available. This comprehensive list of books and publications was compiled for the Eco-villages & Sustainable Communities gathering at Findhorn in October, 1995. Includes many items from Europe and Australia. Also included is a list of the many audio and video tapes available from the conference.

New Society Publishers
PO Box 189, Gabriola Island, British Columbia V0R 1X0, Canada
Tel: +1 800 567 6772
Books to build a new society. Their quarterly catalogue is always full of wonderful articles along with many titles important to sustainable communities.

Permanent Publications
Hyden House Ltd., the Sustainability Centre, East Meon
Hampshire GU32 1HR, England
Tel: +44 (0)1730 823311
Fax: +44 (0)1730 823322
Permanent Publications are publishers and book distributers specialising in books and videos on permaculture, alternative technology, organic gardening, revitalising community and other related subjects compiled in their *Earth Repair Catalogue* which is available free of charge or can be viewed in colour on the World Wide Web, address as above.

Urban Ecology Annotated Bibliography
Edited by Paul F Downton & David Munn, 1993
Urban Ecology Australia, PO Box 3040, Grenfell Street, Adelaide
Tandanya Bioregion, SA 5000, Australia
Tel: +61 8 232 4866
This 165 pages of resources for sustainable community building from throughout the world. $25.

The Whole Co-op Catalog
Co-op Resource Center, 1442A Walnut Street, #415, Berkeley
CA 94709, USA
A co-op education just to read it. 43 pages of co-op resources. Send $1.

Places to Learn

Auroville
Repos, Auroville 605 101, Tamil Nadu, India

Campus Center for Appropriate Technology
Humboldt State University (CCAT, HSU), Arcata, CA 95521, USA
Tel: 707/826–3551
Email: ccat@axe.humboldt.edu

Commonground
PO Box 474, Seymour, Victoria 3660, Australia
Offers training in conflict resolution, consensus decision-making and communal living.

Crystal Waters Permaculture Village
Queensland 4552, Australia
Tel: +61 74 944 741
Fax +61 74 944 578
Email: ecosol@peg.apc.org

Earth Restoration Corps
PO Box 118, Crestone, CO 81131, USA
Tel: +1 719 256 426
Fax: +1 719 256 4266
Email: erc@manitou.com

The Eco-village Training Center
The Farm, PO Box 90, Summertown, TN 38483, USA
Tel: +1 615 964 4324
Email: thefarm@gaia.org
A full range of hands-on eco-village immersion experiences, workshops, courses.

The Eco-village Training Center
Lebensgarten, Ginsterweg 5, D–31595 Steyerberg, Germany
Email: agni@gaia.org
Eco-village design and living in community workshops; training in fundraising; mediation and practical hands-on permaculture, etc.

Federation of Damanhur
Via Pramar 20/3, 10080 Baldissero, Italy
Tel: +39 0124 5127 512226
Email: damankur@damankur.it

Findhorn Foundation
Forres IV36 0RD, Scotland
Training in group living, spiritual development and ecological movement. University accreditation available.

Folkecentre for Renewable Energy
Contact: Preben Maegaard, Kammersgaards 16, 7760 Hurrap, Denmark

Gaia Education Outreach Institute
Derbyshire Farm, Temple, NH 03084, USA
Tel/Fax: +1 603 654 6705
Email: geo@igc.org
Offers eco-village training through class travel and work in sustainable communities around the world.

The Global Village
Bagno di Lucca, Nittamo Monteucco, Villa Demidoff 55201
Bagni di Lucca, Italy
Tel: +39 583 86 404
Email: village@cia.it

Ladakh
Contact: Helena Norberg-Hodge
Apple Barn, Week, Dartington, Devon TQ9 6JP, England
Tel: +44 (0)1803 868650
Fax: +44 (0)1803 868651

The Sarvodaya Movement
Dam Sak Mandira, 98 Rawatawatta Road, Moratuwa, Sri Lanka
Email: ssmplan@sri.lanka.net

We Gratefully Acknowledge Contributions From:

Bay View Crescent, Dunsborough, Western Australia 6281
Email: warwick.rowell@eepo.com.au

Communities – Journal of Cooperative Living. A quarterly magazine, published by the Fellowship for Intentional Community, 290 McEntire Road, Tryon, NC 28782, USA

Context Institute, PO Box 10818, Bainbridge Island, WA 98110, USA

Guy Dauncey, 2069 Kings Road, Victoria, BC V8R 2P6, Canada
Tel/Fax: +1 604 592 4473
Email: gdauncey@islandnet.com

Lois Arkin, 3551 White House Place, Los Angles, CA 90004, USA
Tel: +1 (213) 738 1254
Email: crsp@igc.apc.org

Warwick Rowell, Permaculture Applications Consultancy & Education.

And many others...

GAIA TRUST

Gaia Trust (*contact address on page 256*) is a Danish charitable entity founded in 1987 with the objective of promoting a global consciousness that experiences the whole planet as a living organism and Mankind as part of that whole.

In practice this has been done primarily through a proactive strategy of defining and carrying out its own initiatives. The two major ones to date have been the Global Eco-village Network and Gaia Technologies A/S. In addition, grants have been given over the years to over 80 projects in 20 countries. Grantgiving activities have now been terminated due to the administrative overload, and the complete focus is on proactive projects.

Gaia Villages, a division of Gaia Trust, acts as International Secretariat for GEN – the Global Eco-village Network, a network of small eco-village projects around the world. Gaia Trust sees the promotion of the eco-village movement as a very important part of the transition to a sustainable and just world society based on a value system that places human values above commercial values, in a radical departure from the dominant paradigm of our times, which is seen as unsustainable. While still embryonic, this movement offers a positive vision for the future and has enormous potential. Eco-villagers are the pioneers of our time, building with few resources and their own lives, a new society, one brick at a time. See *www.gaia.org* for over 1,500 pages of information.

The power of this vision should not be underestimated. Sociologist Ted Trainer of the University of New South Wales, Australia, wrote recently: "Would it be an exaggeration to claim that the emergence of the eco-village movement is the most significant event in the twentieth century? I don't think so."

Gaia Technologies is a venture capital firm that invests in small Danish companies, whose products and production methods are ecologically sustainable. The portfolio includes companies in dry goods, organic cereals, alternative banking, organic meats, solar cell panels, and small wind mills.

Gaia Trust is self-financing thanks to daughter company Gaiacorp, which was formed at the same time as Gaia Trust by founder/chairman J T Ross Jackson for the specific purpose of funding its activities, as Ross, whose background is in economics and operations research, saw that his research in the foreign currency market had great earnings potential. Fortunately that turned out to be true, and Gaiacorp has since become a well-known and successful currency fund manager.

Ross Jackson's inspiration and vision was based to a great extent on a deep spiritual experience in India in 1982, which is described in his book, *Kali Yuga Odyssey: A Spiritual Journey*. In his second book, *And We ARE Doing It: Building an Eco-village Future*, Ross describes how and why he got involved in the eco-village movement. It includes a devastating critique of commercial globalisation as well as a vision of what a radically different society might look like. The book's title comes from the GEN rallying cry:

We CAN do it!
We WILL do it!
And we ARE doing it!

Permanent Publications

Permanent Publications (*contact address on page 267*) is a small independent publishing company which started life in 1990 in the spare bedroom of Tim and Maddy Harland's cottage. The mission was to publish practical books to help people live more healthy and self-reliant lives. Permaculture design, a synthesis of useful practises such as low maintenance organic gardening, alternative technology, ecological house design, sustainable agriculture and community economics, quickly became the central focus of the company.

The name 'Permanent' was given to the project because it championed sustainability and a more durable, less throw-away, 'Permanent Culture'; but it was also positive 'tongue in cheek' mantra to aid survival in the hostile world of business... With no external funding or resources except for a passion for the subject, an unbending commitment and agile wits, the early years of the company life were, to say the least, precarious.

In 1992, Permanent Publications began publishing *Permaculture Magazine – Solutions For Sustainable Living* to complement its books on the subject. What started life as an alternative UK based newsletter was quickly to become a popular magazine read on all continents of the world by thousands of people.

Today, the spare bedroom is happily no longer inhabited by computers but a member of the family and the company has moved to a local environmental centre, at a former military base, run by the Earthworks Trust. The centre's mission is to demonstrate and promote the knowledge, skills and technologies that improve people's lifestyles without damaging the local and global environment. Permanent Publications have been allies in this project from its earliest beginnings.

Permanent Publications now publishes books on permaculture in its widest sense and produces the *Earth Repair Catalogue*, offering books and videos by mail on every subject from mulching to mediation and solar heating to spirituality. They also have an information service on the World Wide Web.

Organic gardening has always been one of Tim and Maddy's passions and their own permaculture garden demonstrates this. Permanent Publications is also working in close association with the Henry Doubleday Research Association, one of Europe's largest organic gardening bodies, designing and producing *The Organic Way*, a new quarterly colour magazine for its members.

These are exciting times and whatever direction the company chooses to take in the future, the original mission remain – to encourage good health, for people and the planet, and to inspire a spirit of interdependence and self-reliance.